T0255289

Lecture Notes in Computer Science 9440

Commenced Publication in 1973
Founding and Former Series Editors:
Gerhard Goos, Juris Hartmanis, and Jan van Leeuwen

Editorial Board

David Hutchison
  Lancaster University, Lancaster, UK
Takeo Kanade
  Carnegie Mellon University, Pittsburgh, PA, USA
Josef Kittler
  University of Surrey, Guildford, UK
Jon M. Kleinberg
  Cornell University, Ithaca, NY, USA
Friedemann Mattern
  ETH Zürich, Zürich, Switzerland
John C. Mitchell
  Stanford University, Stanford, CA, USA
Moni Naor
  Weizmann Institute of Science, Rehovot, Israel
C. Pandu Rangan
  Indian Institute of Technology, Madras, India
Bernhard Steffen
  TU Dortmund University, Dortmund, Germany
Demetri Terzopoulos
  University of California, Los Angeles, CA, USA
Doug Tygar
  University of California, Berkeley, CA, USA
Gerhard Weikum
  Max Planck Institute for Informatics, Saarbrücken, Germany

More information about this series at http://www.springer.com/series/7410

Stefan Mangard · Patrick Schaumont (Eds.)

Radio Frequency Identification

Security and Privacy Issues

11th International Workshop, RFIDsec 2015
New York, NY, USA, June 23–24, 2015
Revised Selected Papers

 Springer

Editors
Stefan Mangard   Patrick Schaumont
Graz University of Technology   Blacksburg
Graz   Virginia
Austria   USA

ISSN 0302-9743   ISSN 1611-3349   (electronic)
Lecture Notes in Computer Science
ISBN 978-3-319-24836-3   ISBN 978-3-319-24837-0   (eBook)
DOI 10.1007/978-3-319-24837-0

Library of Congress Control Number: 2015949479

LNCS Sublibrary: SL4 – Security and Cryptology

Springer Cham Heidelberg New York Dordrecht London
© Springer International Publishing Switzerland 2015
This work is subject to copyright. All rights are reserved by the Publisher, whether the whole or part of the
material is concerned, specifically the rights of translation, reprinting, reuse of illustrations, recitation, broadcasting, reproduction on microfilms or in any other physical way, and transmission or information storage
and retrieval, electronic adaptation, computer software, or by similar or dissimilar methodology now known
or hereafter developed.
The use of general descriptive names, registered names, trademarks, service marks, etc. in this publication
does not imply, even in the absence of a specific statement, that such names are exempt from the relevant
protective laws and regulations and therefore free for general use.
The publisher, the authors and the editors are safe to assume that the advice and information in this book
are believed to be true and accurate at the date of publication. Neither the publisher nor the authors or the
editors give a warranty, express or implied, with respect to the material contained herein or for any errors or
omissions that may have been made.

Printed on acid-free paper

Springer International Publishing AG Switzerland is part of Springer Science+Business Media
(www.springer.com)

Preface

Welcome to the 11th International Workshop on RFID Security (RFIDsec), held at the NYIT Auditorium on Broadway in New York City, NY, USA, during June 22–24, 2015. RFIDsec has been the main venue for new results in RFID system and implementation security for over a decade. The event has travelled to many different places all over the world. Driven by the positive experience of 2014, we co-located RFIDsec for the second time with WiSec, and we created a tightly integrated program that allowed attendees to hop from one event to the other.

RFIDsec 2015 assembled four sessions with exciting results in RFID security. The four sessions collect ten regular papers, which were selected by the Program Committee after a rigorous review process out of 23 submissions. The review procedure included an individual review phase followed by a collective online discussion by the 22 members of the Technical Program Committee with the program chairs. The Program Committee members were supported by 30 external reviewers.

Besides the ten accepted papers, the workshop also included a shared keynote with WiSec, an RFIDsec keynote talk and two tutorials. The shared keynote talk was given by Srdjan Capkun from ETH Zurich. In his talk "Why We Should Build a Secure Positioning Infrastructure," Dr. Capkun discussed the main challenges in designing and building new positioning infrastructures that offer security and privacy by design. The keynote talk of RFIDsec 2015, "Hardware Trojans for ASICs and FPGAs," was given by Christof Paar from Ruhr University Bochum and University of Massachusetts Amherst. Hardware Trojans is a topic of rapidly increasing importance in modern complex digital eletronics, especially for those that have a trustworthy function. Dr. Paar shared his insights and latest research results into this problem. The first tutorial was on Contactless Payments, and it was given by Joeri de Ruiter from the University of Birmingham. The contactless environment comes with very challenging problems in power provisioning and communications. Dr. de Ruiter explained the unique solutions that are enabled by sound cryptographic engineering. The second tutorial was on Anonymous Based Credentials (ABCs) in Theory and Practice, and it was given by Gergely Alpar from Radboud University. As explained by Dr. Alpar, ABCs handle the important issue of user authentication and authorization while at the same time ensuring the user's privacy.

The program chairs would like to thank the general chairs, Paolo Gasti and Ramesh Karri, for their support in hosting RFIDsec 2015 in the Big Apple. We are also greatly indebted to the 22 members of the Technical Program Committee, who provided valuable technical insights in the assembly of the program. Finally, we would like to thank the RFIDsec Steering Committee members for their guidance in setting up the 11th edition of this exciting workshop series, and for opening the path to the next decade of RFIDsec.

July 2015   Stefan Mangard
                                                           Patrick Schaumont

Organization

Program Committee

Frederik Armknecht	Universität Mannheim, Germany
Gildas Avoine	INSA Rennes, France and UCL, Belgium
Lejla Batina	Radboud University Nijmegen, The Netherlands
Srdjan Capkun	ETH Zurich, Switzerland
Rajat Subhra Chakraborty	IIT Kharagpur, India
Thomas Eisenbarth	Worcester Polytechnic Institute, USA
Martin Feldhofer	NXP Semiconductors, Germany
Aurélien Francillon	Eurecom, France
Gerhard Hancke	City University of Hong Kong, SAR China
Julio Hernandez	Kent University, UK
Daniel E. Holcomb	University of Michigan, USA
Michael Hutter	Cryptography Research Inc., USA
Stefan Mangard	TU Graz, Austria
Daisuke Moriyama	NICT, Japan
Christof Paar	Ruhr University Bochum, Germany and University of Massachusetts, USA
Axel Poschmann	NXP Semiconductors, Germany
Bart Preneel	KU Leuven, Belgium
Matt Robshaw	Impinj, USA
Kazuo Sakiyama	The University of Electro-Communications, Japan
Nitesh Saxena	University of Alabama at Birmingham, USA
Patrick Schaumont	Virginia Tech, USA
Erich Wenger	TU Graz, Austria
Avishai Wool	Tel Aviv University, Israel

Additional Reviewers

Becker, Georg T.	Herbst, Christoph
Bilgin, Begül	Hermans, Jens
Boehl, Florian	Hiller, Matthias
Budhathoki, Parshuram	Joye, Marc
Chen, Cong	Komano, Yuichi
Chmielewski, Lukasz	Korak, Thomas
Delvaux, Jeroen	Krasnova, Anna
Forte, Domenic	Lamberger, Mario
Gross, Hannes	Li, Yang

Mohamed, Manar
Mukhopadhyay, Dibya
Nikova, Svetla
Phuong Ha, Nguyen
Saha, Sayandeep
Sahoo, Durga Prasad

Schlösser, Alexander
Shirvanian, Maiheh
Shrestha, Babins
Taha, Mostafa
Wang, Chao
Yamamoto, Dai

Contents

PUFs and Applications

Security Evaluation and Enhancement of Bistable Ring PUFs 3
    Xiaolin Xu, Ulrich Rührmair, Daniel E. Holcomb,
    and Wayne Burleson

On the Scaling of Machine Learning Attacks on PUFs with Application
to Noise Bifurcation 17
    Johannes Tobisch and Georg T. Becker

ReSC: RFID-Enabled Supply Chain Management and Traceability for
Network Devices 32
    Kun Yang, Domenic Forte, and Mark Tehranipoor

Side-Channels and Countermeasures

Side-Channel Assisted Modeling Attacks on Feed-Forward Arbiter
PUFs Using Silicon Data 53
    Raghavan Kumar and Wayne Burleson

Sharing is Caring—On the Protection of Arithmetic Logic Units against
Passive Physical Attacks 68
    Hannes Gross

RFID System Attacks

Practical Experiences on NFC Relay Attacks with Android:
Virtual Pickpocketing Revisited 87
    José Vila and Ricardo J. Rodríguez

Algebraic Cryptanalysis and RFID Authentication 104
    Carlos Cid, Loic Ferreira, Gordon Procter, and Matt J.B. Robshaw

An RFID Skimming Gate Using Higher Harmonics 122
    René Habraken, Peter Dolron, Erik Poll, and Joeri de Ruiter

Efficient Implementations

Efficient E-cash with Attributes on MULTOS Smartcards 141
    Gesine Hinterwälder, Felix Riek, and Christof Paar

Efficient and Secure Delegation of Group Exponentiation to a Single
Server 156
    *Bren Cavallo, Giovanni Di Crescenzo, Delaram Kahrobaei,
    and Vladimir Shpilrain*

Author Index 175

Part I

PUFs and Applications

Security Evaluation and Enhancement
of Bistable Ring PUFs

Xiaolin Xu[1], Ulrich Rührmair[2], Daniel E. Holcomb[1], and Wayne Burleson[1]

[1] ECE Department, University of Massachusetts Amherst
{xiaolinx,dholcomb,burleson}@umass.edu
[2] Horst Görtz Institute for IT-Security, Ruhr Universität Bochum
ruehrmair@ilo.de

Abstract. The Bistable Ring (BR) Physical Unclonable Function (PUF) is a newly proposed hardware security primitive in the PUF family. In this work, we comprehensively evaluate its resilience against Machine Learning (ML) modeling attacks. Based on the success of ML attacks, we propose XOR strategies to enhance the security of BR PUFs. Our results show that the XOR BR PUF with more than four parallel BR PUFs is able to resist the ML modeling methods in this work. We also evaluate the other PUF metrics of reliability, uniqueness and uniformity, and find that the XOR function is also effective in improving the uniformity of BR PUFs.

1 Introduction

In the last ten years, physical unclonable functions (PUFs) have established themselves as an alternative to conventional security approaches [4][11]. In a nutshell, a PUF is a disordered, at least partly randomly structured physical system. Due to its random structure that is caused by uncontrollable, small-scale manufacturing variations, it is physically unclonable, i.e., no two specimens can be produced that are physically exactly identical. This limitation applies to both the original manufacturer and to other, potentially adversarial, parties. All PUFs have one basic functionality in common, namely some *challenge-response* mechanism: They can be triggered or excited by signals that are commonly denoted as *challenges* C_i. Upon excitation by a challenge C_i, they react by producing a response R_{C_i} that depends on their internal disorder and usually also on the challenge itself. The tuples $(C_i, R(C_i))$ are called the *challenge-response pairs (CRPs)* of the PUF.

Over the years, different variants or types of PUFs have emerged (see [12] for an overview). They all share the above features of being a disordered structure, possessing physical unclonability, and exhibiting some form of challenge-response mechanism. However, their other security features, together with their intended applications and associated attack scenarios, notably differ. This makes it useful in scientific works to explicitly distinguish these types from each other [12].

© Springer International Publishing Switzerland 2015
S. Mangard, P. Schaumont (Eds.): RFIDsec 2015, LNCS 9440, pp. 3–16, 2015.
DOI: 10.1007/978-3-319-24837-0_1

The two main PUF-types are often denoted as weak and strong PUFs. Weak PUFs possess essentially a single, fixed challenge C, as for example in the case of SRAM PUFs. They are mainly used for internal key derivation in security hardware. The underlying security assumption is that attackers must not be able to access the internal response of the PUF, for example by reading out the power-up state of the SRAM PUF [5][6]. In opposition to that, strong PUFs are PUFs that have a very large number of possible challenges, too many to read out all corresponding CRPs in feasible time. Their challenge-response mechanism should be complex in the sense that it is hard to derive unknown CRPs from a set of known CRPs. In particular, strong PUFs should not allow *"modeling attacks"*, in which an adversary collects a subset of CRPs, uses them to train a machine learning (ML) algorithm, and later employs the model produced by the ML algorithm to predict unknown CRPs.

Strong PUFs are usually employed with a publicly accessible CRP interface, i.e., anyone holding the PUF or the PUF embedding hardware can apply challenges and read out responses. The lack of access restriction mechanisms on strong PUFs is therefore a key difference from weak PUFs. In recent years, strong PUFs have turned out to be a very versatile cryptographic and security primitive: First of all, by using a fixed set of challenges, they can be employed for internal key derivation, just like weak PUFs. But they can do more: They can also implement a host of advanced cryptographic protocols, ranging from identification [11][9] to key exchange [20][1] to oblivious transfer [1].

Their many possible applications make the secure construction of secure strong PUFs a worthwhile and rewarding research target. Unfortunately, it is a nontrivial one, too: A large number of powerful attacks on some first-generation electrical strong PUFs have been published recently. They include the above mentioned modeling attacks [13][14]; side channel attacks [15]; and also optical characterization techniques [19]. Most of these attacks target the first electrical strong PUF, the so-called Arbiter PUF [4][11] and variants thereof, for example XOR Arbiter PUFs and Feed-Forward Arbiter PUFs. For this reason, alternative silicon architectures have been proposed in recent years. One such alternative is the *"Bistable Ring PUF" (BR PUF)* [2][3], which was designed to have a more complex internal response-generating mechanism in hopes of making ML attacks harder.

At TRUST 2014, Hesselbarth and Schuster [16] succeeded in revealing some basic vulnerabilities of the BR PUF against ML techniques. They proved that BR PUFs can be attacked by a single layer artificial neural network (ANN) with prediction errors between close to 0% and 20%, varying from hardware instance to instance. Among the 20 FPGA instances examined, 14 could be predicted with errors less than 10%. This puts close limits on the security usability of the BR PUF on FPGAs. Schuster and Hesselbarth subsequently proposed a small design improvement, so-called twisted BR PUFs (TBR PUFs), which they conjectured to possess better security. Using their own ANN algorithm, they were also able to attack TBR PUFs again. However, the TBR PUF shows average higher prediction errors with respect to ANNs, indicating that TNR PUFs has some improvements over plain BR PUFs. It remained open in the work of Schuster and Hesselbarth whether said improvement is sufficient for secure practical usage of the TBR PUF.

Our Contributions. In this paper, we re-examine the security of the BR PUF and TBR PUF closely, again using FPGA implementations. We thereby make the following new contributions:

- We implement 8 instances of the BR PUF and the TBR PUF on FPGA. To achieve a more comprehensive ML analysis, we implement bitlengths other and larger than 64, namely also 32, 128 and 256. These bitlengths had never before been implemented in silicon and studied in the literature.
- We develop the first analytical models for the BR PUF and the TBR PUF.
- We use these new models in order to apply, for the first time, support vector machines (SVMs) to the BR PUF and the TBR PUF. This more powerful ML-tool drastically improves the ML predication rates relative to previous work. None of our 8 instances has a prediction error exceeding 5%. This result answers the open question of Hesselbarth and Schuster whether certain individual and particularly hard instances of the BR PUF or TBR PUF could be used securely in practice: In our findings, this was not the case.
- We then propose a new, efficient strategy for the secure practical use of the BR PUF: namely the employment of l instances in parallel, whose l outputs are XORed at the end in order to produce one single-bit PUF-response. We call the resulting structure XOR BR PUF. We show that even for small values of l such as 4, this structure cannot be machine learned by our current techniques, while it is still sufficiently stable in practice. This work is the first study of XOR BR PUFs in the literature.

Organization of This Paper. This paper is organized as follows. Section 2 discusses our attacks on the BR PUF, while Section 3 details our attacks on the TBR PUF. Section 4 suggests the use of XOR BR PUFs and evaluates their performance improvement. Section 5 concludes the paper.

2 SVM Attack on BR PUFs

2.1 Mechanism of BR PUF

A ring oscillator (RO) is a device composed of an odd number of logically-inverting delay elements. Since the output of the last element is always the logical "NOT" of the first input, an RO will continually oscillate. Derived from the non-settling structure of RO, BR PUF is a ring comprising an even number of inverting cells. Such a design behaves like a memory cell and will fall into one of two possible stable states: either "101010..." or "010101...".

As depicted in Fig. 1, a 64-bit BR PUF is composed of 64 stages, where each stage has two inverting delay elements (NOR gates as an example). A challenge vector $C = \{c_1, c_2, \ldots, c_n\}$ selects the NOR gates used in each bistable ring configuration by providing values to the MUX and DEMUX gates of the stages. Since each NOR gate has unique process variation, each different challenge vector creates a unique bistable ring configuration, and in total 2^{64} different configurations can be created. A common "RESET" signal is added to each stage to establish a known "all-0" state before letting the ring stabilize to produce its response. Evaluation of the response begins when "RESET" is released and the ring starts to oscillate through the selected NOR gates. Once a stable state is reached, the outputs of any two adjacent stages will be logical compliments of each other, either "10" or "01". The choice among the two possible stable states of the ring depends on noise and the process variation of the NOR gates used in the ring configuration. Any interconnection node between two stages can be used as an output port, and in this work we use the half bit-length port to read out the response (Fig. 1).

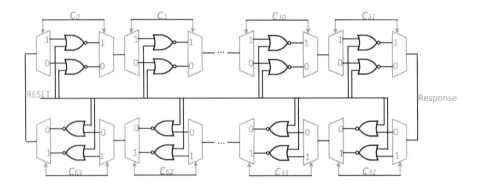

Fig. 1. Schematic of a single BR-PUF with 64 stages

2.2 Intuition for Modeling BR PUF

The intuition for our modeling attack is that the response can predicted based on a summation of weights. Such an additive model is commonly used for predicting the responses of Arbiter PUFs, where the weights represent stage delays [8]. An additive model has also been used for predicting the resolution of metastability [7], with weights representing the strength with which different cells pull toward a particular outcome. We similarly use an additive model in this work; the weight we associate with each gate represents the difference between its pull-up strength and pull-down strength. The weights are summed across all gates used by a challenge to find the overall favored response for that challenge; a positive sum indicates a preference for the positive response. Note that the summation of weights requires negative and positive polarities because the positive overall response is favored by the pull-up strength of even stages and the pull-down strength of odd stages.

2.3   Model

Let the difference between the pull-up and pull-down strength of the top NOR gate in the ith stage be represented by t_i, and in the bottom NOR gate in the ith stage be represented by b_i. The even stages will contribute toward the positive response with strength t_i (or b_i if the challenge bit selects the bottom NOR gate of the stage), and the odd stages will contribute toward the positive response with strength $-t_i$ (or $-b_i$). To account more generally for even-ness or odd-ness, the strength of the ith stage toward the positive response can be written as $-1^i t_i$ if the challenge bit is 0, and $-1^i b_i$ if the challenge bit is 1. For a given 64-bit challenge, the total strength pulling toward the positive response is the summation of 64 t_i and b_i weights.

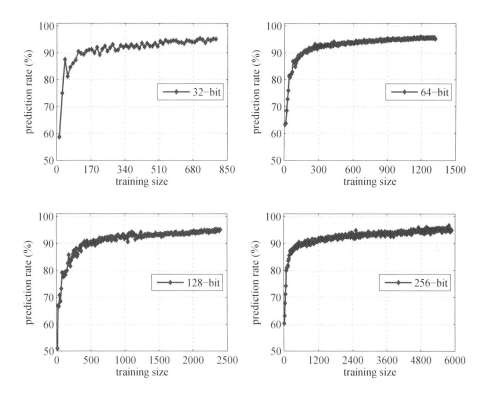

Fig. 2. Prediction rate of SVM modeling attacks on BR PUFs. When the length of the BR PUF increases, more CRPs are required to train the model to achieve 95% prediction. Note that the scale of the x-axes are not consistent across the subfigures.

For convenience we define α_i and β_i (Eq. 1) such that $\alpha_i + \beta_i = -1^i t_i$ and $\alpha_i - \beta_i = -1^i b_i$. This notation allows the pull of the ith stage toward the positive response to be written generally as $\alpha_i + c_i \beta_i$ with challenge bit $c_i \in \{-1, 1\}$. The summed strengths toward the positive response for any challenge vector C is

$r(C)$ as shown in Eq. 2. According to our formulation, if the t_i and b_i weights were known explicitly, then the response could be predicted by the sign of $R(C)$ (Eq. 2).

$$\alpha_i = -1^i \left(\frac{t_i - b_i}{2} \right) \qquad \beta_i = -1^i \left(\frac{t_i + b_i}{2} \right) \qquad (1)$$

$$R(C) = sgn(\sum_{i=0..n-1} \alpha_i + c_i \beta_i) \qquad (2)$$

Given that weights are not known, since there are only two possible responses of BR PUFs, based on the model above, we can convert the response prediction of BR PUFs into a classification problem. Support Vector Machines (SVM) are powerful learning tools that can perform binary classification of data, the classification is realized with building a hyperplane separating surface. While digesting the known input and output data sets, the hyperplane separating surface will be curved to minimize the error of predicted values.

Known CRPs are used to train the classifier to predict responses from challenges. In the SVM formulation, first note that the α_i terms in Eq. 2 can be discarded because they are constant for a given PUF instance across all challenges. Only $c_i \beta_i$ terms remain, and from these terms the response must be predicted. Given a set of challenges and associated responses, the training examples therefore have as their feature vector an applied challenge $C_j \in \{-1, 1\}^n$ and as their labels the observed response $R(C_j) \in \{-1, 1\}$ to challenge C_j. Note that β_i terms do not appear explicitly in the SVM formulation as the classifier simply works to find the maximum margin hyperplane to separate the challenges into two classes according to their responses.

2.4   SVM Attacks on BR PUFs

To explore the effectiveness of SVM attacks, we implemented on a Xilinx Spartan-VI FPGA board, 8 BR PUFs with lengths of 32-, 64-, 128- and 256 bits, and collected 1,000,000 CRPs from each of them (to decrease the impact of measurement noise, all of the final CRPs are formulated by majority voting from 11 repeated measurements). SVM attacks are implemented with a linear kernel to mimic the operation of single BR PUFs (note that to attack XOR BR PUFs, SVM model with a polynomial kernel is utilized, where the poly-order of the model is set as the XORing complexity of BR PUFs). The results of SVM attacks are shown as Fig. 2. To demonstrate the relationship between prediction rate and CRPs used for different PUF lengths, we utilize 95% as a threshold prediction rate. It is clear that while the size of BR PUF is increasing, the demand for CRPs is also increasing to build its ML model. However, for any tested size of BR PUF, the SVM modeling attack is successful in predicting responses. This means a single BR PUF is not secure, even if it has a large number of stages.

3   Twisted BR PUFs Attack

3.1   Model of TBR PUFs

Uniformity, or fractional Hamming weight, is an important feature of PUFs. A good PUF that produces an equal number of 0 and 1 responses will have a uniformity of around 0.50. However, the uniformity of CRPs of BR PUF implementations has been found to be biased in previous work [16] (see also Sec. 4.3 in this work). To compensate for this drawback, TBR-PUF was proposed in [16]. Compared to the BR PUF, the TBR-PUF has a more compact design; when applying a challenge vector to the TBR PUF, all of its $2n$ inverting elements are used in the ring. By contrast, in the standard BR PUF, half of the NOR gates in the circuit are unused for any given challenge. Taking the TBR PUF in Fig. 3 as an example, using challenge bit $c_0 = 1$ or $c_0 = 0$ will change the location of D_0^0 and D_1^0 in the ring, but in either case D_0^0 and D_1^0 will both contribute in some polarity to the response.

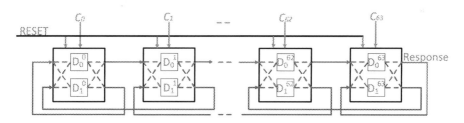

Fig. 3. Schematic of a single TBR-PUF with 64 stages

From Sec. 2, we know that a ring composed of an even number of inverting elements will stabilize according to the summed strength of the pull-up and pull-down strengths of each gate. The TBR PUF uses pull-up and pull-down strengths of all inverting components in the circuit, but only the polarity (i.e. even-ness or odd-ness) of each element toward the overall ring response changes with the challenge vector. According to the interconnections of the 64-bit TBR PUF, the two NOR gates in the ith stage are the ith and $127 - i^{th}$ element in the overall ring. Because one element is odd in the overall ring, and one is even, the pull-up strength of the top and bottom gates in each stage are working against each other. Therefore, the overall contribution toward the positive response is β_i (Eq. 3), or $-\beta_i$ if the ith challenge bit is negative. The overall sum of weights pulling toward the positive response for challenge C is therefore $R(C)$ (Eq. 4). Eq. 2 and Eq. 4 differ only in in the physical meaning of β_i, and in Eq. 2 having an additional offset term of $\sum_i \alpha_i$, but in terms of ML modeling they are actually the same identical model. Therefore, the complexity of ML attacks on the TBR PUF is the same as the complexity of attacking the BR PUF.

$$\beta_i = -1^i(t_i - b_i) \tag{3}$$

$$R(C) = sgn(\sum_{i=0...n-1} c_i \beta_i) \tag{4}$$

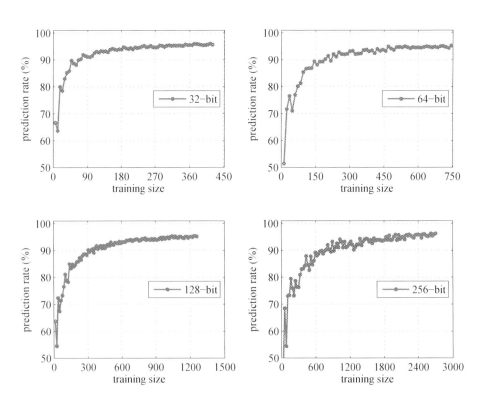

Fig. 4. Prediction rate of SVM modeling attacks on TBR PUFs of different bit lengths. As in Fig. 2, to achieve same prediction rate, a larger PUF requires more CRPs.

3.2   SVM Attacks on TBR PUFs

Given that we have shown the model of a TBR PUF to be the same as that of a BR PUF, we can again train an SVM classifier to predict its responses to each challenge. Eight TBR PUFs are implemented with Spartan-VI FPGA boards, and 1,000,000 CRPs are collected from each of them. For each CRP, majority voting over 11 repeated measurements of the response to a challenge are performed in order to reduce the impact of noise.

Following the experiment in Sec. 2.4, SVM attacks with polynomial kernel are applied on TBR PUFs of 32-, 64-, 128- and 256 bit-length (the poly-order of the model is set as the XORing complexity). The results in Fig. 4 show that the modeling attacks succeed in modeling all different sizes of the TBR PUF, with prediction rate no lower than 95%.

4 XORing BR PUFs to Enhance the Security

It is possible using ML to model the behavior of a single strong PUF like the Arbiter PUF [8]. To thwart modeling attacks, an XOR function was proposed as a way to enhance security of Arbiter PUFs [17] and lightweight PUFs [10]. In an XOR PUF, the same challenge vector is applied to l single PUFs in parallel, and their outputs are XORed together to form a one-bit response. XORing is an efficient method to enhance the security of strong PUFs, because the XOR function obfuscates the CRPs of the individual PUFs [17]. Inspired by this idea, we propose to use XOR strategies on BR PUFs to improve their resistance to modeling attacks.

4.1 Review of Existing Attacks on XOR PUFs

The addition of XOR functions increases the resistance of strong PUF against modeling attacks. Both the training time and number of CRPs required to train a model increase exponentially with the number of XORed PUFs [13]. Attacking XOR-based Arbiter PUFs with more than five parallel Arbiter PUFs was stated as difficult based on pure ML modeling [14]. Later works devised a more powerful class of hybrid attacks that combine side channels with ML [15,21]. Power and timing side-channels allow information about the sub-responses (i.e. the responses of single PUFs before the final XOR) of XORed PUFs to be extracted and used to improve the prediction rate of ML models. In light of these hybrid attacks, if the side-channel information of BR PUFs can also be measured, then the use of XOR will not be an effective way to enhance the security.

4.2 SVM Modeling Attacks on XORed BR PUF

Adopting the model of single BR PUF in Sec. 2, for an XOR BR PUF employing l BR PUFs, the XORed response to a challenge C can be described by Eq. 5. Note the similarity between this formula and the formula of the single BR PUF (Eq. 2). The only modification is that now each stage has l different α and β terms, one for each of the PUFs. The overall response is based on how many of the individual PUFs have a positive response.

$$R(C) = sgn\left(\prod_{j=0}^{l-1}\left(\sum_{i=0}^{n-1}\alpha_{i,j} + c_i\beta_{i,j}\right)\right) \tag{5}$$

In applying SVM to XOR BR PUF, it is found that we can only break the complexity up to 2 XOR for 128-bit length and 3 XOR for 64-bit length. The number of CRPs and runtime[1] for SVM modeling attacks against XOR BR PUFs are listed in Tab. 1. We can surmise that XOR BR PUFs with 4 or more XORed outputs are beyond the reach of current SVM modeling attacks.

---

[1] The computer used has a common Intel 3630QM quadcore processor.

Table 1. The run times and number of CRPs that are required for SVM attacks on the XOR BR PUFs of different sizes. Prediction rates around 50% imply that the SVM model can not break XOR BR PUFs of these complexity. *Note that the training time is greatly determined by the computational systems.

No. of XORs	Bit Length	CRPs ($\times 10^3$)	Predict. Rate	Training* Time
2	32	0.8	95%	3 sec
	64	4	95%	10 sec
	128	18	95%	6 mins
	256	——	50.8%	——
3	32	1.2	95%	5 sec
	64	7.2	95%	24 sec
	128	——	50.1%	——
	256	——	50.1%	——
4	32	——	50.1%	——
	64	——	50.3%	——
	128	——	49.8%	——
	256	——	50.1%	——

4.3   Performance Evaluation of XORed BR PUF

While the basic motivation of XORing BR PUF is to resist modeling attacks, the impact of the XOR on other key metrics must also be considered. In this section, we evaluate the impact of the XOR function on reliability, uniqueness, and uniformity.

Reliability. Reliability is the ratio of consistent CRPs when a PUF is operating in different environment conditions such as temperature. To evaluate the reliability of XOR BR PUFs, 8 BR PUFs are measured across different temperatures between 27°C and 75°C, with a 4°C step, using a Sun Electronics EC12 Environmental Chamber [18] to control the temperature (Fig. 5a). Reliability is evaluated by comparing CRPs collected at 27°C to CRPs collected at other temperatures. For a XOR PUF, any unstable sub-response can cause the XORed response to be unreliable. Therefore, the reliability at any temperature will decrease with the number of PUFs that are XORed together (Fig. 5b). According to the first BR PUF paper [3], an effective solution to solve this problem is employing CRPs that settle down quickly, since those CRPs are less sensitive to noise.

Uniqueness. Uniqueness is the capability of a PUF to distinguish itself from other instances. Uniqueness is quantified as the fraction of responses that are

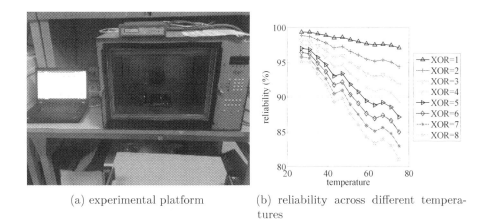

(a) experimental platform

(b) reliability across different temperatures

Fig. 5. Evaluating reliability across different temperatures. Because the reliability of each single BR PUF decreases with temperature, the reliability of the XOR BR PUF results degrade significantly.

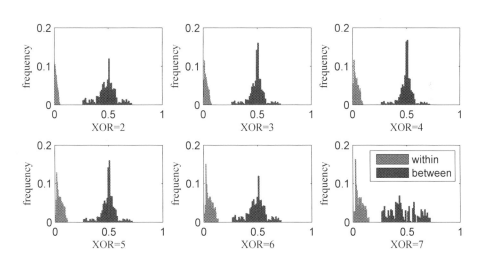

Fig. 6. The between-class and within-class Hamming distance of XOR PUFs. Even when XORing together more BR PUFs, the within-class and between-class Hamming distances can still be differentiated. The results are based on 8 BR PUFs, thus there is only one 8 XOR BR PUF and no uniqueness is formulated for it.

different across instances when the same challenges are applied. Thus for m PUF instances, a total of $\frac{m*(m-1)}{2}$ uniqueness values are obtained. To better explore the uniqueness of XOR BR PUF, we compute its within-class (response flipping by noise, temperature noise here) and between-class uniqueness (response difference between instances), these results are depicted in Fig. 6.

Uniformity. Uniformity denotes the average response of a PUF, the ideal value of which is 0.5, meaning equal amount of "1" and "0" responses. Uniformity that is far away from 0.5 will have less response entropy and be easier to attack with modeling [22]. In our experiment, the uniformity of a single BR PUF is found to be highly biased, and this phenomenon was also reported in [16] [22]. The XOR function helps to remove this bias. To validate the uniformity improvement from the XOR function, we collected the CRPs from eight 64-bit BR PUFs from FPGA (without CRP majority voting). It is found that some PUF instances show extreme bias, but XORing more single BR PUFs together decreases response bias (Fig. 7).

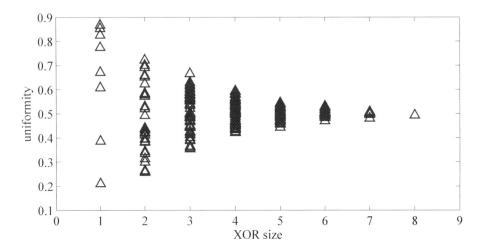

Fig. 7. The response uniformity of a single BR PUF (represented by "XOR=1" in plot) is highly biased. When more BR PUFs are XORed together, the uniformity is closer to 0.5.

5   Conclusion and Future Works

In this work, we studied two relatively new PUF variants: BR PUF and its derived architecture TBR PUF. Their resilience against ML modeling attacks is explored and it is shown that their response can be predicted with success rate exceeding 95% using reasonable runtime and less than 10k CRPs in all cases. Our work confirms that neither a single BR, nor TBR, PUF is secure.

To strengthen the BR PUF against modeling attacks, we proposed and evaluated an XOR BR PUF variant. It is found that XORing 4 or more BR PUFs together produces a behavior that is beyond the modeling capability of current SVM ML attacks, and also improves other key PUF metrics like uniformity. Future work will explore the effectiveness of other modeling attacks, like Evolutionary Strategy and Logistic Regression methods.

References

1. Brzuska, C., Fischlin, M., Schröder, H., Katzenbeisser, S.: Physically unclone-able functions in the universal composition framework. In: Rogaway, P. (ed.) CRYPTO 2011. LNCS, vol. 6841, pp. 51–70. Springer, Heidelberg (2011)
2. Chen, Q., Csaba, G., Lugli, P., Schlichtmann, U., Ruhrmair, U.: The bistable ring puf: A new architecture for strong physical unclonable functions. In: 2011 IEEE International Symposium on Hardware-Oriented Security and Trust (HOST), pp. 134–141. IEEE (2011)
3. Chen, Q., Csaba, G., Lugli, P., Schlichtmann, U., Ruhrmair, U.: Characterization of the bistable ring puf. In: 2012 Design, Automation & Test in Europe Conference & Exhibition (DATE), pp. 1459–1462. IEEE (2012)
4. Gassend, B., Clarke, D., Van Dijk, M., Devadas, S.: Silicon physical random functions. In: Proceedings of the 9th ACM Conference on Computer and Communications Security, pp. 148–160. ACM (2002)
5. Guajardo, J., Kumar, S.S., Schrijen, G.-J., Tuyls, P.: FPGA intrinsic pUFs and their use for IP protection. In: Paillier, P., Verbauwhede, I. (eds.) CHES 2007. LNCS, vol. 4727, pp. 63–80. Springer, Heidelberg (2007)
6. Holcomb, D.E., Burleson, W.P., Fu, K.: Power-up SRAM State as an Identifying Fingerprint and Source of True Random Numbers. IEEE Transactions on Computers (2009)
7. Holcomb, D.E., Fu, K.: Bitline PUF: building native challenge-response PUF capability into any SRAM. In: Batina, L., Robshaw, M. (eds.) CHES 2014. LNCS, vol. 8731, pp. 510–526. Springer, Heidelberg (2014)
8. Lim, D. Extracting secret keys from integrated circuits, MSc Thesis (2004)
9. Lofstrom, K., Daasch, W.R., Taylor, D.: Ic identification circuit using device mismatch. In: 2000 IEEE International Solid-State Circuits Conference, Digest of Technical Papers, ISSCC 2000, pp. 372–373. IEEE (2000)
10. Majzoobi, M., Koushanfar, F., Potkonjak, M.: Lightweight secure PUFs. In: Proceedings of the 2008 IEEE/ACM International Conference on Computer-Aided Design, pp. 670–673. IEEE Press (2008)
11. Pappu, R., Recht, B., Taylor, J., Gershenfeld, N.: Physical one-way functions. Science 297 5589, 2026–2030 (2002)
12. Rührmair, U., Holcomb, D.E.: PUFs at a glance. In: Proceedings of the conference on Design, Automation & Test in Europe, p. 347. European Design and Automation Association (2014)
13. Rührmair, U., Sehnke, F., Sölter, J., Dror, G., Devadas, S., Schmidhuber, J.: Modeling attacks on physical unclonable functions. In: Proceedings of the 17th ACM Conference on Computer and Communications Security, pp. 237–249. ACM (2010)
14. Rührmair, U., Sölter, J., Sehnke, F., Xu, X., Mahmoud, A., Stoyanova, V., Dror, G., Schmidhuber, J., Burleson, W., Devadas, S.: PUF modeling attacks on simulated and silicon data. IEEE Transactions on Information Forensics and Security (2013)

15. Rührmair, U., Xu, X., Sölter, J., Mahmoud, A., Majzoobi, M., Koushanfar, F., Burleson, W.: Efficient power and timing side channels for physical unclonable functions. In: Batina, L., Robshaw, M. (eds.) CHES 2014. LNCS, vol. 8731, pp. 476–492. Springer, Heidelberg (2014)
16. Schuster, D., Hesselbarth, R.: Evaluation of bistable ring pUFs using single layer neural networks. In: Holz, T., Ioannidis, S. (eds.) Trust 2014. LNCS, vol. 8564, pp. 101–109. Springer, Heidelberg (2014)
17. Suh, G.E., Devadas, S.: Physical unclonable functions for device authentication and secret key generation. In: Proceedings of the 44th Annual Design Automation Conference, DAC 2007, pp. 9–14. ACM (2007)
18. Sun Electronic Systems, I. Model EC1X Environmental Chamber User and Repair Manual (2011)
19. Tajik, S., Dietz, E., Frohmann, S., Seifert, J.-P., Nedospasov, D., Helfmeier, C., Boit, C., Dittrich, H.: Physical characterization of arbiter PUFs. In: Batina, L., Robshaw, M. (eds.) CHES 2014. LNCS, vol. 8731, pp. 493–509. Springer, Heidelberg (2014)
20. Van Dijk, M.E.: System and method of reliable forward secret key sharing with physical random functions, US Patent 7,653,197, January 26, 2010
21. Xu, X., Burleson, W.: Hybrid side-channel/machine-learning attacks on PUFs: a new threat. In: Proceedings of the Conference on Design, Automation & Test in Europe, p. 349. European Design and Automation Association (2014)
22. Yamamoto, D., Takenaka, M., Sakiyama, K., Torii, N.: Security evaluation of bistable ring PUFs on FPGAs using differential and linear analysis. In: Federated Conference on Computer Science and Information Systems (FedCSIS), pp. 911–918. IEEE (2014)

On the Scaling of Machine Learning Attacks on PUFs with Application to Noise Bifurcation

Johannes Tobisch and Georg T. Becker

Horst Görtz Institute for IT Security
Ruhr-University Bochum, Germany

Abstract. Physical Unclonable Functions (PUFs) are seen as a promising alternative to traditional cryptographic algorithms for secure and lightweight device authentication. However, most strong PUF proposals can be attacked using machine learning algorithms in which a precise software model of the PUF is determined. One of the most popular strong PUFs is the XOR Arbiter PUF. In this paper, we examine the machine learning resistance of the XOR Arbiter PUF by replicating the attack by Rührmaier *et al.* from CCS 2010. Using a more efficient implementation we are able to confirm the predicted exponential increase in needed number of responses for increasing XORs. However, our results show that the machine learning performance does not only depend on the PUF design and and the number of used response bits, but also on the specific PUF instance under attack. This is an important observation for machine learning attacks on PUFs in general. This instance-dependent behavior makes it difficult to determine precise lower bounds of the required number of challenge and response pairs (CRPs) and hence such numbers should always be treated with caution.

Furthermore, we examine a machine learning countermeasure called noise bifurcation that was recently introduced at HOST 2014. In noise bifurcation, the machine learning resistance of XOR Arbiter PUFs is increased at the cost of using more responses during the authentication process. However, we show that noise bifurcation has a much smaller impact on the machine learning resistance than the results from HOST 2014 suggest.

Keywords: Physical Unclonable Function, Machine Learning Attacks, Arbiter PUF, Noise-Bifurcation.

1 Introduction

Physical Unclonable Functions have gained a lot of research interest in the last years. In Physical Unclonable Functions (PUFs), the inherent process variations of a computer chip are used to give every chip a unique and unclonable identity. The first electrical PUF, the Arbiter PUF, was introduced by Gassend *et al.* in 2002 [1]. A challenge is sent to the Arbiter PUF and each PUF instance answers with a unique response. This way the Arbiter PUF can be used in a simple

© Springer International Publishing Switzerland 2015
S. Mangard, P. Schaumont (Eds.): RFIDsec 2015, LNCS 9440, pp. 17–31, 2015.
DOI: 10.1007/978-3-319-24837-0_2

authentication protocol. The secret information in a PUF are the process variations of the chips and not a digital key. In theory it should not be possible to create an exact clone of a PUF and hence it should be "unclonable". However, for existing electrical strong PUFs such as the Arbiter PUF it is possible to model the PUF in software. The parameters needed for such a software model can be approximated using machine learning techniques given enough challenge and response pairs (CRPs). Different variants of the Arbiter PUF have been proposed to increase the resistance against machine learning attacks, e.g., the Feed-Forward Arbiter PUF [2], the controlled PUF [3], the XOR Arbiter PUF [4] and the Lightweight PUF [5]. From these solutions the XOR Arbiter PUF has gained the most attention. In an XOR Arbiter PUF, the responses of several Arbiter PUFs are XORed to increase the machine learning complexity. However, while there are many papers discussing PUFs, relatively few directly examine machine learning algorithms against PUFs. The most prominent work on machine learning attacks on PUFs is the 2010 CCS paper by Rührmaier et al. [6]. They demonstrated that XOR Arbiter PUFs can be attacked using a Logistic Regression based machine learning algorithm. The initial results were based on simulated data, but follow-up work using silicon data confirmed the simulation results [7].

While their results showed that XOR Arbiter PUFs can be attacked using Logistic Regression, they also showed that the required number of responses grows exponentially with the number of XORs. Hence, in theory it would be possible to build an XOR Arbiter PUF that is resistant against logistic regression machine learning attacks if the PUF parameters are large enough. However, large PUF parameters contradict the lightweight nature of PUFs and each additional XOR increases the unreliability of the PUF. Hence, the number of XORs that can be used is limited in practice. In addition to different PUF constructs, several PUF protocols based on Arbiter PUFs have been proposed, such as the reverse fuzzy extractor protocol [8] or the Slender PUF protocol [9]. A good analysis of different PUF protocols and their weaknesses can be found in [10].

Recently, at HOST 2014, a new machine learning countermeasure called noise bifurcation was introduced by Yu et al. [11]. In noise bifurcation it is assumed that during the set-up phase a verifier builds a precise software model of the PUF that can be used to authenticate the PUF. At the cost of increasing the number of needed response bits, the machine learning resistance is increased without adding additional XORs, unreliability or area overhead, which makes this technique very interesting.

1.1   Our Contribution

In this paper we use an efficient implementation of the Logistic Regression (LR) machine learning algorithm to replicate the results presented by Rührmair et al. for PUFs with a larger number of XORs. Our results suggest that the exponential increase in CRPs needed for a LR machine learning attack claimed by Rührmair et al. holds for larger PUF instances. However, our results show that the success probability of a machine learning attack does not only depend on the PUF parameters and the number of responses. Instead, our results suggest that some PUF instances are easier to attack using machine learning than others. This makes it very difficult to make precise statements about the machine learning resistance of a PUF, since some PUF instances might be less resistant against machine learning attacks than others. This is an important observation that should be kept in mind when evaluating results of machine learning attacks.

Furthermore, we used our efficient implementation to examine the machine learning complexity of the noise bifurcation technique. Our results are in contrast to the results presented in [11]. While the machine learning complexity increases when noise bifurcation is used, we show that the increase due to noise bifurcation is significantly less than the results in [11] suggest.

2   Background

The main idea behind Arbiter PUFs is that the performance of every CMOS gate is slightly different, even if the exact same layout and mask are used. Hence, every CMOS gate will have slightly different timing characteristics. In the Arbiter PUF, these timing differences are used to generate a device-specific response for a given challenge. The idea is to apply a race signal to two identical signal paths. Which of the two paths is faster is determined only by the process variations, which are unique for every device. Both paths end in an arbiter, which generates the response by determining which of the two signals arrived first. In order to make the paths depend on a challenge, both signals are sent through a set of delay stages. Each of these delay stages can be configured to take two different paths. If the challenge bit for a delay stage equals zero, both signals are passed to their corresponding outputs. If the challenge bit of a delay stage is set to one, both signals are crossed. Figure 1 shows an example Arbiter PUF consisting of four stages. Each of the delay stages is realized in practice using two multiplexers as depicted in Figure 2.

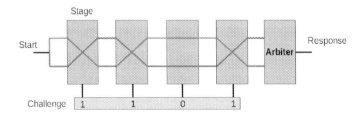

Fig. 1. Schematic of a four-stage Arbiter PUF

2.1   Modeling an Arbiter PUF

If the internal parameters of the PUF are known it is possible to build a precise software model of an Arbiter PUF. Each delay stage adds a delay to the two

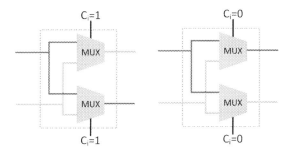

Fig. 2. Schematic of a single stage of an Arbiter PUF for both possible cases, $c_i = 1$ and $c_i = 0$

race signals. Since we are only interested in the relative delays between the top and bottom signal, we do not need the delay added to each signal but only the added delay difference between the top and bottom signal. A delay stage i can therefore be expressed using two parameters, the delay differences $\delta_{0,i}$ and $\delta_{1,i}$, corresponding to the added delay difference when the challenge bit is '0' and '1', respectively. If these two parameters are known for every delay stage, the final delay difference for every challenge can be computed. However, the fact that the paths are crossed in stages where the challenge bit is '1' needs to be considered in this computation. Switching the top and bottom signal effectively turns a positive delay difference (the top signal is faster up to this point) into a negative delay difference (the top signal becomes the bottom signal and hence the bottom signal is now faster). Hence, switching the top and bottom signal is equivalent to changing the sign of the delay difference. The delay difference ΔD_i after the ith stage can be computed recursively according to the following equation, where c_i denotes the ith challenge bit:

$$\Delta D_i = \Delta D_{i-1} \cdot (-1)^{c_i} + \delta_{c_i,i} \tag{1}$$

The final response r can be computed given the delay difference ΔD_n after the last delay stage n by evaluating the sign of ΔD_n:

$$r = \begin{cases} 1 & \text{if} \quad \Delta D_n > 0 \\ 0 & \text{if} \quad \Delta D_n < 0 \end{cases} \tag{2}$$

However, in practice there is a more efficient method to model an Arbiter PUF with only $n+1$ parameters as opposed to the $2 \cdot n$ parameters needed in this recursive method. For this, one needs to compute the delay vector $\boldsymbol{w} = (w_1, ..., w_{n+1})$:

$$\begin{aligned} w_1 &= \delta_{0,1} - \delta_{1,1} \\ w_i &= \delta_{0,i-1} + \delta_{1,i-1} + \delta_{0,i} - \delta_{1,i} \\ w_{n+1} &= \delta_{0,n} + \delta_{1,n} \end{aligned} \tag{3}$$

Additionally, the challenge vector $c = c_1, ..., c_n$ has to be transformed into the feature vector $\boldsymbol{\Phi} = (\Phi_1, .., \Phi_{n+1}) \in \{-1, 1\}^{n+1}$:

$$\Phi_i = \prod_{l=i}^{n} (-1)^{c_l} \quad \text{for} \quad 1 \leq i \leq n$$
$$\Phi_{n+1} = 1 \tag{4}$$

These transformations allow us to compute the delay difference ΔD_n with a simple scalar multiplication:

$$\Delta D_n = \boldsymbol{w}^{\mathsf{T}} \boldsymbol{\Phi} \tag{5}$$

This representation has two tremendous advantages. First, the number of model parameters is reduced to $n + 1$ and, second, the scalar multiplication is an operation that can be implemented efficiently.

2.2   XOR Arbiter PUF

As shown by Rührmair *et al.* in [6], Arbiter PUFs are susceptible to machine learning attacks. These attacks usually require a certain amount of recorded CRPs and allow the adversary to predict the responses for new challenges. To improve the resistance against these attacks, Suh and Devadas [4] proposed a design in which the results of several Arbiter PUFs are combined by XORing them. While this additional non-linearity does not completely prevent machine learning attacks, it does increase the complexity significantly. The model for an XOR Arbiter PUF builds upon the model for the single Arbiter PUF described in the previous section. Assuming the XOR Arbiter PUF has l different Arbiter PUFs which share the same challenges $\boldsymbol{\Phi}$ and each PUF has a unique delay vector $\boldsymbol{w}_j$, then the response r_{XOR} can be computed according to the following equation:

$$\Delta D_{\mathrm{XOR}} = (-1)^{l+1} \prod_{j=1}^{l} \boldsymbol{w}_j^{\mathsf{T}} \boldsymbol{\Phi} \tag{6}$$

$$r_{\mathrm{XOR}} = \begin{cases} 1 & \text{if} \quad \Delta D_{\mathrm{XOR}} > 0 \\ 0 & \text{if} \quad \Delta D_{\mathrm{XOR}} < 0 \end{cases} \tag{7}$$

Please note that the absolute value of ΔD_{XOR} has no meaning in the context of the model. Only its sign carries significant information.

It should also be noted that reliability is a valid concern for XOR Arbiter PUFs. Parameters such as the supply voltage or temperature can have negative effects on the reliability of Arbiter PUFs [12]. An XOR Arbiter PUF aggregates the unreliability of its underlying Arbiter PUFs. Thus, its reliability decreases exponentially with the number of XORs.

3   Scaling of Machine Learning Attacks on XOR Arbiter PUFs

In our machine learning attacks we used logistic regression, together with the RPROP (LR-RPROP) optimization algorithm as proposed by Rührmair et al. [6]. In [6] the largest attacked PUF design was a 5 XOR, 128 stage Arbiter PUF using 500,000 CRPs. In order to test how the machine learning attack scales for larger instances we made a speed and memory optimized implementation of the LR-RPROP algorithm. We used Matlab for the non-time-critical parts of the machine learning algorithm and MEX C functions for the time-critical operations such as computing the gradient of the cost function. Our experiments were conducted using an AMD Opteron cluster, which consists of 4 nodes, each with 64 cores and 256 GB of memory. To make use of the many cores available on the cluster we used OpenMP in the MEX C functions for parallel processing. Due to the diminishing return in our parallelization, we only used 16 cores for each run and instead started several attacks at the same time. Hence, up to 16 machine learning attacks were executed on the cluster[1].

We followed the approach in [6] and used one set of challenges and responses during the training phase of the machine learning algorithm and a second reference set of challenges and responses to determine the resulting model accuracy. For modeling the PUFs we assumed a Gaussian distribution of the PUF delay parameters δ and generated the PUF instance using the Matlab normrand() function. The challenges were also generated randomly. The required training set size grows with increased security parameters of the PUF, that is the number of stages and XORs. This, in turn, increases the runtime of the attack. The runtime of the whole attack is also influenced by the number of runs required. An unsuccessful run occurs when the RPROP algorithm gets stuck in a local minimum of the cost function. Such a run has *not converged*. In this case the RPROP algorithm needs to be restarted with a different start parameter. Each restart is denoted as a *run*. In our implementation we use randomly generated start parameters when restarts are required. Please note that in such a restart, the same challenges and responses are used.

It is well known that the probability of a run not converging decreases with larger training sets [6]. However, the question is what else effects the convergence rate. To test this, in a first experiment 1000 machine learning attacks on the same PUF instance of a 4 XOR, 64 stage Arbiter PUF with 14,000 responses were performed. A different set of challenges and responses was used in each iteration of the attack and the percentage of runs that converged, i.e., that achieved a model accuracy of more than 98%, was determined. The results can be found in Figure 3(a). The average convergence rate for this PUF instance and 14,000 responses was 0.4, i.e., in average 200 out of the 500 runs converged. If a particular set of challenges does not have an impact on the convergence rate, then the chance that of a run converging should be the same for all runs, i.e.,

---

[1] Please note that we did not have exclusive access to the cluster and hence other computations were performed in parallel to our attacks.

the runs should be independent and identically distributed (i.i.d.). We call this distribution the *ideal distribution*. As a reference, the ideal distribution for 1000 attacks with 500 runs each is depicted in Figure 3(a). There is no significant difference between the ideal distribution and the results of the machine learning attack. Hence, one can assume that, if chosen randomly, the challenge set has negligible influence on the convergence rate. In the next experiment, the same challenge set was used for all 1000 attacks but a different, randomly generated PUF instance was used in each attack. The results of this experiment can be found in Figure 3(b).

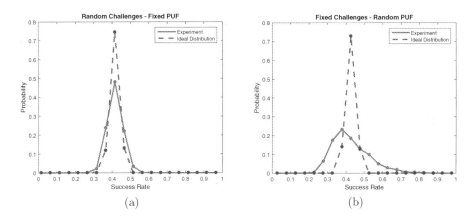

Fig. 3. Histogram of 1000 machine learning attacks on a 4 XOR, 64 stage Arbiter PUF with 500 runs each. The X-axis depicts the achieved convergence rate and the Y-axis is the probability with which such a convergence rate occurred. In (a) the same PUF instance was attacked in all 1000 attacks but a different challenge set was used each time. In (b) the same challenge set but a different PUF instance was used for each attack. The ideal distribution represents the expected distribution if each attack is independent and identically distributed (i.i.d.).

One can clearly see that the convergence rate distribution of this experiment does not follow the ideal distribution anymore. Some PUF instances have a considerably lower or higher convergence rate than any trial in the ideal distribution. Hence, one can conclude that the PUF instance has direct impact on the machine learning complexity. This is a very important result. The worst and best case convergence rates can differ significantly for different instances of the same PUF design. This observation makes it difficult to determine a precise number of needed responses for a given PUF design, since this number is not consistent across different instances of the same PUF design.

To determine the machine learning complexity for different PUF designs, we aimed to limit the influence of the different instances on the results. Therefore we chose a simulation approach which uses a new PUF instance for each run. I.e., for each try we perform 100 machine learning attacks with different challenges and PUF instance in each run. This way we limit the impact of outliers, i.e., PUF instances that are extremely hard or easy to model, on our measured success rate and estimated training time. We used a test set of 10, 000 CRPs to validate the success of the learning. We counted a prediction rate of above 98% as a success. Unsuccessful tries, which did not achieve a prediction rate of above 98% on the training set, were stopped after 800 RPROP iterations. The number of RPROP iterations had to be lowered to 400 for large instances due to limited computational resources. In Table 1, the results for attacks on XOR Arbiter PUFs with different parameters are summarized. For each tested PUF construct the optimal number of challenges and responses in terms of machine learning attack time is determined. For a smaller number of CRPs, less runs converge and hence more need to be restarted. This increases the machine learning attack time. On the other hand, if more challenges and responses are used, then a single run takes longer since more challenges need to be evaluated in each step. However, if the attacker is willing to invest more computation time, he can attack the PUF instance with much fewer challenges than the optimal number. On the right side of Table 1 one can see the minimum number of challenges for which at least one of the 200 runs converged. Please note that this number is not the smallest number for which a machine learning attack can be successful. For one, an attacker might be willing to try much more than 200 runs. Furthermore, as discussed earlier, some PUF instances are easier to model than others. Hence, it might be possible to attack some PUF instances with less challenges and responses. Nevertheless, the results are a good indication of how many challenges are enough to attack the XOR Arbiter PUF with Logistic Regression. Please also note that for large PUF instances we were not able to run as many tries as for small instances and hence the numbers become less reliable for large instances. As can be seen, we were able to attack instances of up to 9 XOR, 64 stage PUFs and 7 XOR, 128 stage PUFs, whereas previously only attacks on instances of 6 XOR, 64 stage PUFs and 5 XOR, 128 stage PUFs have been published. In order to predict the machine learning complexity for increasing XORs, we tried to empirically find an approximate factor for the increase in required CRPs. As mentioned, it is hard to define the required number of challenges to attack an XOR Arbiter PUF. To get a fair comparison, we tried to determine the number of challenges for different Arbiter PUF designs so that a convergence rate of ca. 25% was reached. The results of this experiment can be seen in Table 2. Unfortunately, for large PUF instances we were not able to determine the number of challenges needed for a 25% convergence rate very accurately due to the large computational complexity of these experiments. However, the results presented in Table 2 indicate that the relative increase in number of challenges seems to be similar for each XOR. Hence, the results suggest that the predictions performed in [6] were accurate and that the needed number of challenges and responses indeed increases exponentially with the number of XORs for a LR-RPROP machine learning attack.

Based on this and the results for large instances from Table 1, we observe that it is not possible with our implementation and hardware to break either 64 stages and 10 XORs or 128 stages and 8 XORs. Assuming a multiplicative

Table 1. The needed number of challenge and response pairs (CRPs) for different XOR Arbiter PUF designs. In the left column the optimal number of CRPs that minimizes the training time is listed while in the right column the minimum number of CRPs in which at least one of the 200 runs converged is shown. The memory consumption includes the challenge and response set and the largest temporary arrays. The training time is estimated on the basis of the average time per RPROP iteration and the convergence rate. For most designs 200 runs were performed. Instances with a lower number of runs are marked with an asterisk.

Stages	XORs	optimal CRP	training time	memory	minimal CRP	training- time	memory
	4	$42 \cdot 10^3$	2 sec	2.1 MB	$10 \cdot 10^3$	16 sec	501 KB
	5	$260 \cdot 10^3$	8 sec	15.1 MB	$45 \cdot 10^3$	2:46 min	2.6 MB
64	6	$1.40 \cdot 10^6$	1:01 min	92.6 MB	$210 \cdot 10^3$	30:24 min	13.9 MB
	7^*	$20 \cdot 10^6$	54:32 min	1.5 GB	$3 \cdot 10^6$	2:43 hrs	220 MB
	8^*	$150 \cdot 10^6$	6:31 hrs	12.3 GB	$40 \cdot 10^6$	6:31 hrs	6.2 GB
	9^*	$350 \cdot 10^6$	37:46 hrs	31.5 GB	$350 \cdot 10^6$	37:46 hrs	31.5 GB
	4	$200 \cdot 10^3$	5 sec	13.2 MB	$22 \cdot 10^3$	2:24 min	1.5 MB
128	5	$2.2 \cdot 10^6$	54 sec	163.1 MB	$325 \cdot 10^3$	12:11 min	24.1 MB
	6^*	$15 \cdot 10^6$	4:45 hrs	1.2 GB	$15 \cdot 10^6$	4:45 hrs	1.2 GB
	7^*	$400 \cdot 10^6$	66:53 hrs	36.1 GB	$400 \cdot 10^6$	66:53 hrs	36.1 GB

factor of 8 for the training set size, 64 stages and 10 XORs would require roughly $2.8 \cdot 10^9$ CRPs, which results in a memory consumption of 275 GB. Similarly, 128 stages and 8 XORs would require roughly $5.4 \cdot 10^9$ CRPs or 530 GB of memory. This is more than the 256 GB of memory that our cluster provides per node. This limitation can be circumvented by adding support for distributed memory to the implementation. Hence, a dedicated attacker can very likely also attack such a PUF.

4   Machine Learning Attacks on Noise Bifurcation

In the previous section, we highlighted the susceptibility of XOR Arbiter PUFs to machine learning attacks. In this context, it is of great interest to find ways to improve the security of XOR Arbiter PUFs without adding more XORs since each additional XOR increases the manufacturing costs and unreliability of the PUF. One such possible improvement, a noise bifurcation architecture, was introduced by Yu *et al.* at HOST 2014 [11].

The main idea behind noise bifurcation is to prevent the attacker from associating challenges and their corresponding responses. Hence, the goal is to obfuscate the responses from an attacker's point of view while a verifier should still be able to authenticate the PUF. In noise bifurcation it is assumed that the verifier has a software model of the PUF under test. To achieve this, in a set-up phase the verifier collects direct responses from each of the individual Arbiter PUFs of the used XOR Arbiter PUF. Using these direct responses, the verifier can use machine learning to derive a precise software model of each individual

Table 2. Scaling of the number of challenge and response pairs (CRPs) that are required to achieve a success rate of around 0.25

Stages	XORs	CRPs	Success Rate	CRP factor
	4	$12 \cdot 10^3$	0.29 (58/200)	-
	5	$90 \cdot 10^3$	0.28 (56/200)	7.5
64	6	$750 \cdot 10^3$	0.26 (52/200)	8.3
	7	$5 \cdot 10^6$	0.31 (10/32)	6.7
	8	$50 \cdot 10^6$	0.5 (14/28)	10
	9	$350 \cdot 10^6$	0.25 (2/8)	7
	4	$65 \cdot 10^3$	0.26 (52/200)	-
128	5	$975 \cdot 10^3$	0.26 (52/200)	15
	6	$22 \cdot 10^6$	0.25 (2/8)	22.6
	7	$400 \cdot 10^6$	0.38 (3/8)	18.2

Arbiter PUF. Once this is done, the set-up phase should be permanently disabled so that direct challenges and responses are not revealed anymore.

The authentication phase is initiated by the server who sends a master challenge C_1 to the PUF token. The PUF token generates a second random master challenge C_2 and applies C_1 and C_2 to the challenge control, which computes m PUF challenges. These m PUF challenges are then applied to the XOR Arbiter PUF to compute m response bits $y_P \in \{0,1\}^m$. However, instead of directly transmitting these m response bits to the server, the PUF device performs a *response decimation*. The m responses y_P are divided into m/d groups of d responses each. From each group one response bit is randomly selected while the others are discarded. These m/d response bits form the actual response string $y'_P \in \{0,1\}^{m/d}$ that is transmitted to the server together with C_2.

The server uses the master challenges C_1 and C_2 to compute the m corresponding challenges and uses its software model of the XOR Arbiter PUF to compute the m corresponding responses y_S. The server also sorts these responses into the m/d groups of length d as done by the PUF device. But the server does not know which response was picked for each group by the PUF device. However, if all responses within a group are identical, i.e., all bits in a group are 1 or 0, the server also knows which value the corresponding bit in y'_P should have. Hence, the server discards all groups in which the bits are not equal and only compares the groups in which all response bits are equal to the corresponding bit of y'_P.

This process is illustrated in Figure 4 for $d = 2$. If the mismatch between these bits is below a threshold, the PUF is authenticated, otherwise authentication fails. While in average 2^{d-1} of the bits in y'_p are discarded, the server can predict the remaining response bits in y'_p with 100% accuracy if the software model is 100% accurate. An attacker on the other hand has to guess which challenge was chosen by the PUF device for each group. For each response bit, the chance that the attacker guesses correctly is $1/d$. If the attacker does not guess the correct challenge, the response bit has a 50% chance of being correct. Thus, while the accuracy for the server is still 100%, the attacker has lost information and hence machine learning attacks should be harder. Please note however, that

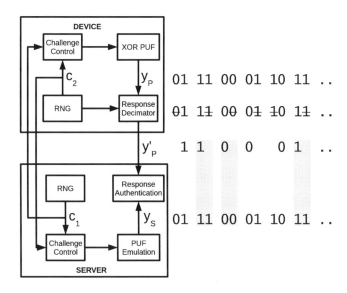

Fig. 4. Illustration of the noise bifurcation scheme with a decimation factor of $d = 2$

the downside of noise bifurcation is that a software model is needed on the server's side. This is a major drawback of the noise bifurcation countermeasure. Furthermore, the noise bifurcation scheme would not be considered a strong PUF according to the formal definition in [13] since the challenges are generated by the device as well as the server and hence the server cannot query the PUF with the same challenge twice.

4.1   Attacking Noise Bifurcation

In order to use logistic regression, one has to build a training set from the set of m challenges and the decimated responses y'_P. Yu *et al.* mention two strategies, namely single-challenge guess and full-response replication [11]. In the first approach, the attacker guesses which challenge was used for each response bit in y'_p. This results in a training set of m/p challenges. In full-response replication, all m challenges are kept and each response bit in y'_p is duplicated $d - 1$ times and associated with all challenges of the same group. We chose the full-response replication strategy for our machine learning attack, since more challenges are kept per protocol execution.

In the following we only consider the case of $d = 2$, where the m responses are divided into $m/2$ groups of size 2. We chose $d = 2$ since this is the only case for which empirical results were presented in [11]. With full-response duplication and $d = 2$, even an attacker with a 100% accurate PUF model would have a mismatch of 75% in average, since in each group of two the attacker would correctly predict one PUF response while the other PUF response would be correct with a probability of 50%. Hence, noise bifurcation with $d = 2$ should be similar to attacking an XOR Arbiter PUF which has a reliability of 75%.

4.2 Results

Yu *et al.* also used logistic regression and the RPROP algorithm to evaluate the resistance of their scheme against machine learning attacks, although some slight alteration might have been made. They used the methodology of assuming a Gaussian distribution of delay values as done in Section 3 and compared their results to those presented by Rührmair *et al.* [6]. With their implementation of the attack, which uses full-response replication, they were only able to attack small instances, i.e., 64 stages and 4 XORs. We had the chance to discuss our contradicting results with the authors of [11] and learned that for their noise bifucation implementation they used an XOR PUF whose individual Arbiter PUFs are each supplied with an independent, random challenge. This design in itself constitutes a countermeasure (cf. attacks on Lightweight PUFs [6]). Hence, their noise bifurcation implementation actually consists of two countermeasures compared to their reference XOR implementation. However, in order to understand the impact of noise bifurcation, these countermeasures need to be examined separately. In the following, we will call an XOR PUF in which the same challenge is applied to all Arbiter PUFs a *classic XOR PUF* and a PUF in which a different challenge is applied to each Arbiter PUF an *enhanced XOR PUF*.

We used our implementation of the LR-RPROP machine learning algorithm from Section 3 without any additional modifications to attack the noise bifurcation countermeasure using the full-response replication strategy. As can be seen in Table 3, we were still able to break classical XOR Arbiter PUFs with noise bifurcation for up to 6 XORs with less than two million CRPs. The number of CRPs does not grow fast enough to gain a reasonable machine-learning resistance. The bigger security gain actually came from using the enhanced XOR PUF. When noise bifurcation and enhanced XOR PUF are combined, the machine learning attack complexity increased significantly. However, we were still able to break such a design with 64 stages and 5 XORs with a reasonable number of CRPs. Attacking 6 XORs does also seem possible with an estimated training set size of $300 \cdot 10^6$ CRPs.

To determine the impact of noise bifurcation on machine learning resistance, we also attacked different PUF instances with a range of varying training set sizes, as can be seen in Table 4. A lower number of CRPs increases the training time because a lot more runs are necessary, as has been discussed in Section 3. This also negatively affects the prediction error on the test set, which can be seen in greater detail in Figure 5(b). The positive trade-off between an increased number of CRPs and a lowered test set error is clearly visible. This effect is also visible for regular XOR Arbiter PUFs without noise, albeit on a smaller scale. As depicted in Figure 5(a), an increase of the training set size is met with a decreased prediction error. However, in this case, the effect of the decrease can be neglected in regard to the very low error rate. In general, the achieved model accuracy in the noise bifurcation attack is significantly lower than in the attack on plain XOR Arbiter PUFs.

The results clearly show that noise bifurcation can be attacked using machine learning and that the increase in needed challenges and responses is not as great

Table 3. Comparison of machine learning attacks on noise bifurcation with results from Yu *et al.* [11] using 64-stage PUFs with respect to the needed number of CRPs. In this table CRPs denote the number of CRPs that are computed by an attacker in the full-response replication strategy as opposed to the number of transmitted CRPs, which are actually half that number. Columns with *classic* denote experiments in which a classic XOR PUF is used while columns with *enhanced* denote experiments in which an enhanced PUF is used. In columns with *noise* the noise bifurcation countermeasure with $d = 2$ was used, i.e., the equivalent of 25% noise was added. The reference values were originally published by Rührmair *et al.* [6] and replicated in [11].

XORs	Yu et al. Reference classic	Yu et al. enhanced + noise	Our Results classic + noise	Our Results enhanced + noise
4	12,000	$1 \cdot 10^6$	$25 \cdot 10^3$	$1 \cdot 10^6$
5	80,000	$>> 2 \cdot 10^6$	$200 \cdot 10^3$	$15 \cdot 10^6$
6	200,000	$>> 2 \cdot 10^6$	$1.5 \cdot 10^6$	-

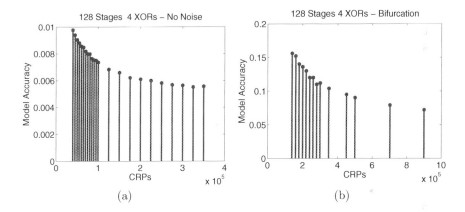

(a)   (b)

Fig. 5. The average prediction error for successfully attacked instances of a 4 XOR, 128 stages Arbiter PUF in relation to the size of the training set. In (a) the plain XOR Arbiter PUF is used, while in (b) the results for an XOR Arbiter PUF in conjunction with noise bifurcation with a decimation factor of $d = 2$ are shown.

if it is not combined with other countermeasures. Nevertheless, the machine learning complexity does increase when noise bifurcation is used compared to plain XOR Arbiter PUFs, although at a much smaller scale. If this increase in machine learning complexity is worth the overhead is an open question. It is clear, however, that noise bifurcation can only be used with PUFs that already have an extremely high machine learning resistance.

Table 4. Our results of the attack on noise bifurcation for different PUF instances and training set sizes. Target is a classical XOR PUF (same challenge for all Arbiter PUFs) with noise bifurcation.

Stages	XORs	CRPs	Mean Runs	Training Time	Test Error
64	4	$25 \cdot 10^3$	29.7	8 min	23%
64	4	$110 \cdot 10^3$	1	<2 min	13%
64	5	$200 \cdot 10^3$	33.1	22 min	14%
64	5	$340 \cdot 10^3$	2.3	<5 min	12%
64	6	$1.5 \cdot 10^6$	15.1	150 min	11%
64	6	$4 \cdot 10^6$	2.4	60 min	12%
128	4	$140 \cdot 10^3$	14.2	5 min	15%
128	4	$240 \cdot 10^3$	2.5	<5 min	12%
128	5	$2 \cdot 10^6$	11.4	144 min	8%
128	5	$4 \cdot 10^6$	2	54 min	7%

5   Conclusion

In this paper we presented a detailed analysis of Logistic Regression machine learning attacks on XOR Arbiter PUFs. We used an efficient implementation to attack larger XOR Arbiter PUFs than has been done previously. Our results show that the machine learning complexity indeed increases exponentially, as predicted by Rührmair *et al.* [6]. We showed that even a 7 XOR, 128 stages PUF can be attacked in less than 3 days using 16 cores of our cluster. Hence, only very large XOR PUF instances could withstand a dedicated attacker.

A very important result in this paper is that not only the PUF design and the number of used responses impact the machine learning algorithm. Some PUF instances are considerably more or less resistant against machine learning attacks than others. Together with the probabilistic nature of these machine learning attacks, this makes it extremely difficult to determine the minimum number of CRPs needed to attack a PUF design. If the goal is to find a strict lower bound on the number of needed CRPs, e.g., to evaluate the resistance of PUF protocols which restrict the number of responses an attacker can collect from the same PUF, it is not enough to test a few PUF instances. Even if all of the tested PUF instances cannot be attacked with a certain number of CRPs, it might be possible that there are some PUF instances that can be attacked. Furthermore, there is a clear trade-off between computational complexity and the number of CRPs. That is, the smaller the number of CRPs, the smaller the convergence rate. Hence, if an attacker is willing to use more computational power and thus to restart the machine learning algorithm more often, the attacker can be successful with a smaller number of CRPs. Together with the fact that the convergence rate also depends on the PUF instance and not only on the design, this makes it extremely difficult to define a minimum number of CRPs an attacker needs to collect for a successful machine learning attack.

Last but not least we showed in this paper that the impact of the recently introduced noise bifurcation countermeasure is significantly smaller than claimed. We could attack a classical 5 XOR, 128 stage Arbiter PUF using 2 million challenges, which corresponds to 1 million transmitted responses in the protocol, in less than three hours. Considering that the number of responses transmitted per protocol execution increases by a factor of 2^{d-1}, it is questionable if this increase in machine learning resistance is worth the introduced overhead. The method does not seem to be suited to turn a PUF design that is hard to attack using machine learning into a design that is computationally infeasible to attack.

References

1. Gassend, B., Clarke, D., van Dijk, M., Devadas, S.: Silicon physical random functions. In: Proceedings of the 9th ACM Conference on Computer and Communications Security, CCS 2002, pp. 148–160. ACM, New York (2002)
2. Lee, J.W., Lim, D., Gassend, B., Suh, G.E., van Dijk, M., Devadas, S.: A technique to build a secret key in integrated circuits for identification and authentication applications. In: 2004 Symposium on VLSI Circuits, Digest of Technical Papers, pp. 176–179, June 2004
3. Gassend, B., Clarke, D., van Dijk, M., Devadas, S.: Controlled physical random functions. In: Proceedings of the 18th Annual Computer Security Applications Conference 2002, pp. 149–160 (2002)
4. Suh, G.E., Devadas, S.: Physical unclonable functions for device authentication and secret key generation. In: 44th ACM/IEEE Design Automation Conference, DAC 2007, pp. 9–14, June 2007
5. Majzoobi, M., Koushanfar, F., Potkonjak, M.: Lightweight secure PUFs. In: Proceedings of the 2008 IEEE/ACM International Conference on Computer-Aided Design, ICCAD 2008, pp. 670–673. IEEE Press, Piscataway (2008)
6. Rührmair, U., Sehnke, F., Sölter, J., Dror, G., Devadas, S., Schmidhuber, J.: Modeling attacks on physical unclonable functions. In: Proceedings of the 17th ACM Conference on Computer and Communications Security, CCS 2010, pp. 237–249. ACM, New York (2010)
7. Rührmair, U., Sölter, J., Sehnke, F., Xu, X., Mahmoud, A., Stoyanova, V., Dror, G., Schmidhuber, J., Burleson, W., Devadas, S.: PUF Modeling Attacks on Simulated and Silicon Data. IEEE Transactions on Information Forensics and Security 8(11), 1876–1891 (2013)
8. Van Herrewege, A., Katzenbeisser, S., Maes, R., Peeters, R., Sadeghi, A.-R., Verbauwhede, I., Wachsmann, C.: Reverse fuzzy extractors: enabling lightweight mutual authentication for PUF-enabled RFIDs. In: Keromytis, A.D. (ed.) FC 2012. LNCS, vol. 7397, pp. 374–389. Springer, Heidelberg (2012)
9. Majzoobi, M., Rostami, M., Koushanfar, F., Wallach, D.S., Devadas, S.: Slender PUF protocol: a lightweight, robust, and secure authentication by substring matching. In: 2012 IEEE Symposium on Security and Privacy Workshops (SPW), pp. 33–44, May 2012
10. Delvaux, J., Gu, D., Schellekens, D., Verbauwhede, I.: Secure lightweight entity authentication with strong PUFs: mission impossible? In: Batina, L., Robshaw, M. (eds.) CHES 2014. LNCS, vol. 8731, pp. 451–475. Springer, Heidelberg (2014)
11. Yu, M.-D., Verbauwhede, I., Devadas, S., M'Raïhi, D.: A Noise bifurcation architecture for linear additive physical functions. In: IEEE International Symposium on Hardware-Oriented Security and Trust (HOST 2014), pp. 124–129 (2014)
12. Gassend, B., Lim, D., Clarke, D., van Dijk, M., Devadas, S.: Identification and Authentication of Integrated Circuits: Research Articles. Concurr. Comput.: Pract. Exper. 16(11), 1077–1098 (2004)
13. Armknecht, F., Maes, R., Sadeghi, A., Standaert, F.-X., Wachsmann, C.: A Formalization of the security features of physical functions. In: 2011 IEEE Symposium on Security and Privacy (SP), pp. 397–412, May 2011

ReSC: RFID-Enabled Supply Chain Management and Traceability for Network Devices

Kun Yang, Domenic Forte, and Mark Tehranipoor

ECE Dept., University of Connecticut, USA
{kuy12001,forte,tehrani}@engr.uconn.edu

Abstract. The supply chains of today are much more complex, global, and difficult to manage than ever before. Disappearance/theft of authentic goods and appearance of counterfeit (cloned, forged, etc.) goods are two major challenges to
address. As a result, owners, manufacturers, distributors, etc. are becoming more
interested in approaches that facilitate greater visibility and enable traceability
of products as they move through the supply chain. One promising approach is
based on Radio-Frequency Identification (RFID) where each product is equipped
with a unique RFID tag that can be read in a contactless fashion to track the move-
ment of products. However, existing RFID tags are simply "wireless barcodes"
that are susceptible to split attacks (i.e., separating tag from product, swapping
tags, etc.) and can easily be stolen or cloned. In this paper, we propose an RFID-
enabled Supply Chain (ReSC) solution specific to network devices (i.e., routers,
modems, set-top boxes, video game consoles, home security devices, etc.) that
addresses the security and management issues of their entire supply chain. By
combining two techniques: one-to-one mapping between tag identity and control
chip identity, and unique tag trace which records tag history information, ReSC is
resistant to counterfeit injection, product theft, and illegal network service (e.g.,
Internet, TV signals, online games, etc.) access. Simulations and experimental
results based on a printed circuit board (PCB) prototype demonstrate the effectiveness of ReSC.

Keywords: Radio-Frequency Identification (RFID), Supply Chain Management,
Traceability, Network Device.

1 Introduction

The security and management issues of today's supply chains have raised serious concerns recently for industry, governments, and consumers. Two major challenges include
disappearance/theft of authentic goods and appearance of counterfeit (cloned, forged,
etc.) goods. Both of these impact the profit and reputations of the owners, manufacturers, and distributors. In 2012, 117 electronic thefts were reported in the US with the
average loss of $382,500 per theft incident [12]. One example is the infamous Cisco
router theft problem [30, 38]. In addition, more than 12 million counterfeit parts were
reported from 2007 to 2012 [6], and this number is on the rise [26]. In most cases, crim-
inals take the risk of theft and/or counterfeiting for nothing more than the economic
gain (i.e., resale values of stolen products, price discrepancy between genuine and fake
goods, etc.). Such criminal activities however could later become aid in tampering and

© Springer International Publishing Switzerland 2015
S. Mangard, P. Schaumont (Eds.): RFIDsec 2015, LNCS 9440, pp. 32–49, 2015.
DOI: 10.1007/978-3-319-24837-0_3

cause of other major security concerns. For example, hackers could invade the internal network of a company if they obtain the branch router using unlawful means [38], confidential data (e.g., trade secrets) could be disclosed if a counterfeit (tampered) device is installed in the information management system of a company, and so forth. Other than theft of product, theft of service draws a great deal of attention from network service providers. For instance, Comcast, AT&T, Charter, Cox, etc. want to authenticate their devices before providing service to customers. By enhancing visibility and traceability of such devices across the entire supply chain, we may be able to overcome and mitigate many of these issues before they have even more significant consequences.

Further, the concept of the Internet of Things (IoTs) has attracted more and more attention over the past few years. The IoTs correspond to the interconnection of uniquely identifiable embedded computing devices within the existing Internet infrastructure. Cisco's Internet Business Solutions Group (IBSG) predicts there will be 25 billion devices connected to the Internet by 2015 and 50 billion by 2020 [11]. Compared with stand-alone devices, the security and management issues of networked devices have raised more concerns, not only because of the rise of the number of networked devices, but also because of the mutual dependence between networked devices. For example, if one device in a network system is tampered, the attacker could send malicious messages to its neighboring devices to obtain secret information [38].

Barcodes have traditionally been used to track and trace commodities in the supply chain [35]. Quick response (QR) codes which can include much more information have also been put into use [19]. However, both barcodes and QR codes are very easy to damage, remove, replace, forge or clone because of visibility of identity information and low technical barrier. Other shortcomings (i.e., requirement of individual scanning, need of direct line-of-sight and close proximity to reader, lack of write capability once printed, etc.) severely impact their access efficiency, thus limiting their utility. More recently, RFID technologies have been proposed to enhance the management of supply chains [10, 16]. Wal-Mart and the United States Department of Defense have published requirements that their vendors place RFID tags on all shipments to improve supply chain management. Compared to barcodes and QR codes, an RFID-based scheme has much more attractive features – possess write capability, support batch scanning, exist in very small factors, and do not require direct line-of-sight for access – making them easier to be embedded in many different products and enable automatic track-and-trace. However, existing RFID tags are simply "wireless barcodes" which lack inherent connection to the objects they are attached to. As a result, they are vulnerable to split attacks (i.e., separating tag from product, swapping tags, etc.).

In this paper, we present an RFID-enabled Supply Chain (ReSC) solution that addresses the security and management issues of network devices in the supply chain. The major features of ReSC and our main contributions are as follows:

– Attack models against RFID-enabled supply chain systems are defined and analyzed. The corresponding mitigation measures have been integrated into the ReSC system.
– By binding the RFID tag and the identified network device together with a one-to-one mapping between tag identity and control chip (i.e., the host processor that is responsible for major functions and coordination between different components on

the board) identity, ReSC is resistant to split attacks. Mismatch between tag and control chip identities will be detected.

– When the network device is distributed in the supply chain, a unique tag trace composed of signatures of readers on the distribution path of that device will be generated and stored in the tag memory. The tag trace is unique for each device, digitally signed by each reader on the tag's path, and thus is resistant to duplication by untrusted entities involved in the supply chain. When the network device is installed at the end-user, service requests will be rejected if the tag trace stored in the tag memory shows that the device has not passed through the valid supply chain. ReSC differs from other supply chain solutions in that: (i) the tag trace is bound to the device and cannot be duplicated to be used for another device; (ii) readers cannot repudiate their signatures; and (iii) ReSC is the first RFID-assisted scheme to prevent fake or stolen products from being used by end-users.

– We implement major functions of ReSC system in a PCB prototype to verify that the system as a whole operates within the pre-defined specification. Our approach is also cost effective in that it takes advantage of existing parts on present network devices and requires only a few extra very low-cost components.

The rest of this paper is organized as follows: Section 2 presents previous work related to ReSC. Section 3 describes the supply chain features specific to network devices, attack models against RFID-enabled supply chain systems, and the hardware architecture of ReSC system. Section 4 elaborates on our proposed authentication procedures (i.e., tag matching with device and valid tag trace) in detail. Section 5 presents the implementation of ReSC prototype. In Section 6, we evaluate ReSC system in terms of performance and security. Finally, we conclude in Section 8.

2   Related Work

Two areas of prior work have particular relevance to our study: digital integrated circuit (IC) identification/authentication and RFID-enabled supply chain management.

Physical Unclonable Functions: Among different digital IC identification/authentication approaches, physical unclonable functions (PUFs) are widely considered to be one of the most promising methods [31,37]. PUFs are more secure than conventional identity storage since they exploit the uncontrollable process variations associated with modern IC fabrication [13]. An ideal PUF produces a unique and reliable response when issued a challenge. A variety of different types of PUFs have been proposed and implemented over the past decade, including arbiter PUF [37], ring oscillator (RO) PUF [28], SRAM PUF [17], butterfly PUF [23], etc. SRAM PUF has become popular due to its convenience of using commonly available and integrated SRAM rather than include a dedicated primitive in the circuit. Comparative analysis of SRAM memories manufactured by different vendors using different technology nodes was conducted by authors in [36] and demonstrated that all of the tested SRAMs can be used as PUFs. Like other PUFs, SRAM PUF is also susceptible to reliability issues. Error Correcting Code (ECC) [8] that corrects the unreliable output bits is widely used to address the reliability issues of SRAM PUF. Neighborhood analysis based bit selection algorithms [18,39] improve the reliability of SRAM PUF by exploring the selection of stable bits through enrollment under different conditions (temperature, voltage, and aging) and exploiting interactions between neighboring SRAM cells. A soft decision helper data algorithm [27] was also presented to deal with the fuzziness of SRAM PUF's responses.

RFID-Enabled Supply Chain Management: RFID technologies have been widely explored to enhance visibility and enable traceability in the supply chain over the past decade [1, 3, 14, 29]. Unidirectional key distribution across time and space [22] was proposed to address the problem of key management in RFID systems. The authors in [24, 41, 42] proposed a tailing mechanism to detect counterfeit goods with cloned or forged tags by writing random numbers to tags as they go through the supply chain and verifying tail (composed of random numbers) divergence between authentic and cloned or forged tags over time. However, this approach has the following limitations: (i) the tags lack inherent connection to the objects they are attached to and thus are vulnerable to split attacks; (ii) the tag trace has no necessary relation to the tag itself and thus is vulnerable to duplication attack (i.e., duplicating tag trace); (iii) readers have to be connected to the database to perform rule verification and clone detection; (iv) this approach does not consider different types of potential attacks (i.e., eavesdropping, denial-of-service attack, replay attack, etc.); and (v) this approach cannot prevent counterfeit or stolen products from being used by end-users.

By combining the features of these two techniques, we propose a new type of supply chain system specific to network devices that addresses most security and management issues of the supply chain.

3   ReSC Framework

Disappearance/theft of authentic goods and appearance of counterfeit (cloned, forged, etc.) goods frequently occur in the global electronics component and system supply chain. There is no effective approach to enhance product traceability, enable counterfeit detection, and prevent theft of product and service simultaneously with low cost. ReSC is the *first* supply chain system specific to network devices that enables product track-and-trace, counterfeit detection, and theft prevention. To do so, it makes use of *offline* and *online* modes (more details below).

3.1   Supply Chain with Transition Points

Figure 1(a) demonstrates our proposed RFID approach aimed at addressing different challenges/issues in the supply chain for network devices. Our proposed RFID system for network devices would consist of the following: (i) a front-end composed of RFID tags and readers; (ii) network devices equipped with RFID tags that include read-only tag identities (*tagIDs*) stored in the locked memories; (iii) locations associated with each reader; (iv) a back-end consisting of a centralized database (DB) that stores information (e.g., tag identities, control chip identities, tag traces, etc.) and authenticates network devices. We divide the supply chain for network devices into three states (S1, S2, and S3) and there are three possible state transitions (T1, T2, and T3) between states. Figure 1(b) illustrates the state transition graph of our proposed scheme.

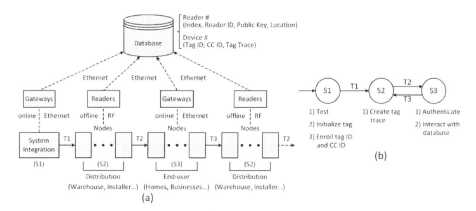

Fig. 1. (a) Supply chain with transition points and (b) State transition graph

S1. System Integration. This state is essentially the start of the network device's life and occurs in a trusted environment. The assumption that manufacturers of RFID tags or system integrators of RFID-enabled devices can be trusted is ubiquitous and has been explicitly or implicitly stated in literature [7, 25, 40]. Functional and reliability testing will be performed to ensure both hardware and software work as expected. Initialization steps are also finished and would include extracting tag identities (*tagIDs*) and control chip identities (*CC IDs*) from RFID tags and control chips separately and storing them in the centralized database. All this information will be used later to track network devices as they move through the supply chain and verify their identities. Network devices would eventually move into the next states which are untrusted (susceptible to attacks). We refer to this as transition T1.

S2. Distribution. In this state, network devices are stored in inventories and transported between supply houses, distributors, retailers, and installers. In an RFID-enabled supply chain, network devices can be tracked using an *offline* (unplugged and disconnected from the network) mode. Tags are powered by the readers and communicate their authentication information (more in Section 4). RFID readers on the distribution path will jointly create a unique tag trace that is stored in the tag memory. When the RFID readers are connected to the network, they can store backups of the current tag trace in the database. Note that each reader can process many network devices almost at the same time [34]. To address the shortcomings of existing protocols as mentioned in Section 2, a more secure and practical tag trace enrollment and validation procedure will be presented in Section 4. Since the communication with RFID tag is done only by readers in the distribution and the devices are unplugged, we refer to this as *offline* mode.

S3. End-User. Eventually, network devices will be installed in the homes or businesses of end-users. We refer to this as transition T2. In this state, the network device will interact over encrypted Ethernet with the centralized database. Since this occurs when the network device is powered in the home or business and operates over cable or wireless WiFi, we refer to this as *online* mode. Authentication procedures (i.e., verification of the matching between tag and device, and validating tag trace) will be performed before network service is available. In more general supply chains, the track-and-trace process would end here. However, in the supply chain for many network devices, the process should continue for several reasons. First, most network devices such as set-top boxes and routers will eventually be returned to network service providers and may re-enter the distribution state. We would refer to this as transition T3 in our notation. Second, some network devices (e.g., stolen devices, expensive devices whose tags have been replaced with tags of much cheaper devices, etc.) may fail the authentication process and have to be recalled. Hence, an improved supply chain management and traceability system would include features to handle tracking at the edges and from edges back to distribution.

3.2 Attack Models

In order to evaluate the security of an RFID-enabled supply chain system, we define some practical attacks in this subsection.

1. Cloning Tag ID: Rogue elements place cloned tags on fake products so as to escape inspection of RFID-based counterfeit detection systems. One main feature of this type of attack is that more than one device will carry tags with exactly the same identity, although those tag identities are indeed recorded in the centralized database.

2. Duplicating Tag Trace: Untrusted entities in the supply chain (e.g., installers) duplicate valid tag traces and store the copies in the tag memories of stolen products so as to spoof authentication of server when the network devices are installed in the homes or businesses of end-users. One main feature of this type of attack is that more than one device will carry tags with exactly the same trace.

3. Denial-of-service Attack: Malicious readers overwrite the tag memory so that the compromised tag cannot authenticate itself to the authorized readers on its distribution path.

4. Replay Attack: Rogue elements eavesdrop on the communication between the authorized reader and the legal tag, intercept the authentication code sent by the legal tag, and replay the authentication code to the authorized reader to obtain copies of reader updates.

5. Man-in-the-middle Attack: Rogue elements intercept the authentication code sent by the legal tag to the authorized reader, change the tag identity contained in the authentication code to any other wanted tag identity, and send the forged authentication code to the authorized reader to obtain reader update associated with that specific tag identity.

3.3 ReSC Hardware Architecture and Constraints

Figure 2 illustrates the hardware architecture of ReSC, including the entities involved and their connections. Central to our approach are two new features: i) the RFID tag and the control chip are bound together with a one-to-one mapping to prevent potential split attacks; ii) tag identity, control chip identity, and tag trace can be sent to the database for authentication over encrypted Ethernet. The constraints of the entities are described as follows:

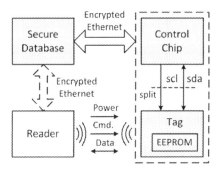

Fig. 2. ReSC hardware architecture

Database: One centralized database stores reader information (i.e., index, identity, public key, location, etc.), tag information (i.e., identity, tag trace, etc.), and device information (i.e., control chip identity, one-to-one mapping between tag and device, etc.). Database can authenticate readers based on their secret identities (would not be transmitted in plaintext). Database can also authenticate devices based on authentication procedures to be discussed in Section 4. We assume that the database could inform the readers of their preceding readers for each tag in the supply chain, which is also assumed in other literature [24,41,42]. This is a fair assumption especially for the supply chain of network devices since its topology is relatively fixed and there are usually limited number of owners, manufacturers, and distributors involved.

RFID Reader: Readers are dispersed at different stages of the supply chain. Readers can jointly create a unique tag trace and store that trace in the tag memory in a secure fashion. To be specific, readers at different locations will write their own signatures (protected by cryptographic hash functions) to the tag memory to make up a unique tag trace. If necessary, the RFID reader could communicate with the database via Ethernet channel to store or retrieve the backup of tag trace. It is a fair and popular assumption that the readers are networked in the RFID-based supply chain solutions [7,24,40]. We assume the communication between database and readers is secure and protected by a strong protocol (e.g., transport layer security (TLS) protocol [2,9]).

RFID Tag: Every tag has a tag memory storing tag identity and tag trace. The size of tag memory is typically several kilo bits. Generally speaking, low-cost RFID tags are not equipped to resist physical tampering. The RFID tag communicates with the RFID reader via RF channel.

Control Chip: The start-up signature (SRAM PUF) of embedded SRAM inside the control chip will be captured and used as its identity. Each SRAM cell consists of two cross-coupled CMOS inverters and two access transistors. Depending on the mismatch between the transistors, each SRAM cell produces a zero or a one after powering up the circuit. Larger mismatch leads to a more stable zero/one output for some SRAM cells. A number of such stable SRAM cells define the output of the SRAM PUF. The SRAM PUF will be used to authenticate the control chip when the network device is installed at the end-user. The control chip communicates with the RFID tag via I2C channel [32] on board. The connection between the RFID tag and the control chip allows the control chip to read out tag trace and transmit the trace to the database for authentication in *online* mode (plugged and connected to the network). We also assume the communication between database and network devices is secure and protected by a strong protocol (e.g., transport layer security (TLS) protocol [2,9]).

4   Authentication

Overall, the authentication procedure of ReSC can be split into two phases: (i) verification of the matching between the tag identity (*tagID*) and the control chip identity (*CC ID*); and (ii) verification of the integrity of tag trace to make sure that the network device has passed through the valid supply chain before arriving at the end-user.

4.1   ReSC I: Tag Matching with Device

At the system integration stage, the control chip identity (*CC ID*) will be generated from the start-up signature (SRAM PUF) of embedded SRAM inside the control chip. The control chip identity together with the tag identity will compose a 2-tuple (*CC ID*, *tagID*) and is stored in the centralized database in *online* mode for future device authentication. The communication between the control chip and the database is assumed protected by cryptographic protocols such as TLS [9]. Potential split attacks can be detected since we bind the RFID tag and the network device together with the one-to-one mapping between the tag identity and the control chip identity. Even if the attacker could probe the I2C channel [32], intercept the packets being transmitted between the tag and the control chip, and program them into the cloned tag, we can still detect this type of eavesdropping since the tag identity stored in the tag memory only matches one specific control chip identity (which is never communicated in plaintext). The tag memory includes two parts: one unique, read-only tag identity and one unique tag trace composed of the signatures of readers on the distribution path of that tag.

4.2   ReSC II: Valid Tag Trace

We define a tag trace as valid when it carries all the necessary signatures of authorized readers on its distribution path. When the network device is distributed in the supply chain, the RFID readers dispersed at different locations will join up to compose a unique tag trace and store that trace in the tag memory. The contents of tag memory include a static read-only tag identity and a unique tag trace composed of the signatures of readers on the tag's distribution path. We assume that the system integrator can be trusted and will perform the tag initialization (i.e., assigning an initial signature ($SIGN_0$)). We also assume that each reader (R_i) knows the public key (pk_{i-1}) of the reader (R_{i-1}) at the previous stage. This is a fair assumption since all the public keys of readers could be uploaded to the cloud and shared among them. The centralized database can also look up the public key (pk_i) of each reader (R_i) using the index ($Index_i$) of that reader. Public key cryptography based digital signature technique (e.g., Merkle signatures [5], Rabin signatures [33], GMR signatures [15], etc.) is used to generate reader's signature. Figure 3 illustrates our proposed light-weight RFID protocol with cyclic redundancy check

(CRC) and XORing with random numbers omitted for brevity of expression. The entire communication flow between RFID reader and RFID tag can be divided into the following three steps:

Step 1: When the network device arrives at the next intermediate stage, the reader R_i at that stage will first issue a *Query* command to the tag.

Step 2: After receiving the *Query* command, the tag will reply with its identity (*tagID*) and current authentication code

$$SIGN_{i-1} = H_{sk_{i-1}}(tagID||Index_{i-1}||timestamp_{i-1}) \tag{1}$$

where $Index_{i-1}$ is the index associated with the $(i-1)_{th}$ reader, $timestamp_{i-1}$ denotes the specific time when reader R_{i-1} updated the tag, $||$ indicates the concatenation operation, and $H_{sk_{i-1}}(X)$ indicates encrypted hash value of input argument X using sk_{i-1} as private key of reader R_{i-1}. Note that $timestamp_{i-1}$ and $Index_{i-1}$ which are contained in the tag's memory will also be sent to verify the hash in the next step.

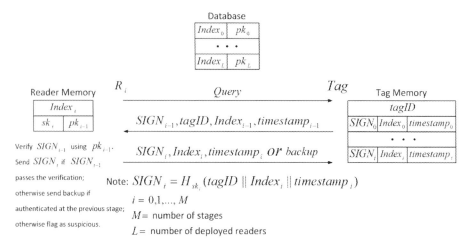

Fig. 3. Light-weight RFID protocol

Step 3: After receiving the quad ($SIGN_{i-1}$, $tagID$, $Index_{i-1}$, $timestamp_{i-1}$), the reader R_i will decrypt $SIGN_{i-1}$ with the public key pk_{i-1} of reader R_{i-1}, and recover the hash value of $tagID||Index_{i-1}||timestamp_{i-1}$. Simultaneously, the reader R_i will generate the hash value of $tagID||Index_{i-1}||timestamp_{i-1}$ locally. By comparing these two hash values, the reader R_i can authenticate the tag. If these two match, the reader R_i will generate its own signature $SIGN_i$ by encrypting the hash value of $tagID||Index_i||timestamp_i$ with its private key sk_i and send the triple ($SIGN_i$, $Index_i$, $timestamp_i$) to the tag to update the tag trace. However, if the old signature fails the verification or there is no old signature stored in the tag memory, the tag may be impersonated or compromised by a rogue reader. The reader R_i will then communicate with the centralized database to determine whether the tag with that specific tag identity has been authenticated at the previous stage. If yes, the reader R_i will extract backup from the centralized database and send the backup to the tag to recover the compromised tag memory contents; otherwise, the reader R_i will simply flag that device as suspicious and report an event to the centralized database. Note that if the old signature passes the verification, the reader R_i does not need to communicate with the centralized database in real-time. Instead, the reader R_i can let the centralized database know that the tag carrying one specific tag identity has passed its authentication when the reader is not busy. The reader signature update process will utilize a wraparound fashion and the tag memory will be regarded as a circular buffer storing 10 reader signatures, which can prevent the tag memory from overflowing.

The above process of updating tag traces has several useful features. The *timestamp* can prevent attackers from replaying a proper supply chain trace in a stolen device's tag. It can also be useful for forensics. For example, if a rogue employee uses an authorized reader to update a stolen device, we can catch him or her since the *timestamp* embedded in the reader's signature could indicate who is on duty at that time. The reader R_i can read out the incomplete tag trace from the tag memory and send the tag identity (*tagID*) associated with its trace to the centralized database for backup. The reader R_i can also retrieve the backup of tag trace from the centralized database to recover the compromised tag trace in the tag memory.

When the network device is installed at the end-user, the control chip will read out the chain of readers' signatures from the tag memory and transfer it to the centralized database for validation in *online* mode. The database has stored the correct supply chain trace (associated with each tag). It will use the index $Index_i$ of each reader to look up its public key pk_i and then validate the signature $SIGN_i$ using that public key pk_i. If the chain of readers' signatures is incomplete or does not match the expected trace (stored in the database), the service request from the suspicious network device will be rejected by the server.

4.3 Authentication at the End-User

The authentication at the end-user involves the following two steps: (i) the control chip authenticates itself to the centralized database based on its identity; and (ii) the control chip reads out the contents of tag memory (i.e., tag identity and tag trace), encrypts them, and transmits them to the centralized database for validation. Both steps are performed in *online* mode. This second step can ensure not only that the device has passed through the legal supply chain (as described above) but also that the tag is genuine and bound to that specific device. Service is only available to the end-user after all the authentication procedures (i.e., tag matching with device, valid tag trace including all the necessary signatures of authorized readers on the distribution path, etc.) are passed. This shall prevent stolen and/or counterfeit products from being used; making them worthless. The authentication procedures can also be performed in retail stores before purchase.

5 Implementation

A PCB prototype has been designed and fabricated to prove the concept of ReSC. In this section, we will briefly introduce the implementation of ReSC prototype. First, we introduce the ICs contained on ReSC prototype and the connections between them. Next, we discuss the PCB slot antenna design to ensure that: (i) it can generate enough bandwidth at the operating frequency specified by the EPC C1G2 standard [21] to guarantee proper communication between the RFID reader and tag; (ii) it can transfer enough power from the RFID reader's RF waves to finish read/write operations towards the RFID tag.

5.1   ICs and Connections between Them

Texas Instruments' (TI's) microcontroller (MCU) MSP430F247 is used as the control chip in the ReSC prototype. We choose one of TI's MSP430 family of microcontrollers because of their popularity, small footprint area, and low power consumption. ReSC itself does not have any special requirements towards the control chip being used so long as it has a large enough embedded SRAM and supports communication with RFID tag. The start-up signature of $4KB$ SRAM embedded inside MSP430F247 is utilized to generate control chip identity. NXP Semiconductors' UCODE I2C SL3S4021 is used as the RFID tag in the ReSC prototype. A 96-bit tag identity ($tagID$) including a 48-bit unique serial number is used to uniquely identify each tag. It is stored in the locked memory and cannot be tampered by the attacker. The 3328-bit user memory is used to store tag trace. I2C channel (serial clock and serial data) [32] is used to connect the control chip and the RFID tag. TI's TPS77601 is used as the voltage regulator to provide stable 3.3V power supply to the control chip and RFID tag in *online* mode. π section filters composed of capacitors and ferrite beads are used to suppress power supply noise in the ReSC prototype. GMR signature scheme [15] is used to generate reader's signature. We assign 20 *bits* for each index which could mark 1 *million* readers. We assign 40 *bits* for each timestamp in the format of yymmddhhmm (i.e., year:month:day:hour:minute). The bit-width of signature depends on the selected signature scheme. For GMR signatures, 10 readers can be visited before the tag's memory is full. To overcome this limitation, the reader signature update process will utilize a wraparound fashion and the tag memory will be regarded as a circular buffer storing 10 reader signatures. Figure 4(a) shows the PCB prototype layout.

5.2   PCB Antenna Design

For the sake of reducing cost and saving assembly space, a PCB slot antenna instead of a discrete antenna component is used in the ReSC prototype. The impedance of the PCB antenna should be matched conjugately to the input impedance of RFID tag chip in order to eliminate the need for matching network and sustain the power supply for RFID tag. Figure 4(b) shows our PCB antenna design and its return loss obtained using the simulation tool Ansoft HFSS 14.0. The PCB antenna arms should be symmetrical to achieve prime performance. FR4 is the dielectric material employed and its thickness is set to 0.5mm. The PCB antenna impedance is designed to be $12.7 + j199 Ohm$ in our prototype. The resonance frequency and $-10dB$ bandwidth are $910MHz$ and $522MHz$ respectively. Simulation results demonstrate that the PCB slot antenna is sufficient to provide enough $-10dB$ bandwidth at the operating frequency. Further, at the wave valley point ($910MHz$) the vast majority of input power is absorbed by the antenna and

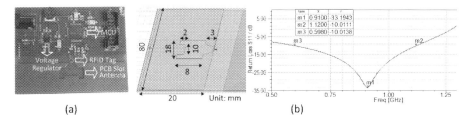

Fig. 4. (a) PCB prototype layout and (b) PCB antenna design and its return loss

only a tiny part is reflected back. Therefore, there will be enough power provided to the tag when the ReSC system is in *offline* mode.

6   Evaluation

In this section, we evaluate the performance and security of ReSC via experiments and theoretical analysis. Experimental results are based on a PCB prototype implementation. Afterwards, we compare ReSC with prior work in terms of overhead and security.

6.1   Performance Evaluation

In this subsection, we evaluate the performance of ReSC in two phases (ReSC I and ReSC II as discussed in Section 4). For ReSC I, we verify the quality of control chip identity (SRAM PUF) in terms of uniqueness. Since tag identity is nothing more than a bitstream stored in the read-only memory block, the issue of uniqueness will not occur and thus there is no need to verify its quality. Discussion on reliability issue is out of the scope of this paper. For ReSC II, we evaluate the performance of ReSC in terms of RF communication efficiency.

Performance of ReSC I.   The essence of ReSC I is the matching between tag identity and control chip identity. Since tag identity is not faced with the issue of uniqueness, we only consider the quality of control chip identity here. The start-up signature (SRAM PUF) of embedded SRAM inside the control chip is used as its identity. Two bit selection algorithms, random bit selection and neighborhood analysis based bit selection [18,39], are respectively employed to pick up the candidate bits for control chip identity from all the stable bits at enrollment phase.

Four prototype boards are employed to analyze the uniqueness of control chip identity. For each board, the entire $4KB$ embedded SRAM is divided into 9 blocks. Each block has the same size (416 *bytes*) and will be used to work as a 128-*bit* identity. Thus, 36 128-*bit* identities will be generated to evaluate the uniqueness of control chip identity. Figure 5 illustrates the hamming distance (HD) distributions of control chip identities based on random bit selection and neighborhood analysis based bit selection respectively. Hamming distance distributions based on both bit selection algorithms appear Gaussian. Both distributions pass the Chi-square goodness-of-fit test at the 5% significance level. The mean values of hamming distances for both bit selection algorithms

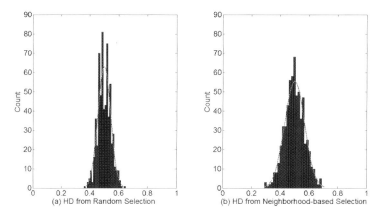

(a) HD from Random Selection   (b) HD from Neighborhood-based Selection

Fig. 5. Hamming distance distributions of control chip identities

are 63.8317 (49.87%) and 63.8381 (49.87%) respectively. Both average inter-die HDs are quite close to the ideal value 64 (50%) out of 128. Experimental results demonstrate that the embedded SRAM PUF is effective at identifying boards.

Performance of ReSC II. The essence of ReSC II is the composition process of unique tag trace based on the signatures of readers at different locations. We evaluate the RF communication efficiency by performing tag access using an actual RFID reader to ensure that the tags can be updated promptly in the supply chain and the tag trace composition process can function correctly. Our experimental platform is set up as shown in Figure 6(a). Figure 6(b) shows the RF communication efficiency. When the reading distance is smaller than 4 meters, the reading rate is larger than $50 reads/sec$, which indicates that the RFID reader can finish reading 50 boards per second. No bit error occurs throughout our experiments. Experimental results demonstrate that the RF communication between the RFID reader and the RFID tag is effective and efficient for implementing track-and-trace in the supply chain.

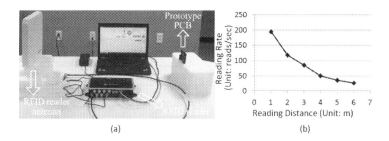

(a)   (b)

Fig. 6. (a) Experimental setup for evaluating RF performance and (b) RF communication efficiency

6.2   Security Evaluation

In addition to the attack models discussed in Section 3.2, several other attacks/risks are also considered in this subsection to perform a comprehensive security evaluation. Table 1 lists the potential system-level attacks/risks associated with general RFID-based systems (including ReSC) and corresponding mitigation methods. We divide all the potential attacks/risks into five categories in terms of attack targets and discuss them respectively. We don't consider sophisticated physical attacks [20] here.

RFID Tag: By binding the RFID tag and the identified network device together with a one-to-one mapping between tag identity (*tagID*) and control chip identity (*CC ID*), cloning tag ID can be detected and service request will be rejected by the server when the cloned network device is installed at the end-user. Since the tag trace of ReSC depends on both reader information (i.e., reader's index and private key), tag information (i.e., tag identity), and the specific time (i.e., *timestamp*) when the tag trace is updated, it is unique for each device and thus is resistant to duplication attack (duplicating tag trace by untrusted entities involved in the supply chain). When a rogue employee uses an authorized reader to update a stolen device, we can catch him or her since the *timestamp* embedded in the reader's signature could indicate who is on duty at that time. Although spoofed reader could overwrite or compromise tag trace stored in the tag memory to perform denial-of-service attack, this type of tampering can be detected by the reader at the next stage. We can restore the compromised tag trace by retrieving backup from the database when the reader is connected to the network. Protecting tag privacy [4] is out of the scope of this paper.

Control Chip: Illegal substitute of control chip (i.e., replacing original control chip with a counterfeit/tampered IC) can be detected with unclonable control chip identity (SRAM PUF).

Network Device: Stolen network devices can be detected since their tag traces are either incomplete or fake and will fail the tag trace validation procedure.

RF Channel: Sensitive information (e.g., reader's private key) is never transmitted in clear and thus is resistant to eavesdropping. Replay attack described in Section 3.2 can be prevented since reader update (i.e., new signature generated by current reader) is generated based on one specific tag identity and cannot be simply duplicated to be used for another tag. To be specific, even if the adversary could eavesdrop on the RF channel, intercept the tag authentication codes (see Section 4.2) sent by legal tags, and replay the tag authentication codes to authorized readers to obtain copies of reader updates. The freshly generated readers' signatures are computed based on the identities of tags under attack and cannot be simply used for counterfeit tags with different identities. In the worst case, even if the adversary performs replay attack and tag ID cloning simultaneously, the copies of reader updates obtained by replay attack could match the cloned tag identities. Those cloned tag identities would not match the control chip identities. ReSC is also resistant to man-in-the-middle attack described in Section 3.2 since the tag authentication code is bound to one specific tag identity and would not match another tag identity. Specifically, when the adversary intercepts the authentication code sent by the legal tag to the authorized reader, changes the tag identity contained in the authentication code to any other wanted tag identity, and sends the forged authentication code to the authorized reader to swindle reader update associated with that wanted tag identity, the forged authentication code will fail the verification by the authorized reader since it does not match the provided tag identity.

RFID Reader: Spoofed tags usually originate from an illegal channel and cannot include valid signatures of previous readers. We can detect spoofed tags by verifying the old signatures stored in the tag memory.

Table 1. System level security evaluation

Attack target	Attack approach	Mitigation
RFID tag	1. Cloning tag ID 2. Duplicating tag trace 3. Denial-of-service attack	1. One-to-one mapping between tag identity and control chip identity. 2. Tag trace is unique to each device and generated based on the tag identity. 3. i) The compromised tag trace can be detected by the reader at the next stage. ii) Backup the tag trace when the reader is connected to the network.
Control chip	Replacing the original chip with an illegal substitute (e.g., a counterfeit IC).	Unclonable control chip identity (SRAM PUF).
Network device	Stealing devices from inventories or shelves.	Verification of the integrity of tag trace.
RF channel	1. Eavesdropping 2. Replay attack 3. Man-in-the-middle attack	1. Sensitive information (e.g., reader's private key) is never transmitted in clear. 2. Reader update is generated based on one specific tag identity and cannot be simply duplicated to be used for another tag. 3. The tag authentication code is bound to one specific tag identity.
RFID reader	Spoofed tag	Authenticate tag by verifying the old signatures stored in the tag memory.

Table 2. Overhead comparison

Metrics	Tailing [41]	Jeongkyn et al. [40]	Hung-Yu et al. [7]	ReSC
# of Hash Operations	0	$2N + 2$	0	1
# of Keyed Hash Operations	0	2	0	1
# of RNG Operations	1	1	6	0
# of Encryptions	0	1	0	1
# of Decryptions	0	1	0	1
# of Messages	4	5	5	3
Required Tag Memory Size	$M \times symbol + pointer + tagID$	$SN+ID+2\ keys$	$EPC + 2\ keys$	$M \times (SIGN + Index + TS) + tagID$
Extra Tag Circuit	No	Yes	No	No
Real-time Interaction with DB	Yes	Yes	Yes	No
Exhaustive Search in DB	No	Yes	Yes	No

Note: 1. M stands for the number of stages on the distribution path.

2. N stands for the number of issued tags.

3. Extra tag circuit indicates the primitive not supported by EPC C1G2.

4. SN: serial number, EPC: electronic product code, and TS: timestamp.

6.3   Comparison with Prior Work

In this subsection, we compare ReSC with prior work in terms of overhead and security. Table 2 compares ReSC with several famous RFID-based techniques in terms of overhead. Table 3 compares ReSC with those techniques in terms of anti-attack capability. Different from tailing mechanism [24, 41, 42], ReSC can verify tag trace without requiring that reader be connected to the database. As a tradeoff, ReSC has to store more authentication information in the tag memory. For ReSC, the tag traces are mostly validated at the end-user. Different from the other three techniques, ReSC prevents tag cloning by binding the tag identity to the unclonable control chip identity. ReSC can address more attacks with a relatively smaller overhead. Among these four approaches under comparison, ReSC is the only one that can prevent counterfeit or stolen products from being used by end-users.

Table 3. Security comparison

Attacks	Tailing [41]	Jeongkyn et al. [40]	Hung-Yu et al. [7]	ReSC
Removing tag	√	√	√	√
Swapping tags	×	×	×	√
Cloning tag ID	√	√	×	√
Forging tag	√	√	√	√
Cloning tag ID + Duplicating tag trace	×	–	–	√
Tracking tag location	×	√	√	×
Spoofed reader	×	√	√	√
Illegal chip replacement	×	×	×	√
Product theft	×	×	×	√
Eavesdropping	×	√	×	√
Replay attack	×	√	√	√
Denial-of-service attack	×	√	√	√
Spoofed tag	×	√	√	√

7 Conclusion

In this paper, we have presented an RFID-enabled Supply Chain (ReSC) solution that addresses the security and management issues of network devices in the supply chain. The practical effectiveness of ReSC system has been verified through simulations, theoretical analysis, and experimental results. Compared with existing approaches, ReSC has the following merits: (1) By binding the RFID tag and the identified device together with a one-to-one mapping, potential split attacks (i.e., separating tag from product, swapping tags, etc.) can be detected; (2) By combining two techniques (i.e., one-to-one mapping between tag identity and control chip identity, and unique tag trace composed of signatures of readers on the distribution path) together, this system is resistant to counterfeit injection, product theft, and illegal network service access; (3) The fabrication cost is quite low since the vast majority of components (e.g., voltage regulator, control chip with embedded SRAM, etc.) in this design already exist in many modern network devices.

References

1. Angeles, R.: RFID Technologies: Supply-chain Applications and Implementation Issues. Information Systems Management 22(1), 51–65 (2005)
2. Armknecht, F., Gasmi, Y., Sadeghi, A.-R., Stewin, P., Unger, M., Ramunno, G., Vernizzi, D.: An efficient implementation of trusted channels based on openSSL. In: Proceedings of the 3rd ACM Workshop on Scalable Trusted Computing, STC 2008, pp. 41–50. ACM, New York (2008)
3. Asif, Z.: Integrating the Supply Chain with RFID: a Technical and Business Analysis. Communications of the Association for Information Systems 15(1), 24 (2005)
4. Avoine, G.: Privacy challenges in RFID. In: Garcia-Alfaro, J., Navarro-Arribas, G., Cuppens-Boulahia, N., de Capitani di Vimercati, S. (eds.) DPM 2011 and SETOP 2011. LNCS, vol. 7122, pp. 1–8. Springer, Heidelberg (2012)
5. Buchmann, J., García, L.C.C., Dahmen, E., Döring, M., Klintsevich, E.: CMSS – an improved merkle signature scheme. In: Barua, R., Lange, T. (eds.) INDOCRYPT 2006. LNCS, vol. 4329, pp. 349–363. Springer, Heidelberg (2006)
6. Carbone, J.: Most Counterfeit Parts Involve Obsolete Semiconductors and Other EOL Components. The Source, August 2012

7. Chien, H.-Y., Chen, C.-H.: Mutual Authentication Protocol for RFID Conforming to EPC Class 1 Generation 2 Standards. Computer Standards & Interfaces 29(2), 254–259 (2007)
8. Devadas, S., Yu, M.: Secure and Robust Error Correction for Physical Unclonable Functions
9. Dierks, T.: The Transport Layer Security (TLS) Protocol Version 1.2
10. Ekinci, Y., Ekinci, O., Giinaydin, U.: The application of UHF passive RFID technology for the effectiveness of retail/consumer goods supply chain management. In: 2007 1st Annual RFID Eurasia, pp. 1–6, September 2007
11. Evans, D.: The Internet of Things: How the Next Evolution of the Internet Is Changing Everything. CISCO white paper 1 (2011)
12. FreightWatch International Supply Chain Intelligence Center. 2013 Global Cargo Theft Threat Assessment (2013)
13. Gassend, B., Clarke, D., Van Dijk, M., Devadas, S.: Silicon physical random functions. In: Proceedings of the 9th ACM Conference on Computer and Communications Security, pp. 148–160. ACM (2002)
14. Gaukler, G.M., Seifert, R.W., Hausman, W.H.: Item-Level RFID in the Retail Supply Chain. Production and Operations Management 16(1), 65–76 (2007)
15. Goldwasser, S., Micali, S., Rivest, R.L.: A Digital Signature Scheme Secure Against Adaptive Chosen-message Attacks. SIAM Journal on Computing 17(2), 281–308 (1988)
16. Hancke, G.P.: RFID and contactless technology. In: Smart Cards, Tokens, Security and Applications, pp. 295–322. Springer (2008)
17. Holcomb, D., Burleson, W., Fu, K.: Power-Up SRAM State as an Identifying Fingerprint and Source of True Random Numbers. IEEE Transactions on Computers 58(9), 1198–1210 (2009)
18. Hosey, A., Rahman, M., Xiao, K., Forte, D., Tehranipoor, M., et al.: Advanced analysis of cell stability for reliable SRAM PUFs. In: 2014 IEEE 23rd Asian Test Symposium (ATS), pp. 348–353. IEEE (2014)
19. Huang, H.-C., Chang, F.-C., Fang, W.-C.: Reversible Data Hiding with Histogram-based Difference Expansion for QR Code Applications 57, 779–787
20. Hutter, M., Mangard, S., Feldhofer, M.: Power and EM attacks on passive 13.56 MHz RFID devices. In: Paillier, P., Verbauwhede, I. (eds.) CHES 2007. LNCS, vol. 4727, pp. 320–333. Springer, Heidelberg (2007)
21. Inc., E. EPC Radio-Frequency Identity Protocols Class-1 Generation-2 UHF RFID Protocol for Communications at 860 MHz-960 MHz Version 1.2.0, May 2008
22. Juels, A., Pappu, R., Parno, B.: Unidirectional key distribution across time and space with applications to rfid security. In: USENIX Security Symposium, pp. 75–90 (2008)
23. Kumar, S.S., Guajardo, J., Maes, R., Schrijen, G.-J., Tuyls, P.: The butterfly PUF protecting IP on every FPGA. In: IEEE International Workshop on Hardware-Oriented Security and Trust, HOST 2008, pp. 67–70. IEEE (2008)
24. Lehtonen, M., Ostojic, D., Ilic, A., Michahelles, F.: Securing RFID systems by detecting tag cloning. In: Tokuda, H., Beigl, M., Friday, A., Brush, A.J.B., Tobe, Y. (eds.) Pervasive 2009. LNCS, vol. 5538, pp. 291–308. Springer, Heidelberg (2009)
25. Lehtonen, M.O., Michahelles, F., Fleisch, E.: Trust and Security in RFID-based Product Authentication Systems. IEEE Systems Journal 1(2), 129–144 (2007)
26. Livingston, H.: Couterfeit Incident Reporting Trends – Observations in Anticipation of Forthcoming Regulations, August 2013.
http://counterfeitparts.wordpress.com/2013/08/06/
counterfeit-incident-reporting-trends-observations-
anticipation-of-forthcoming-regulations/
27. Maes, R., Tuyls, P., Verbauwhede, I.: Low-overhead Implementation of a soft decision helper data algorithm for SRAM PUFs. In: Clavier, C., Gaj, K. (eds.) CHES 2009. LNCS, vol. 5747, pp. 332–347. Springer, Heidelberg (2009)

28. Maiti, A., Schaumont, P.: Improved Ring Oscillator PUF: an FPGA-friendly Secure Primitive. Journal of Cryptology 24(2), 375–397 (2011)
29. Michael, K., McCathie, L.: The pros and cons of RFID in supply chain management. In: International Conference on Mobile Business, ICMB 2005, pp. 623–629. IEEE (2005)
30. Mitchell, B.: Network Engineer Charged in Multi-Million Dollar Cisco Equipment Theft, December 2011. `http://compnetworking.about.com/b/2011/12/10/ network-engineer-charged-in-multimillion-dollar-cisco-equipment-thef.htm`
31. Mukhopadhyay, D., Chakraborty, R.S., Nguyen, P.H., Sahoo, D.P.: Tutorial T7: Physically unclonable function: A promising security primitive for internet of things. In: 28th International Conference on VLSI Design (VLSID), pp. 14–15. IEEE (2015)
32. NXP Semiconductors. I2C Bus Specification and User Manual, April 2014
33. Rabin, M.O.: Digitalized Signatures and Public-key Functions as Intractable as Factorization. Tech. rep., DTIC Document (1979)
34. Roberti, M.: How Can an RFID Reader Interrogate Multiple Tags Simultaneously? September 2010. `http://www.rfidjournal.com/blogs/experts/entry?7853`
35. Rocholl, J., Klenk, S., Heidemann, G.: Robust 1D barcode recognition on mobile devices. In: 2010 20th International Conference on Pattern Recognition (ICPR), pp. 2712–2715, August 2010
36. Schrijen, G.-J., van der Leest, V.: Comparative analysis of SRAM memories used as PUF primitives. In: Proceedings of the Conference on Design, Automation and Test in Europe, EDA Consortium, pp. 1319–1324 (2012)
37. Tariguliyev, Z., Ors, B.: Reliability and Security of Arbiter-based Physical Unclonable Function Circuits. International Journal of Communication Systems 26(6), 757–769 (2013)
38. Waters, A.: The Case of the Great Router Robbery, May 2011. `http://resources.infosecinstitute.com/router-robbery/`
39. Xiao, K., Rahman, T., Forte, D., Tehranipoor, M., Huang, Y., Su, M.: Bit Selection algorithm suitable for high-volumn production of SRAM PUF. In: 2014 IEEE International Symposium on Hardware-Oriented Security and Trust (HOST) (2014)
40. Yang, J., Park, J., Lee, H., Ren, K., Kim, K.: Mutual authentication protocol. In: Workshop on RFID and Lightweight Crypto (2005)
41. Zanetti, D., Capkun, S., Juels, A.: Tailing RFID tags for clone detection. In: Network and Distributed System Security Symposium (2013)
42. Zanetti, D., Fellmann, L., Capkun, S.: Privacy-preserving clone detection for RFID-enabled supply chains. In: IEEE International Conference on RFID, pp. 37–44. IEEE (2010)

Part II

Side-Channels and Countermeasures

Side-Channel Assisted Modeling Attacks on Feed-Forward Arbiter PUFs Using Silicon Data

Raghavan Kumar and Wayne Burleson

Department of Electrical and Computer Engineering
University of Massachusetts Amherst, Amherst, Massachusetts, USA
{raghavan,burleson}@engin.umass.edu

Abstract. Physically Unclonable Functions (PUFs) are used for generating unique signatures from the complex manufacturing variations in integrated circuits. However, the majority of PUFs have been shown to be vulnerable to modeling attacks. In this work, we take a closer look at the vulnerability of feed-forward arbiter PUFs towards a combined side-channel and modeling attack using data measured from our 32nm test chips. The side-channel information from the feed-forward PUF construction is used as a catalyst for improving the performance of modeling attacks. This hybrid attack helps to push the prediction accuracies to very high limits ($> 98.5\%$), especially for larger PUF circuits. The hybrid attack yields around 7% improvement in prediction rates when compared to a conventional modeling attack mounted under the presence of error-inflicted challenge-response pairs.

Keywords: Physically Unclonable Functions, Hardware security, Modeling attacks, Fault-injection attacks.

1 Introduction

The trend of *ubiquitous computing* is gaining significant attention in the digital world. Embedded systems are frequently used for performing security related tasks in day-to-day life. The era of ubiquitous computing has also led to the concept of *Internet of Things*, where the devices have communication ability in addition to computation power. However, this also brings out security and privacy issues, as these devices serve as an ideal target for attackers. In particular, protection of sensitive data stored on the devices has gained significant attention and the sensitive data often demands cryptographic protection.

The majority of embedded systems pose tight constraints on area and energy. Hence, the trend towards lightweight cryptographic primitives is becoming extremely popular in the design market. The majority of classical cryptographic primitives are based on the concept of a *secret binary key* embedded on the device. The digital storage of a secret key poses some security vulnerabilities, especially against physical and software attacks [14]. The fact that the key has to be stored in a non-volatile memory further aggravates the problem. All these

© Springer International Publishing Switzerland 2015
S. Mangard, P. Schaumont (Eds.): RFIDsec 2015, LNCS 9440, pp. 53–67, 2015.
DOI: 10.1007/978-3-319-24837-0_4

issues have served as one of the major motivations towards the development of Physically Unclonable Functions (PUFs).

PUFs are partially disordered systems that map an external input known as a "challenge" to an output known as a "response". A challenge associated with its response is referred to as a challenge-response pair (CRP). In silicon-based PUFs, the mapping function is determined by the process variations arising during the manufacturing process of an integrated circuit (IC). As the manufacturing process is extremely complicated in sub-nm regime, even the manufacturer cannot produce an identical tuple of ICs that have the same layouts due to molecular level variations. This property is exploited in PUF designs to generate unique signatures. PUFs can be broadly classified into "strong" and "weak" PUFs based on the number of independent responses that it can generate [13]. A strong PUF produces a large number of responses and can be used in security protocols, key establishment and device authentication. A classical example for a strong PUF is an arbiter PUF [14]. A weak PUF, on the other hand, has a highly reduced challenge-response space [13]. The weak PUFs can be used in classical cryptosystems for deriving the secret key. One of the typical examples for a weak PUF is an SRAM PUF [4].

PUF circuits find applications in device authentication, identification, secret key generation, etc. These applications require that any two responses from two different PUFs should have a significant difference. This property of PUFs is referred to as uniqueness. To ensure stable authentication, PUFs are expected to produce the same response for a particular challenge under any operating condition, which is measured in terms of reliability. Finally, a PUF should be unpredictable such that an attacker possessing a subset of CRP pairs should be unable to predict the response for a challenge outside that subset. Among these performance metrics, security has gained significant attention and considerable amount of effort has been put to make and break a PUF. Modeling attacks have been proposed as a major threat to PUF circuits, especially for those architectures with a linear challenge-response relationship [7–9, 12, 13]. Recently, unreliable CRP data has been shown to be a catalyst for aiding modeling attacks [1, 3]. Power and timing-side channels can also be used to extract more device-dependent information for breaking PUF circuits [10].

In this paper, we take a closer look at the security vulnerabilities of feed-forward arbiter PUFs, which is one of the "strong" PUF circuits. The challenge-response pairs are collected from test chips fabricated using IBM 32nm silicon-on-insulator (SOI) process. Evolution strategies (ES) based attacks show that the feed-forward PUF construction is highly vulnerable to modeling attacks. However, the performance of modeling attacks is impacted by the presence of error-prone CRPs in the training set. To that extent, we explore the technique that exploits fault-injection to push the prediction accuracies achieved by machine learning algorithms in the presence of error-inflicted CRPs. The side-channel information obtained from the fault-injection attack helps to extract more data-dependent information from the PUF circuit and is used along with a modeling attack framework. This hybrid attack (modeling attack combined with side-channel analysis (SCA)) achieves very high prediction accuracies especially for larger PUFs that are typically unattainable by conventional modeling attacks in the presence of error-prone CRPs. The terms "error-prone" and "error-inflicted" refer to the same set of CRPs. To the best of our knowledge, this is the first work that reports hybrid attacks on feed-forward arbiter PUFs using silicon data.

The rest of the paper is organized as follows. Section 2 describes the related work. The methodology adopted for CRP extraction from the test chip is presented in section 3. The attack results on feed-forward arbiter PUFs using evolution strategies are presented in section 4. Section 5 presents the hybrid attacks on feed-forward arbiter PUFs. Finally, concluding remarks are presented in section 6.

2   Background and Related Work

2.1   Attacks on PUFs

Numerous attacks on PUFs have been reported in recent years. Most of the attacks are specific to the PUF architecture being targeted, while some of them are generic. Some of the attacks include modeling, side-channel, fault attacks, etc. Among this group, the most prominent one is the modeling attack, which employs a Machine Learning (ML) algorithm. ML attacks are more specific to strong PUFs, as the weak PUFs have very few CRPs or a single CRP. The collection of various modeling attacks on some of the popular implementations of strong PUFs can be found in [7, 12, 13]. As simple arbiter PUFs have shown increased vulnerability towards modeling attacks, variants such as feed-forward arbiter PUFs [6], XOR arbiter PUFs [13] have been proposed in the literature. However, those variants also exhibit vulnerabilities towards different types of ML algorithms and interested readers are referred to [12, 13] for more details.

Recently, attacks on PUFs that exploit data-dependent information in addition to CRP pairs have been demonstrated [2, 3, 5, 15]. The attacks use the inherent instability in PUF responses due to thermal noise in [2] and the instability due to external noise from environmental conditions in [3]. A similar work on attacking controlled arbiter PUFs through fault- and power side-channels is presented in [1]. In parallel to [1], Mahmoud et al. have proposed a combined ML and side-channel (power and timing) for XOR arbiter PUFs [10]. Hybrid attacks on current-based PUFs were first reported by Kumar et al. in [5]. Although the hybrid attack framework is similar to the one presented in this work, the modeling attacks in [5] were performed using statistical simulation data and some of the performance metrics were slightly optimistic when compared to the attack's performance obtained from silicon data. However, none of the above mentioned attacks look at exploiting the side-channels exhibited by a feed-forward arbiter PUF for improving the performance of modeling attacks. To the best of our knowledge, this is the first work that reports modeling and hybrid attack results on feed-forward arbiter PUFs using silicon data from 32nm test chips.

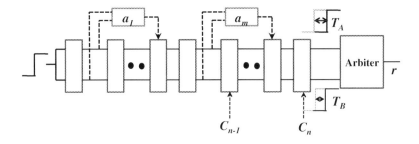

Fig. 1. Feed-forward arbiter PUF

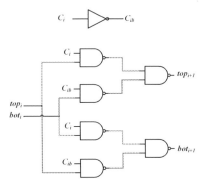

Fig. 2. Individual delay path implementation

2.2   Feed-Forward Arbiter PUFs

A feed-forward arbiter PUF exploits delay variations in CMOS gates and interconnects to extract unique signatures as in an arbiter PUF [6]. However, some of the challenge bits in a feed-forward PUF are determined as a result of racing conditions at intermediate stages with the help of arbiters. The construction of a feed-forward arbiter PUF is shown in Figure 1. The intermediate arbiters $a_1..a_m$ generates the additional challenge bits apart from the user specified challenge $C_1..C_n$. The challenge bits $C_1..C_n$ decide the path of propagation through the delay paths whose gate-level implementation is shown in Figure 2. For example, if the challenge bit $C_i = 1$, then the signals pass directly to output $(top_{i+1} = top_i, bot_{i+1} = bot_i)$ and the signals gets switched when $C_i = 0$ $(top_{i+1} = bot_i, bot_{i+1} = top_i)$. The rising pulse applied at the input undergoes different delays as it gets propagated through the delay paths and the total delay difference $(\Delta t_n = T_A - T_B)$ generated is sampled at the output with the help of an arbiter to generate the response bit r. The condition for response generation is given by the equation 1.

$$r = \begin{cases} 0 & \text{if } T_A > T_B \\ 1 & otherwise \end{cases} \qquad (1)$$

Fig. 3. Die micrograph (left) and Packaged die (right)

3   CRP Collection from ASIC

The feed-forward arbiter PUF described in section 2.2 was fabricated using the 32nm SOI process available from IBM. The dies were packaged and the packaged versions were used for post-silicon measurements. The micrograph of the chip along with the packaged versions are shown in Figure 3. As the focus of this work is on modeling attacks, we skip the physical design and power consumption details of the feed-forward arbiter PUFs and they will be presented in our future publications.

The challenges for the PUF circuit were generated using an on-chip linear feedback shift register (LFSR). As the hybrid attacks described in this work require fault injections, the measurements were conducted at extreme conditions ($V_{dd}\pm0.1$V and 75°C) apart from the nominal conditions (0.9V and 25°C). The terms "nominal" and "extreme" operating conditions further in this paper refer to these voltage and temperature values used in post-silicon measurements. The block diagram of the chip measurement setup is shown in Figure 4. A standard QFN56 test socket was used to mount the packaged die. Spartan-3E FPGA that operates at a voltage of 2.5V was used for post-silicon validation setup. An off-chip bi-directional voltage converter (TXB0104) between 2.5V and 1.8V was used for interfacing the FPGA and ASIC. I/O cells were available on the test chip for bi-directional voltage level translation between 1.8V and 0.9V for the signals (clock, configuration bits and output). The FPGA helps in loading the configuration bits into the chip and reading out the response bits from the chip. The configuration bits are used to select the type of PUF among the other PUF implementations and also to choose a particular instance of the selected PUF circuit. Once the responses are available, the FPGA dumps the data into the host computer via UART communication.

4   Attacks on Feed-Forward PUF

In this work, evolution strategies (ES) have been used for breaking feed-forward arbiter PUFs. They have been shown to be efficient for breaking feed-forward arbiter PUFs, especially for the constructions with number of loops more than

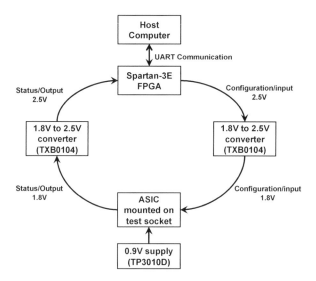

Fig. 4. Post-silicon measurement flow

2 [13]. In this section, we report the results of ES based attacks on feed-forward PUFs using silicon data from our 32nm test chip measurements. First, we describe the design strategy that was adopted to choose the optimal number of loops and stages/loop in section 4.1.

4.1 Performance Evaluation of Feed-Forward Arbiter PUFs

It is highly essential to validate the performance of PUF circuits before mounting an attack. There are different configurations possible to implement feed-forward PUFs. Some of the variable design parameters include number of feed-forward loops, number of stages/loop, dependency between loops, etc. Assuming the loops are symmetric, if the external challenge is k bits wide and the number of loops is l, then the total number of delay stages is $k + l$ and the number of stages/loop is k/l. As the variable design parameters impact the performance of a PUF, they were analyzed through statistical circuit simulations and post-silicon measurements from the test chip. In statistical circuit simulations, different PUF instances were created through Monte Carlo (MC) simulations. For MC simulations, threshold voltage variations were assigned to the transistors from a Gaussian distribution with 3σ deviation of 90mV, as specified in the transistor's technology library. IBM 32nm transistor models were used in simulations. The feed-forward PUFs were implemented in such a way that the number of loops and number of stages/loop can be altered using the configuration bits during post-silicon measurements. The different configurations were analyzed for different performance metrics such as uniqueness, reliability, uniformity and bit-aliasing probability, as per the framework described in [11]. For evaluating PUF's uniqueness, inter-class hamming distance(HD) was used. Intra-class HD

Table 1. Summary of Feed-forward arbiter PUF's performance metrics from statistical circuit simulations and post-silicon measurements

Type of analysis	# Bits in challenge (k)	# Loops (l)	# PUF instances	Inter-class HD	Intra-class HD	Uniformity	Bit aliasing HD
Statistical circuit simulations	64	6	200	0.48	0.05	0.48	0.49
		7		0.485	0.052	0.485	0.48
		8		0.47	0.055	0.47	0.485
	80	6		0.485	0.055	0.49	0.49
		7		0.48	0.0575	0.48	0.475
		8		0.47	0.059	0.49	0.48
	128	6		0.475	0.052	0.48	0.47
		7		0.48	0.056	0.47	0.48
		8		0.48	0.06	0.49	0.49
Post-silicon measurements	64	6	200	0.42	0.074	0.42	0.41
		7		0.425	0.076	0.41	0.415
		8		0.415	0.08	0.415	0.42
	80	6		0.41	0.077	0.42	0.42
		7		0.42	0.079	0.42	0.415
		8		0.415	0.0881	0.425	0.42
	128	6		0.43	0.076	0.43	0.42
		7		0.425	0.079	0.435	0.43
		8		0.415	0.0882	0.42	0.425

was used to capture the PUF's reliability. Around 3 million CRPs were collected from 20 different PUF instances and uniqueness was analyzed. For measuring PUF's reliability, the experiments were conducted at nominal and extreme operating conditions and the number of bit-flips were observed. The results are shown in Figure 5 and also tabulated in Table 1. The distributions from the post-silicon measurements are only shown for the sake of brevity. It can be observed that the design strategy has a significantly higher impact on reliability than uniqueness. As expected, reliability decreases with the number of loops. So, it is highly necessary to choose the number of loops and number of stages/loop such that an optimal design is achieved in terms of reliability and unpredictability. For the feed-forward PUFs (64, 80 and 128 stage PUFs) considered in modeling attacks, the number of loops were set at 8 ($l = 8$) as they exhibit decent performance metrics and they should exhibit better unpredictability (intuitively) when compared to designs with lower l values.

4.2   Evolution Strategies Based Attacks

Evolution strategies are used for black-box optimization problems and are shown to be efficient for breaking PUF circuits [1, 13]. They are based on creating random models in several iterations also known as *generations* from a *parent*. The sample models are also known as offsprings. Only the offsprings that are deemed fit based on some fitness tests are selected and used as parents for the

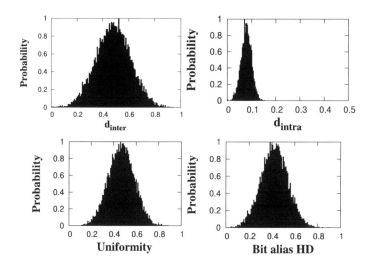

Fig. 5. Feed-forward arbiter PUF's performance metrics distribution from post-silicon measurements (a) Inter-class HD (b) Intra-class HD (c) Uniformity and (d) Bit-aliasing probability

next generation. The process is repeated until optimal prediction accuracies are reached. The major advantage of ES is that it is completely randomized and can be parameterized [13]. For our experiments based on ES, we set $(\mu, \lambda) = (6,36)$ and the mutation parameter $\tau = \frac{1}{\sqrt{n}}$ as in [13]. However, we evaluated the performance of attacks with and without recombination. The performance improvement with recombination ($\rho < 6$) was very marginal with respect to the attack without recombination.

ES attacks were performed over 20 different PUF instances (2 instances/die). Around 3 Million CRPs were collected for modeling attacks. A subset of CRPs was used for training the ES predictor and the rest were used for evaluating its performance. The prediction errors as a function of the number of training CRPs for different PUF configurations are shown in Figure 6. The plot shows the prediction errors for the PUF configurations with number of loops set to 8. It can be observed that the prediction accuracies as high as 97% can be achieved with around 80,000 CRPs. The attack results represent the best case out of 100 random trials unless mentioned otherwise further in the paper. The attack results along with the time overheads (for a single trial) are shown in Table 3. The attack results agree well with the modeling attack results on 45nm feed-forward arbiter PUFs presented in [12].

4.3   Impact of Error-Inflicted CRPs

As the PUFs are not 100% reliable, there is a high probability that some of the CRPs are error-prone. The bit-flip in response happen when the polarity of

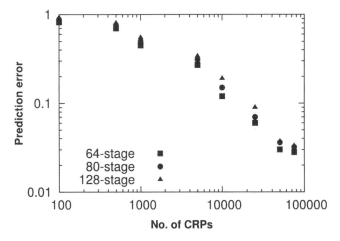

Fig. 6. Prediction errors from ES attacks on 64, 80 and 128 stage feed-forward arbiter PUFs

Table 2. Bit flips measurements for Feed-forward PUFs from 32nm test chip

# Stages	Type of Noise	# CRPs	# Bit flips	% Bit flips
64			81,200	2.7
80	Intrinsic		81,650	2.72
128		3M	80,800	2.69
64			263,900	8.8
80	Extrinsic		264,200	8.81
128			264,500	8.82

delay difference is reversed. These bit-flips can happen due to the impacts of intrinsic and extrinsic noise sources. The intrinsic noise includes the substrate and thermal noise, which are routinely observed in an integrated circuit. On the other hand, extrinsic noise source includes voltage and temperature fluctuations, which impact the operating conditions of a circuit. The amount of bit-flips from intrinsic and extrinsic noise sources in feed-forward PUFs are shown in Table 2. The amount of bit-flips are shown for feed-forward PUFs with $l = 8$. Similar results were observed for other PUF configurations as well. For observing the impact of intrinsic noise, the measurements were conducted at nominal conditions for 5 times and the number of bit-flips for the same challenges was observed. We can observe that the maximum bit-flips induced by intrinsic noise sources is around 2.7%. For observing the impact of extrinsic noise, the measurements were conducted at extreme operating conditions and the bit-flips were collected. From table 2, we can observe that the maximum bit-flips induced by extrinsic noise is around 9%.

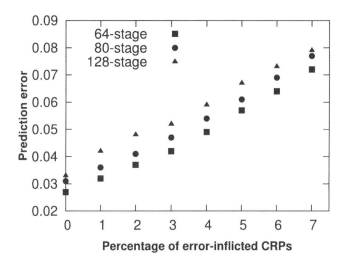

Fig. 7. Impact of error-inflicted CRPs on the prediction accuracies of ES attacks

Table 3. Summary of ES attacks on Feed-forward PUFs using silicon data

Type of attack	# Stages	# Training CRPs	Prediction accuracy (%)	Attack time
ES with stable CRPs	64	75,000	97.4	55:10min
	80		97.1	55:10min
	128		96.7	55:10min
ES with 7% error-inflicted CRPs	64	100,000	93.1	66:30min
	80		92.8	66:30min
	128		92.4	66:30min

The impact of error-inflicted CRPs on the performance of ES attacks is shown in Figure 7. The best-case prediction accuracies under 7% error-inflicted CRPs are tabulated in Table 3. Although ES based attacks are highly tolerant to errors in CRPs, there is a slight drop in prediction accuracy (around 7%). As the error-inflicted CRPs have a reversed polarity in delay difference, the learning phase of the modeling attack is impacted. However, not all the CRPs suffer from polarity reversal. Only the challenges for which the delay difference is lower than a threshold are susceptible. This threshold delay difference can leak some data-dependent information and can be used along with the training set CRPs to improve the prediction accuracies. The details are described in the next section.

5   Hybrid Attacks on Feed-forward Arbiter PUFs

In this section, we present the vulnerabilities of feed-forward PUFs to hybrid attacks, where a fault-injection attack is used along with a ML algorithm to improve the prediction accuracies. The injected faults into the PUF circuit reveal data-dependent information about the device under attack, which is exploited by the modeling attack framework. As side-channels from fault attacks are used in conjunction with a modeling attack, the new attacks are referred to as hybrid attacks.

There are several techniques to inject faults into a circuit. Among them, one of the popular techniques is voltage and temperature (V/T) manipulation. Altering the environmental conditions causes the circuit to deviate from its nominal operation and results in malfunction. Apart from environmental fluctuations, PUF based circuits also suffer from substrate noise as described in the previous section. This means that the PUF circuit may produce a different response for a particular challenge when measured at a different point of time under the same operating conditions. An attacker can degrade the reliability of a PUF circuit by manipulating the V/T conditions. Although this is detrimental to a PUF's operation, some data (input) dependent information can be extracted. One such information is the range of delay difference that is highly sensitive to V/T variations. This range is referred to as threshold delay difference (Δt_{min}) further in the paper.

It is highly difficult to measure the absolute Δt_{min} from post-silicon measurements and hence statistical circuit simulations are used to determine approximate Δt_{min} for the given technology node. To determine Δt_{min}, Monte Carlo simulations were performed using the IBM 32nm SOI transistor models. For each PUF instance, 1 Million CRPs were collected through statistical circuit simulations under nominal and extreme operating conditions along with the corresponding delay difference values (Δt_n). The error-prone response bits under extreme conditions were mapped to the corresponding Δt_n values. Figure 8 shows the distributions of delay-difference values for error-free and error-prone CRPs observed under nominal and extreme operating conditions. The plot shows the distributions for a 128-stage PUF with $l = 8$ and similar characteristics were observed for 64- and 80-stage PUFs. For majority of the flipped bits, Δt_n was less than $5ps$. The number of flipped bits whose delay differences were less than $5ps$ is shown in Figure 9. As some of the bit-flips are caused by device mismatches in the arbiter, the amount of bit flips with Δt_n less than $5ps$ is lower than the intra-class HD shown in Table 1. This analysis shows that when a bit flip is observed, then it is highly likely that the delay difference for the response bit is less than $5ps$. This value is taken as Δt_{min} and is used along with modeling attacks for improving the prediction accuracies. However, please note that, not all the CRPs with Δt_{min} less than $5ps$ are susceptible to bit-flips (from Figure 8), as some of the bit-flips might be caused by instabilities in the output arbiter. So, the threshold information is an approximate indicator for susceptible CRPs with a certain probability.

In hybrid attacks, the ES algorithm with the same parameters described in section 4.2 was used. But, the threshold Δt_{min} data obtained from circuit simulations was used to filter out the bad PUF models. In normal ES attacks, the filtering process is based on the number of correct responses predicted by the model. But, by using fault data, more stable and accurate PUF models were

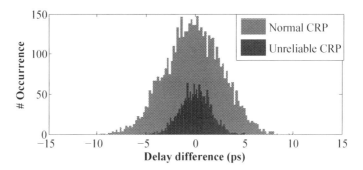

Fig. 8. Delay difference distributions for normal and unreliable CRP pairs

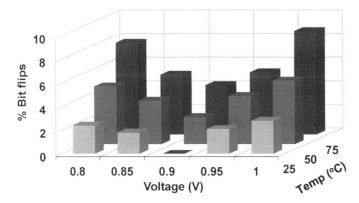

Fig. 9. Percentage of bit flips with Δt_n less than $5ps$ for a 128 stage Feed-forward arbiter PUF with $l = 8$. Nominal operating conditions (0.9V and 25°C) were used as the reference point to measure bit-flips.

obtained for each generation. This is due to the fact that the fault data contains circuit-specific information (Δt_{min}) in addition to CRPs unlike a simple ES attack which involves only the CRPs. In order to incorporate the fault-injection data, the PUF models were tested for their fitness by evaluating the correlation-coefficient between a hypothesis vector and the golden vector obtained from measured CRPs as in [1]. The hypothesis vector is obtained from the PUF model by computing the delay-difference for a given challenge (Δt_H). The hypothesis vector F_H is given by,

$$F_H = \begin{cases} 1, \text{if}|\Delta t_H| < \Delta t_{min} \\ 0, \text{if}|\Delta t_H| > \Delta t_{min} \end{cases} \tag{2}$$

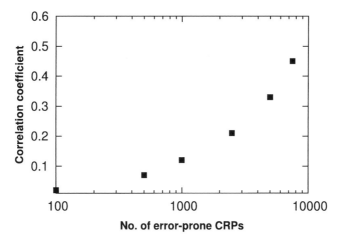

Fig. 10. Impact of the number of error-inflicted CRPs on the strength of PUF models

The same process is repeated to obtain the golden vector F over the measured CRPs from the test chip. If the response bit r_i got flipped under extreme conditions, then F_i is assigned to 1, else F_i is assigned to 0. By evaluating the correlation-coefficient between F and F_H, the strength of the hypothesis vector is obtained. The models which yield the best fit in terms of the number of correct response bits predicted and correlation co-efficient are passed onto the next generation. Better models were obtained by increasing the number of unstable CRPs in the training set as shown in Figure 10.

Hybrid attack experiments were performed over the same 20 PUF instances from the test chips. The attacks were performed using 100 sets of random CRPs picked from the global pool (3 million) and the results were averaged. In the training set, around 8% of the CRPs were error-inflicted which were obtained from fault-injection attacks. The performance of hybrid attacks over feed-forward arbiter PUFs are shown in Figure 11. The best-case prediction accuracy achieved from hybrid attacks is over 99% for around 100,000 CRPs. This represents around 7% improvement in performance over the simple ES attack with error-inflicted CRPs. The major advantage with hybrid attacks is that better prediction accuracies are achieved with almost the same number of CRPs as in simple ES attacks. The best-case prediction accuracies from hybrid attacks along with attack time overheads are shown in Table 4. The Δt_{min} obtained from circuit simulations may be slightly off when compared to actual Δt_{min} observed in the test chip. But, as mentioned earlier, it is highly difficult to observe the Δt_{min} from post-silicon measurements. The Δt_{min} observed from circuit simulations can be altered slightly around $5ps$ value to determine the best-case value for the given PUF instance on the given die. The analysis of the impacts of varying Δt_{min} on the attack's performance is part of the future work.

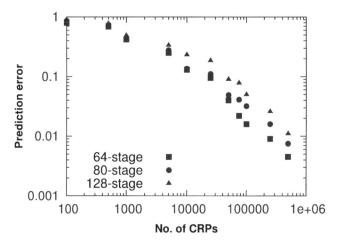

Fig. 11. Performance of hybrid attacks on Feed-forward PUFs with 7% error-prone CRPs

Table 4. Performance of hybrid attacks with 7% error-inflicted CRPs

# Stages	# Training CRPs	Prediction accuracy (%)	Attack time
64		99.5	75:20min
80	100,000	99.1	75:20min
128		98.8	75:20min

6   Future Work and Conclusion

We presented the modeling and hybrid attack results on feed-forward arbiter PUFs using post-silicon measurements from our 32nm test chips. In particular, we presented a technique that exploits unreliability in PUF responses to extract data dependent information. The side-channel information when used in conjunction with a machine learning algorithm improves the prediction accuracies to very high limits. The improvement in prediction rates is obtained with a minimal increase in the number of training CRPs. Although the techniques have been presented for feed-forward arbiter PUFs, they can be modified with minimal effort to attack other arbiter PUF implementations. As the side-channel information is obtained from circuit simulations, future work includes extensive analysis of the impacts of varying Δt_{min} on the performance of modeling attacks.

Acknowledgments. This work was supported by Semiconductor Research Corporation (SRC) task # 1836.074. The authors would like to thank the anonymous reviewers for their valuable comments and suggestions.

References

1. Becker, G., Kumar, R.: Active and Passive Side-Channel Attacks on Delay based PUF Designs. Cryptology ePrint Archive, Report 2014/287 (2014)
2. Delvaux, J., Verbauwhede, I.: Side channel modeling attacks on 65nm arbiter PUFs exploiting CMOS device noise. In: Hardware-Oriented Security and Trust (HOST), pp. 137–142, June 2013
3. Delvaux, J., Verbauwhede, I.: Fault Injection Modeling Attacks on 65nm Arbiter and RO Sum PUFs via Environmental Changes. IEEE Transactions on Circuits and Systems I: Regular Papers 61(6), 1701–1713 (2014)
4. Holcomb, D.E., Burleson, W.P., Fu, K.: Power-up SRAM State as an Identifying Fingerprint and Source of True Random Numbers. IEEE Transactions on Computers 58(9), 1198–1210 (2009)
5. Kumar, R., Burleson, W.: Hybrid modeling attacks on current-based PUFs. In: IEEE International Conference on Computer Design (ICCD), pp. 493–496, October 2014
6. Lee, J.W., Lim, D., Gassend, B., Suh, G.E., van Dijk, M., Devadas, S.: A Technique to build a secret key in integrated circuits for identification and authentication applications. In: Proc. Symposium on VLSI Circuits, pp. 176–179 (2004)
7. Lim, D.: Extracting secret keys from integrated circuits. Master's thesis, Massachusetts Institute of Technology, Dept. of Electrical Engineering and Computer Science (2004)
8. Lin, L., Holcomb, D., Krishnappa, D.K., Shabadi, P., Burleson, W.: Low-power sub-threshold design of secure physical unclonable functions. In: Proc. International Symposium on Low Power Electronics Design, pp. 43–48, August 2010
9. Lin, L., Srivathsa, S., Krishnappa, D.K., Shabadi, P., Burleson, W.: Design and Validation of Arbiter-based PUFs for Sub-45-nm Low-Power Security Applications. IEEE Trans. on Information Forensics and Security 7(4), 1394–1403 (2012)
10. Mahmoud, A., Rührmair, U., Majzoobi, M., Koushanfar, F.: Combined Modeling and Side Channel Attacks on Strong PUFs. Cryptology ePrint Archive, Report 2013/632 (2013)
11. Maiti, A., Gunreddy, V., Schaumont, P.: A Systematic method to evaluate and compare the performance of physical unclonable functions. In: Athanas, P., Pnevmatikatos, D., Sklavos, N. (eds.) Embedded Systems Design with FPGAs, pp. 245–267. Springer, New York (2013)
12. Rührmair, U., Sölter, J., Sehnke, F., Xu, X., Mahmoud, A., Stoyanova, V., Dror, G., Schmidhuber, J., Burleson, W., Devadas, S.: PUF Modeling Attacks on Simulated and Silicon Data. IEEE Transactions on Information Forensics and Security 8(11), 1876–1891 (2013)
13. Rührmair, U., Sehnke, F., Sölter, J., Dror, G., Devadas, S., Schmidhuber, J.: Modeling attacks on physical unclonable functions. In: Proc. ACM Conference on Computer and Communications Security, pp. 237–249 (2010)
14. Suh, G.E., Devadas, S.: Physical unclonable functions for device authentication and secret key generation. In: Proc. Design Automation Conference, pp. 9–14 (2007)
15. Xu, X., Burleson, W.: Hybrid side-channel/machine-learning attacks on PUFs: a new threat? In: Proceedings of the Conference on Design, Automation & Test in Europe, DATE 2014, pp. 349:1–349:6 (2014)

Sharing is Caring—On the Protection of Arithmetic Logic Units against Passive Physical Attacks

Hannes Gross

Institute for Applied Information Processing and Communications (IAIK),
Graz University of Technology, Inffeldgasse 16a, 8010 Graz, Austria
hannes.gross@iaik.tugraz.at

Abstract. Embedded systems are often used in security-critical scenarios where physical access of an adversary cannot be prevented. An attacker with unrestricted physical access to an embedded device could thus use observation-based attacks like power analysis or chip probing techniques to extract chip-internal secrets. In this work, we investigate how to counteract first-order passive physical attacks on an embedded microcontroller. In particular, we focus on the protection of the central point of data processing in the microcontroller design—the arithmetic logic unit (ALU)—with the provably secure threshold implementation (TI) masking scheme. Our results show that the amount of required fresh random bits—a problem many masked implementations suffer from—can be reduced to only one bit per ALU access and clock cycle. The total chip area overhead for implementing the whole microcontroller of our case study as a three-share TI is about a factor of 2.8.

Keywords: secure ALU, threshold implementation, masking, side-channel analysis, DPA, chip probing.

1 Introduction

Throughout the last decades, our understanding of the term "security" became much broader. In the beginning of cryptographic research almost the whole security problematic was somehow narrowed down on finding mathematical problems that are hard to solve without the knowledge of some secret information or trapdoor function. As it turned out, physical systems are usually easier to attack through the back door than by attacking the mathematical approach that protects the front door.

In particular, when an attacker has unrestricted access to a device—for example, because she is the holder of the device or the device is operated in an area that can hardly be secured—physical attacks become a serious threat. An unprotected hardware implementation reveals its secrets through, e.g., its power consumption [8], the electromagnetic emanation [13], or an attacker could even use needles to eavesdrop on the chip internal data exchange [6].

Protecting cryptographic hardware against physical attacks is now for more than 15 years an ongoing research topic. Many different masking schemes were proposed, but because of the possible occurrence of glitches caused by the combinatorial logic in hardware, the security of the masking schemes were jeopardized. Since the introduction

© Springer International Publishing Switzerland 2015
S. Mangard, P. Schaumont (Eds.): RFIDsec 2015, LNCS 9440, pp. 68–84, 2015.
DOI: 10.1007/978-3-319-24837-0_5

of threshold implementations (TI) by Nikova et al. [10] in 2006, a big step towards provable protection of hardware implementations was taken. However, until now this approach was only used to protect cryptographic hardware implementations against passive physical attacks.

In order to protect a whole system against these observation-based attacks, all components of the system that touch the assets of the system need to be considered. In the case of an embedded system, the data is usually processed by a microcontroller. More precisely, every information that is processed has to pass the arithmetic logic unit (ALU) of the microcontroller. The ALU is thus the most attractive and also the most vulnerable point to be attacked by an adversary that can physically observe a device. It is therefore crucial for the security of such a system to have an ALU protected against these kind of attacks.

Our Contribution. In this work, we show how a general purpose ALU design can be secured against first-order passive physical attacks. Therefore, the functionality of a typical ALU is considered and its functionality is transformed step-by-step in order to fulfill the requirements of the threshold implementation scheme. Considering each function separately is of course not enough. By carefully bringing these functions together, the chip area and the number of required fresh random bits per clock cycle can be reduced. The final ALU TI design requires about 1.1 kGE of chip area and only one random bit per clock cycle. The protected ALU is then integrated in a case study microcontroller and the required changes to the microcontroller design are discussed. Finally, the protected and unprotected hardware implementations are compared on three different levels: (1) on gate level—by comparing standard cell library gates to the TI of the gates required by the functionality of the ALU—, (2) the resulting costs of the standalone ALU TI are considered in relation to the unshared ALU, and (3) the comparison is done for the case study microcontroller. It is shown that the area overhead in the latter case is about a factor of 2.8, and the power consumption is increased by a factor of 2.3.

The rest of the paper is organized as follows: In Section 2, an overview of the threshold implementation scheme is given. In Section 3, the considered attack scenario is explained briefly. Afterwards, in Section 4, a look into the functionality provided by a general purpose ALU is given, and the functionality is then transformed in accordance with the requirements of the threshold implementation scheme. In a case study (Section 5), the integration of the protected ALU into a microcontroller design is described before the results are discussed in Section 6. Closing remarks are given in Section 7.

2   Threshold Implementations

The threshold implementation (TI) masking scheme was introduced by Nikova et al. in 2006 [10]. In contrast to many existing masking schemes, TIs are provably secure against first-order passive physical attacks—like differential power analysis attacks or chip probing—even in the presence of glitches. In the past, the TI scheme was mainly used to protect cryptographic circuits in order to make them side-channel resistant (e.g. Keccak [2], AES [9], Present [12]). The basis of TI is a technique well known from

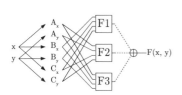

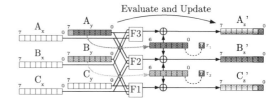

Fig. 1. Example for a shared function   **Fig. 2.** Resharing of a nonuniform function

multi party computations named *secret sharing* which breaks the data dependency of the computation. As it was shown by Barak et al. [1] a calculation can never be totally independent from its underlying data, but the complexity—the order of the attack—can be increased. In the subsequent sections the term sharing and threshold implementations are used interchangeably. The secret sharing principle is illustrated in Figure 1 for a bivariate function based on the TI scheme with three shares.

Before the shared function F is applied to the two variables, the variables themselves need to be shared. In this paper we use the same notations as Bilgin et al. [2]. Accordingly, a variable x is shared with three shares A, B, and C so that Equation 1 is valid at any time.

$$x = A_x \oplus B_x \oplus C_x \tag{1}$$

In order to have a shared implementation that is called a valid TI, the sharing must fulfill the following three requirements: *correctness*, *non-completeness*, and *uniformity*. A sharing of a function F is said to be correct if the sum of the output shares equals F applied to the sum of the input shares (see Equation 2).

$$F_{(A_x \oplus B_x \oplus C_x)} \Leftrightarrow F1_{(B_x, C_x)} \oplus F2_{(A_x, C_x)} \oplus F3_{(A_x, B_x)} \tag{2}$$

The non-completeness property requires that each of the component functions of a function F is independent from at least one input share like it is shown in Figure 1 and Equation 2. Fulfilling the uniformity property is usually the hardest task, because a uniform sharing of F requires that under the assumption of a uniformly distributed input sharing, the resulting output shares of the component functions are again uniformly distributed.

Even for a simple boolean function, like *AND* or *OR*, no uniform sharing exists for a three-share TI as it was shown by Nikova et al. In this case, additional random bits are required to recover the uniformity of the output shares. As an alternative, a higher amount of shares could be used, but this has the drawback of a higher resource footprint. However, the requirement of many high-quality fresh random bits with a high entropy at each clock cycle is also not quite practical. In 2013, Bilgin et al. [2] showed that the majority of the required random bits for the Keccak TI can be taken from independent shares by using Lemma 1.

Lemma 1 *(Simplified version from [2]). Let (A, B, C) be n-bit shares (not necessarily uniform). Let (D, E, F) be uniform n-bit shares statistically independent of (A, B, C). Then, (A+D, B+E, C+F) are uniform n-bit shares.*

Figure 2 shows how the uniformity of a nonuniformly shared function F—where each of the component functions are not uniform—can be repaired according to Lemma 1, when F is a bit-wise function. Since each of the bits of the shares A, B, and C are independent from the bits with a different index, the bits from the input shares of F can be used to reshare the output of the component functions of F. This is done by adding uniformly distributed and statistically independent bits—from the input shares and the two random bits—to the resulting output shares. The random bits are necessary to avoid dependencies between the bits. The result is a correct and uniform sharing at the output. When only one or two of the component functions are not uniform, it is enough to apply Lemma 1 to only two of the component functions which then requires just one high-quality random bit.

3 Attack Scenario

Figure 3 shows a typical embedded system scenario—considered to be integrated on a single microchip. The illustrated system could be, e.g., part of a technical process, and interacts with its direct environment through sensors and actuators. The core of the embedded system is a microcontroller that exchanges data with other modules connected to the I/O bus.

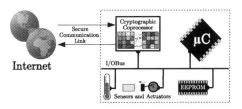

Fig. 3. Embedded system scenario

When a message is received or needs to be sent—e.g. to a server on the Internet—the cryptographic coprocessor handles security services like authentication, confidentiality protection, message integrity, et cetera. Therefore, the communication channel is considered to be secure. However, in this scenario we assume a powerful attacker that can not only spy on the network communication of the embedded system, but can also physically observer the device. Such an attacker could measure the power consumption of the system, place an electromagnetic probe on the device, or even put a needle on the I/O bus or on any other of the system's component in order to reveal any data flowing inside the system. Nevertheless, the adversary is assumed to be constraint in its observations and attacks to first-order scenarios. The attacker could thus either probe a single chip wire or execute a first-order power analysis attack. This is a typical assumption one has to make, because the costs for protecting the device, the attack costs, and the value of the protected assets should be considered to find adequate countermeasures.

The information an attacker is interested in could be, e.g., the communicated message between the system and the outside world, configuration parameters or cryptographic keys stored inside the non-volatile memory, et cetera. Regardless of the origin of the data, as soon as the data is processed inside the system it needs to pass the ALU of the microcontroller.

Protecting the system with the TI scheme hinders an attacker—limited to first-order attacks—to succeed. In the following it is assumed that security-critical data is either stored in the system or transported inside the system—e.g. over the I/O bus—in shared form. The targeted representation of the data input and output signals for the TI of the ALU is thus a uniform sharing. The number of used shares thereby determine the overhead of the TI relative to the unshared implementation, because the number of registers increases linearly with the number of required shares. Therefore, it is desirable to have an implementation with only three shares, which is the minimum number for first-order secure TIs. For a more sophisticated attacker the approach could be extended to higher-order threshold implementations like it was shown by Bilgin et al. [3] on the costs of higher hardware requirements. As a precondition, it needs to be considered that at no point of the system the data signal sharing is violated (demasking of the data), because an attacker could exploit this signal, e.g., for a simple probing attack. This condition leads to the requirement that all data input signals are already uniformly shared before they are handed to the ALU.

4   Protection of the Arithmetic Logic Unit

Since the arithmetic logic unit (ALU) is the central point of computation in all processor designs—like embedded microcontrollers—it is also the most vulnerable point for attacks on security-critical data. In the following, the typical functionality of a general purpose ALU is described in detail. The remainder of this section is then spent on answering the question how the ALU functionality can be implemented according to the threshold implementation (TI) masking scheme, and how these functions can be efficiently put together.

4.1   ALU Description

Figure 4 shows an ALU like it is used in similar form in many common processor architectures. The ALU basically consists of three stages. At first, the operands are selected from the ALU inputs. Then a preprocessing stage optionally inverts, shifts, or rotates an operand. Additionally, individual bits of the operands can be picked by using *bit-select* masks. Finally, the selected operands are applied to a so-called *functions array* that then executes the selected arithmetic or logic function.

In general there are two types of signals the ALU has to deal with: the control signals (red) and the data signals (black). The majority of signals are originated from data. The operands of the ALU can either be one or two selected registers, constants (from the program memory), the internally generated bit-select mask value, or the carry bit. For unary operations there is also a *"0"* operand selectable by the first operand multiplexer. Additionally, the first operand can also be inverted before it is applied to the

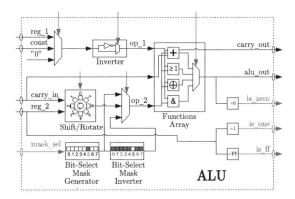

Fig. 4. Overview of the considered ALU (signals colored in red are control signals)

functions array of the ALU. The second operand can be either shifted or rotated before the two operands are combined. In order to test or set a single bit of a register value, the *bit-select mask generator* provides a one-hot or one-cold encoded bit vector. The core functionality of the ALU is built by the functions array which consists of an arithmetic adder, and the three logic operations *AND*, *OR*, and *XOR*. The computed value is then available at the output of the ALU. Control signals, on the other hand, are either used by the controller to select the desired functionality of the ALU or are generated by the ALU to inform the controller about certain events, like data overflows or comparison results.

4.2 Sharing of the ALU

In the following the sharing of the ALU functions is explained in detail. Therefore, it is assumed that all data input signals of the ALU are uniformly shared. This requirement is decisive for the correctness of the TI implementation.

Functions Array, Inverter, and Shift/Rotate. Sharing of the bit inverter and the *XOR* function of the *functions array* is straight-forward and was already shown before, e.g., by Nikova et al. [10]. For the inverter, it is sufficient to invert one of the shares of the selected operand. The logic *XOR* of two shared operands can be calculated by applying a logic *XOR* operation pairwise on the shares, e.g., $x \oplus y = (A_x \oplus A_y) \oplus (B_x \oplus B_y) \oplus (C_x \oplus C_y)$. The uniformity in both cases is not violated, and a resharing of the result is thus not required. Since, shifting and rotating also does not produce any new data the uniformity is guaranteed as long as the input is shared uniformly.

Sharing of the logic *AND* and *OR* operation is somewhat trickier. To the best of our knowledge, there exists no work that lists or analyzes all possibilities for sharing the logic *AND* and *OR* operations with three shares. In order to find the sharings, either a mathematical approach can be taken, like it was shown by Bilgin et al. [4], or an exhaustive search can be performed to search through all possibilities. It was shown by Nikova et al. [11] that for nonlinear functions, no uniform sharing with three shares exists. However, if a nonuniform sharing is found, it can be repaired by using so-called virtual variables. The equations for the shared functions is then extended by terms that contain random bits in such a manner that the uniformity is given again.

The exhaustive search approach used for this work to find the sharing with the lowest hardware costs for the logic *AND* and *OR* is described in Appendix A. In total eight possible (non equivalent) sharings for the logic *AND* and *OR* functions were found as it is listed in Table 1 and Table 2, respectively.

Table 1. Sharings for a logic *AND* function: $F_{(A_x \oplus B_x \oplus C_x, \, A_y \oplus B_y \oplus C_y)}$

	$F1_{(B_x.B_y.C_x.C_y)}$	$F2_{(A_x.A_y.C_x.C_y)}$	$F3_{(A_x.A_y.B_x.B_y)}$
AND-Sharing #1	0000001101010110	1001010100110000	**0001110110111000**
AND-Sharing #2	0000001101010110	**1101000101110100**	0101100111111100
AND-Sharing #3	0000001101011001	1101000101111011	0101100111111100
AND-Sharing #4	0000001110101001	**1101000110001011**	0101100111111100
AND-Sharing #5	0000110010101001	1101111010001011	0101100111111100
AND-Sharing #6	**0001110110111000**	1101111010001011	0101100111110011
AND-Sharing #7	0011111110011010	1101111010001011	0101100100000011
AND-Sharing #8	0111101111011110	1101111010001011	0101011000000011

Table 2. Sharings for a logic *OR* function: $F_{(A_x \oplus B_x \oplus C_x, \, A_y \oplus B_y \oplus C_y)}$

	$F1_{(B_x.B_y.C_x.C_y)}$	$F2_{(A_x.A_y.C_x.C_y)}$	$F3_{(A_x.A_y.B_x.B_y)}$
OR-Sharing #1	0000001101010110	1001101011000000	**0111010000101110**
OR-Sharing #2	0000001101010110	**1101111010000100**	0011000001101010
OR-Sharing #3	0000001101011001	1101111010001011	0011000001101010
OR-Sharing #4	0000001110101001	1101111001111011	0011000001101010
OR-Sharing #5	0000110010101001	1101000101111011	0011000001101010
OR-Sharing #6	**0001110110111000**	1101000101111011	0011000001100101
OR-Sharing #7	0011111110011010	1101000101111011	0011000010010101
OR-Sharing #8	0111101111011110	1101000101111011	0011111110010101

Each entry in these tables shows the output bit combination that appears when iterated over the input variables. Some of the component functions are already uniform (emphasized in the table). In this case only the two non-uniform component functions need to be repaired by simply adding one random bit as a virtual variable to the output of the nonuniform functions (see Figure 2). For the case where all three component functions are non-uniform, either two virtual variables could be used, or a nonlinear combination of one virtual variable with other variables leads to a uniform sharing. Anyway, as it turns out in our hardware implementation evaluation (see Section 6), these sharings are always more hardware demanding than the sharings with already one uniform component function. The extension of the 1-bit shared logic operations to the required n-bit is trivial, since the bits are independent and hence the shared gates can be put in parallel.

Adders and the "0" Operand. A simple half-adder takes per definition two input bits and calculates one sum bit and further on a carry bit. The implementation of a half-adder can be realized by using an *XOR* gate for the resulting sum bit and an *AND* gate to calculate the carry. Full-adders—as they are required for the ALU design—which also take a carry bit as an input, can be built of two half-adders and an *OR* gate (see Figure 5).

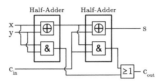

Fig. 5. Schematic of a full-adder built from two half-adders and one logic *OR*

A straightforward way of implementing a shared full-adder would be to use the already obtained shared logic gates to implement the half-adders and the logic *OR*. However, this would require fresh random bits for each of the full-adders in the design to guarantee uniformity. Nevertheless, Figure 5 shows that for the calculation of the sum bit "s" only *XOR* gates are required, and thus the corresponding *s*-bit output sharing is already uniform if the inputs are uniformly shared. The carry bit on the other hand can be realized by Equation 3.

$$
\begin{aligned}
c_{out} &= (x \wedge y) \vee (x \oplus y \wedge c) \\
&= (x \wedge y) \vee (x \wedge c) \vee (y \wedge c)
\end{aligned}
\tag{3}
$$

The shared form of this equation is presented in Equation 4, and is obtained by using a direct sharing approach.

$$
\begin{aligned}
(A_{Cout} \oplus B_{Cout} \oplus C_{Cout}) =& \big((A_x \oplus B_x \oplus C_x) \wedge (A_y \oplus B_y \oplus C_y) \big) \vee \\
& \big((A_x \oplus B_x \oplus C_x) \wedge (A_c \oplus B_c \oplus C_c) \big) \vee \\
& \big((A_y \oplus B_y \oplus C_y) \wedge (A_c \oplus B_c \oplus C_c) \big)
\end{aligned}
\tag{4}
$$

By dissolving the brackets and by grouping the terms according to the non-completeness rule, the sharing of the carry results in Equations 5-7.

$$
\begin{aligned}
A_{Cout} =& (B_x \wedge B_y) \oplus (B_x \wedge C_y) \oplus (B_y \wedge C_x) \oplus \\
& (B_x \wedge B_c) \oplus (B_x \wedge C_c) \oplus (B_c \wedge C_x) \oplus \\
& (B_c \wedge B_y) \oplus (B_y \wedge C_c) \oplus (B_c \wedge C_y)
\end{aligned}
\tag{5}
$$

$$
\begin{aligned}
B_{Cout} =& (C_x \wedge C_y) \oplus (A_x \wedge C_y) \oplus (A_y \wedge C_x) \oplus \\
& (C_x \wedge C_c) \oplus (A_x \wedge C_c) \oplus (A_c \wedge C_x) \oplus \\
& (C_c \wedge C_y) \oplus (A_y \wedge C_c) \oplus (A_c \wedge C_y)
\end{aligned}
\tag{6}
$$

$$C_{Cout} = (A_x \wedge A_y) \oplus (A_x \wedge B_y) \oplus (A_y \wedge B_x) \oplus$$
$$(A_x \wedge A_c) \oplus (A_x \wedge B_c) \oplus (A_c \wedge B_x) \oplus \qquad (7)$$
$$(A_c \wedge A_y) \oplus (A_y \wedge B_c) \oplus (A_c \wedge B_y)$$

The sharing of the carry bit is again uniform, and does not require additional random bits. The question that still remains is whether or not the joint distribution of the shared sum and carry bits are uniform. A nonuniform joint distribution would leak information about the operands and could thus be considered in a power model. By iterating over all input share combinations for each pair of the component functions of the sum and carry bits, it can be shown that also the joint distribution of these bits are also uniform. The shared implementation of the full-adder can therefore be realized without using any additional random bits at all if the input shares are uniform.

From 1-bit Adders to n-bit Adders. The circumstance that an addition—in contrast to the boolean operations—needs to consider all bit positions together to calculate the correct sum, leads to the observation that the calculations cannot be performed in a single clock cycle—like it was shown recently by Schneider et al. [14]. Putting a series of shared full-adders together to from an n-bit adder violates the independence requirement of the TI, because the calculations then no longer depend on only two shares. The consequences could be data dependent power glitches that lead to a vulnerability to first-order attacks. Consequently, the calculations of the component functions must be separated by register stores.

While there exist many possible adder designs with different benefits and drawbacks—Schneider et al. [14] showed two possible realizations—, we decided on a straight-forward iterative approach, because of the rather low data width of the targeted ALU design. The shared 8-bit adder design is shown in Figure 6.

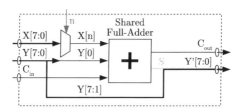

Fig. 6. Iterative Shared 8-bit Adder (upper case variables are shared)

At the input, the multiplexer selects one bit of the shared operand X beginning with the least-significant bit. The source of the Y operand is always a register which also servers as the destination for the result. The two shared operand bits and the carry are then applied to the shared full-adder. The calculated carry is stored and then reused in the subsequent iteration. For the new register content, only the current bit position of the shared operand is overwritten with the resulting sum bit S and the bits are reordered in each iteration. The number of required clock cycles thus increase linearly with the number of used bits. However, the benefits of this approach are the very low area footprint and that no additional random bits are required.

Increment and Decrement. A special case of the addition operation are the increment and the decrement instructions. In this case the first operand is set to zero and the inverter control signal and the carry input bit are set accordingly. Setting the first operand and the carry to a fixed value seems to be a violation against the uniformity requirement at first sight. Nevertheless, by doing this the right way the uniformity property can be saved.

For a uniform implementation of the increment instruction, the shares of the first operand (A_x, B_x, and C_x) are set to zero, the inverter control is set to "by-pass", and all bits of the *carry_in* shares (A_c, B_c, and C_c) are set to one. The uniformity of the sum bit is given, since for its calculation only the shares of the second operand (A_y, B_y, and C_y) are inverted because of the carry bit shares. The carry output bit, however, only depends on the value of the second operand which can be demonstrated by inserting the afore mentioned changes into Equations 5-7. Since the output of the first full-adder is uniform, so is the output of the next full-adder, et cetera.

For the decrementation instruction, the first operand's shares (A_x, B_x, and C_x) are again set to zero but then inverted by setting all bits of the A_x share to one through the inverter. Furthermore, the A_c share of the *carry_in* is set to zero and all other shares to one.

Bit Set/Bit Clear and the Bit-Select Mask Generator. In the unshared design, the *Bit-Select Mask Generator* basically performs a one-hot encoding of the *mask_sel* value. This mask is then used to set or clear one specific bit. Setting one bit high is then performed by selecting the logic *OR* operation from the functions array. For clearing one bit, the inverse mask is used. The selected register is finally combined with the mask by using the *AND* operation.

Applying the same operations on shared values requires some changes in the ALU. One possibility for implementing shared n-bit select masks is shown in Equation 8.

$$
\begin{aligned}
M_1 &= 000 \cdots (A_x \oplus B_x) \cdots 000_n \\
M_2 &= 000 \cdots (A_x \oplus [1]) \cdots 000_n \\
M_3 &= 000 \cdots B_x \qquad\quad \cdots 000_n
\end{aligned}
\tag{8}
$$

First of all, the bit-select mask value generation already needs to take the desired operation into account. This is done by adding an additional "1" to the desired bit position for M_2 when the bit needs to be set. All other bits of the shares are set to zero. The resulting bit-select mask is then applied to the operand by using the *XOR* operation of the functions array in either case. For the output sharing, only the targeted bit position changes.

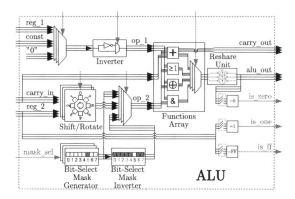

Fig. 7. Overview of the TI of the ALU

Sharing of Control Signals. The ALU usually generates some control signals required for the control unit of a processor to handle, e.g., conditional branch instructions. These instructions compare the output of the ALU or the content of one register to a fixed value (e.g., the zero and overflow flags). This could be realized by bringing the comparison equation to a disjunctive normal form. In so doing, this results in a cascaded network of logic *AND* gates with a gate count of $n - 1$ and a delay path depth of $log_2(n)$—for a comparison equation with n (= power of two) variables. Even though it is possible to share these control signals, it was shown in the past that branches can be detected quite easily by an attacker. Branches can be detected through changes in the program flow structure which affect the power traces or the execution time of the program. It is thus essential to avoid branches or conditional code execution which depend on the data one wants to protect. Cryptographic software implementations, e.g. for the AES, could use table lookups either in the program memory or the data memory to speed up their implementation. These issues are well know and are therefore usually avoided by programmers aware of side-channel attacks (see e.g., Käsper et al. [7]). Sharing of control signals will thus not lead to a better protection and can thus be excluded from the TI of the ALU. The software developers are responsible to program the software in a way that it is free of branches which rely on security critical data. However, it needs to be ensured that the creation of data dependent control signals is suppressed when critical data is processed, e.g., by using operand isolation techniques in case a branch instruction is fetched.

Bringing the Findings Together. Besides the described shared implementation of the functions and the tripled signal paths, some new components are introduced in the final design of the ALU (see Figure 7). A new module called *reshare unit* is added which does the repairing of the non-uniform boolean functions by adding the virtual variables to the output of the functions array. Since, only one of the functions from the functions array is executed at a time, the reshare unit needs to be implemented only once. Therefore, only one fresh random bit is required—for the reparation of the *OR* and *AND* function—, and the rest of the virtual variables are taken from independent shares similar to Figure 2. So, the TI of the ALU requires one fresh random bit in each clock cycle to guarantee uniformity at the output. Furthermore, in order to thwart an unintended unmasking of the shared data, the comparison units are isolated from the operands in any case other than a branch instruction is fetched. This is done by gating the input signal of the comparison units which is controllable by a single input control signal. In the next section, the protected ALU is integrated into a case study microcontroller design and the required implications are discussed.

5   Case Study: Microcontroller

The microcontroller used in the case study of this paper is illustrated in Figure 8. It is an 8-bit microcontroller with a Harvard architecture design and has a separate storage for program code and data, accordingly. Instructions from the program memory are decoded in the *control FSM* unit that generates the control signals for the ALU, the *register file*—consisting of up to 64 registers—, and the *program counter* (PC). Overall, there are just about 30 instructions available in the standard instruction set. However, the microcontroller is completely configurable in terms of program memory size, size of the register file, and also the instruction set can be extended or reduced easily to the needs of certain applications. The register file has three special purpose registers, and a configurable size of general purpose (GPR) and I/O registers. I/O registers have an additional external feedback path that is used to extend the microcontroller with peripherals, or an additional RAM, or a cryptographic coprocessor.

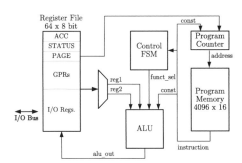

Fig. 8. Overview of the used 8-bit microcontroller

Figure 8 also shows how the ALU from Section 4 is integrated into the microcontroller design. All data inputs of the ALU need to be shared before the processing in the ALU is performed. For data that needs to be protected, it is assumed that this data is either stored (and updated) on-chip in a shared representation—e.g. in a non-volatile memory—or that the data is transported into the microcontroller in a uniformly shared way.

The origin of the data input signals of the ALU can either be the internal registers or the I/O registers, or the program memory. The internal registers are successively filled with the shared data output of the ALU or with data provided by the I/O modules.

The register file size is therefore tripled, and I/O modules connected to the microcontroller need to be prepared for handling shares. For example, if the microcontroller is connected to a cryptographic coprocessor that secures the external communication, the design of the coprocessor also needs to be a TI. The data between the microcontroller and the cryptographic coprocessor is then exchanged in a shared form over the I/O bus.

For the sake of simplicity it is assumed that data inside program memory is shared and updated accordingly. The program memory therefore needs to be writable and non volatile. One possible realization is the usage of ferroelectric RAM (FRAM) like it is used in the MSP430F microcontroller family. FRAM is extremely fast—50 ns for writing, according to [5]—and has a very low power consumption. How the program memory sharing and the updating is managed is out of scope for this work. In this case study we are mainly interested in estimating the overhead for implementing the core of the microcontroller as a threshold implementation, since the program memory requirements vary from application to application.

6   Results

In this section, the impact of the shared components of the threshold implementation is investigated on three different abstraction levels. At first the influence of the TI on gate level is considered which shows how the sharing changes the requirements regarding chip area, power consumption, and timing constraints. In a more macroscopic juxtaposition the costs for the ALU described in Section 4 are then considered. Finally, the microcontroller of the case study in Section 5 is compared with and without shared components. All results are collected for a 90 nm UMC Standard Performance Low-K ASIC library from Faraday for a global clock of 10 MHz and a 1 V power supply. For the synthesis step, the Cadence Encounter RTL Compiler Version v08.10-s28 and for the routing the Cadence NanoRoute v08.10-s155 are used.

Comparison on Gate Level. Table 3 shows the costs for a sharing of the *XOR*, *AND*, *OR* and *full-adder* cells relative to the costs of the standard-cell library gates. The required chip area is measured in multiples of a gate equivalent (= the size of a single two-input NAND gate). The maximum clock frequency is calculated on the basis of the remaining slack for the longest combinatorial path in the circuit at the targeted clock period. Therefore, it should not be seen as a total maximum but only with regard to the used gates. Gates with a higher driving strength would of course increase the maximum possible clock frequency, but this would also influences the chip area and power consumption. The power consumption is estimated with Cadence Encounter which only allows a rough estimation of the power consumption, because no transistor-level power information is considered. However, since these values are only compared in relation to each other, it should be sufficient and accurate enough to show how a sharing influences the power consumption.

Since the shared *XOR* gate requires only two additional XOR gates in parallel, the overall size triples but the propagation delay stays unchanged. The effect on the consumed power is with an overhead factor (OHF) of almost 36 more noticeable. In the case of a logic *AND* the best results in all categories are obtained from implementation #1 of

Table 3. Comparison of standard library cells and their shared implementations

Function	Implementation	Area [GE]	Area OHF	max. Frequency [GHz]	Delay OHF	Power [nW]	Power OHF
XOR	std-cell	2.50	3.00	22.73	1.00	22.73	35.94
	shared	7.50		22.73		816.77	
AND	std-cell	1.25	13.40	27.03	3.54	57.50	25.93
	shared	16.75		7.63		1,491.21	
OR	std-cell	1.25	12.80	23.26	2.88	140.14	11.64
	shared	16.00		8.06		1,631.40	
Full-Adder	std-cell	8.25	10.67	6.58	1.94	777.00	11.93
	shared	88.00		3.39		9,268.83	

Table 1. The area overhead factor is in this case 13.4 which means that a standard cell library *AND* gate is 13.4 times smaller. Due to the cascaded combination of the gates in the shared *AND* gate, the delay path increases only to a factor of 3.54, and therefore also the maximum possible clock frequency is just lowered according to this factor. In terms of power, the shared variant consumes almost 26 times more power because of the increased gate count on one side but also due to the higher capacitances at the load side of the gates. Compared to the shared logic *AND*, the shared logic *OR* implementation is a bit cheaper with an area OHF of 12.8, but also the propagation delay and the power increase is comparably smaller. Whats also very interesting, is the fact that the variants of the shared logic gates where already one component function is uniform result in a smaller design than the variants with three nonuniform component functions[1]. The area overhead factor of the logic *AND* variant #1 and variant #3 of Table 1 is 13.4 and 17.4, respectively.

The most complex shared function is the full-adder. Nevertheless, the sharing requires "only" 10.7 times more area than the standard cell, and lowers the maximum clock frequency to a factor of 1.9. Also the effect on the power is relatively small compared to other shared gates.

Comparison of the ALU Designs. Table 4 shows a comparison between the shared and unshared ALU. It can be seen that the size of the ALU changes from 249 GE to 1.14 kGE. The area OHF in this case is about 4.56. The longest combinatorial path, however, is reduced because of the iterative adder design. Please note that additions take now eight cycles instead of one. Furthermore, the power increases to a factor of almost five.

Table 4. Comparison of the shared and unshared ALU

Component	Implementation	Size [GE]	Area OHF	max. Frequency [MHz]	Delay OHF	Power [μW]	Power OHF
ALU	unshared	249	4.56	725.69	0.99	34.60	4.98
	shared	1.135		731.53		172.40	

---

[1] Please note that only the best candidates for each shared gate are considered in the respective tables for brevity and clarity reasons.

Comparison of the Microcontroller Designs. In this comparison the costs for the shared microcontroller core including the ALU, the register file, the control FSM, and the program counter are evaluated. This comparison interestingly shows how the influence of the TI to the resource costs is relativized compared to Tables 3 and 4. The influence of the program memory and peripherals connected to the microcontroller are left out for this considerations, because they strongly vary from application to application. Table 5 shows that the relative area increase in the shared case sinks below a factor of three. The reason for this is the still relatively small size of the ALU compared to the rest of the microcontroller. A bigger influence to the overall size has the shared register file which is almost twelve times bigger than the shared ALU. The maximum working frequency of the shared microcontroller is still 191 MHz. Also the relative power consumption overhead is not as highly influenced as in the previous comparison with a factor of about 2.3.

Table 5. Comparison of the shared and unshared Microcontroller

Component	Implementation	Size [GE]	Area OHF	max. Frequency [MHz]	Delay OHF	Power [μW]	Power OHF
Microcontroller	unshared	5,216	2.80	198.14	1.04	246.88	2.27
	shared	14,605		191.09		560.65	

7 Conclusions

In this work, we showed how a general purpose arithmetic logic unit (ALU) can be implemented in a way that it resists first-order passive physical attacks. Therefore, we looked at the functionality of a typical ALU and discussed then how this functionality can be realized in accordance to the provably secure threshold implementation (TI) scheme. While the protection of cryptographic implementations with the TI scheme was already addressed in the literature, the shared implementation of the more versatile functionality provided by an microcontroller has not yet been researched. A problem that often limits the usability of masked implementations is the required amount of fresh random bits. It was shown that by combining the ALU functions in an efficient way, the number of required random bits can be reduced to only a single bit per clock cycle. The protected ALU was finally integrated into a case-study microcontroller design and the impact of the sharing on other modules of the microcontroller investigated. Nevertheless, the shared implementation of the microcontroller should not be considered as an all-round carefree package for software designers. There are some pitfalls one can run into, like branches depending on security sensitive data, table lookups, et cetera. The whole spectrum of implications that result from a shared microcontroller design as well as a side-channel evaluation is part of future research.

Acknowledgements. This work has been supported by the Austrian Science Fund (FWF) under the grant number TRP251-N23 (Realizing a Secure Internet of Things - ReSIT) and the FFG research program SeCoS (project number 836628).

References

1. Barak, B., Goldreich, O., Impagliazzo, R., Rudich, S., Sahai, A., Vadhan, S., Yang, K.: On the (Im)Possibility of Obfuscating Programs. J. ACM 6, 6:1–6:48 (2012)
2. Bilgin, B., Daemen, J., Nikov, V., Nikova, S., Rijmen, V., Assche, G.V.: Efficient and first-order DPA resistant implementations of keccak. In: Smart Card Research and Advanced Applications - 12th International Conference, CARDIS 2013, Berlin, Germany, November 27–29, Revised Selected Papers, pp. 187–199 (2013)
3. Bilgin, B., Gierlichs, B., Nikova, S., Nikov, V., Rijmen, V.: Higher-order threshold implementations. In: Sarkar, P., Iwata, T. (eds.) ASIACRYPT 2014, Part II. LNCS, vol. 8874, pp. 326–343. Springer, Heidelberg (2014)
4. Bilgin, B., Nikova, S., Nikov, V., Rijmen, V., Stütz, G.: Threshold Implementations of All 3 ×3 and 4 ×4 S-Boxes. In: Prouff, E., Schaumont, P. (eds.) CHES 2012. LNCS, vol. 7428, pp. 76–91. Springer, Heidelberg (2012)
5. Instruments, T.: FRAM FAQs (2014) (accessed February 10, 2015)
6. Ishai, Y., Sahai, A., Wagner, D.: Private circuits: Securing hardware against probing attacks. In: Boneh, D. (ed.) CRYPTO 2003. LNCS, vol. 2729, pp. 463–481. Springer, Heidelberg (2003)
7. Käsper, E., Schwabe, P.: Faster and timing-attack resistant AES-GCM. In: Clavier, C., Gaj, K. (eds.) CHES 2009. LNCS, vol. 5747, pp. 1–17. Springer, Heidelberg (2009)
8. Kocher, P.C., Jaffe, J., Jun, B.: Differential power analysis. In: Wiener, M. (ed.) CRYPTO 1999. LNCS, vol. 1666, pp. 388–397. Springer, Heidelberg (1999)
9. Moradi, A., Poschmann, A., Ling, S., Paar, C., Wang, H.: Pushing the limits: a very compact and a threshold implementation of AES. In: Paterson, K.G. (ed.) EUROCRYPT 2011. LNCS, vol. 6632, pp. 69–88. Springer, Heidelberg (2011)
10. Nikova, S., Rechberger, C., Rijmen, V.: Threshold implementations against side-channel attacks and glitches. In: Ning, P., Qing, S., Li, N. (eds.) ICICS 2006. LNCS, vol. 4307, pp. 529–545. Springer, Heidelberg (2006)
11. Nikova, S., Rijmen, V., Schläffer, M.: Secure Hardware Implementation of Nonlinear Functions in the Presence of Glitches. Journal of Cryptology 24(2), 292–321 (2011)
12. Poschmann, A., Moradi, A., Khoo, K., Lim, C.-W., Wang, H., Ling, S.: Side-Channel Resistant Crypto for Less than 2, 300 GE. J. Cryptology 24, 322–345 (2011)
13. Quisquater, J.-J., Samyde, D.: ElectroMagnetic analysis (EMA): measures and counter-measures for smart cards. In: Attali, S., Jensen, T. (eds.) E-smart 2001. LNCS, vol. 2140, pp. 200–210. Springer, Heidelberg (2001)
14. Schneider, T., Moradi, A., Gneysu, T.: Arithmetic Addition over Boolean Masking - Towards First- and Second-Order Resistance in Hardware. Cryptology ePrint Archive, Report 2015/066 (2015)

A   Searching for Efficient TI Realizations of Boolean Functions

In Section 4.2, we mentioned our approach for finding possible realizations of shared boolean functions based on an exhaustive search. Since, the results in Table 1 and Table 2 can be interpreted more easily if the underlying approach is clarified, we briefly step through the search strategy in the following.

The exhaustive search approach used for this paper to find the sharing with the lowest hardware costs for the logic *AND* and *OR* is based on the simple observation that the structure of the component functions is defined by the requirements for TIs: (1) each of the three component functions of F for a three-share TI can have at most four input bits from two independent sharings (non-completeness), (2) the output of the component functions is always one bit, and (3) added together these functions must output the same value as the original function (correctness). A shared boolean function with three shares can therefore be fully described by the following truth tables.

B_x	B_y	C_x	C_y	$F1$		A_x	A_y	C_x	C_y	$F2$		A_x	A_y	B_x	B_y	$F3$
0	0	0	0	b_0		0	0	0	0	b_0		0	0	0	0	b_0
0	0	0	1	b_1		0	0	0	1	b_1		0	0	0	1	b_1
0	0	1	0	b_2		0	0	1	0	b_2		0	0	1	0	b_2
0	0	1	1	b_3		0	0	1	1	b_3		0	0	1	1	b_3
0	1	0	0	b_4		0	1	0	0	b_4		0	1	0	0	b_4
:	:	:	:	:		:	:	:	:	:		:	:	:	:	:
1	0	1	1	b_{11}		1	0	1	1	b_{11}		1	0	1	1	b_{11}
1	1	0	0	b_{12}		1	1	0	0	b_{12}		1	1	0	0	b_{12}
1	1	0	1	b_{13}		1	1	0	1	b_{13}		1	1	0	1	b_{13}
1	1	1	0	b_{14}		1	1	1	0	b_{14}		1	1	1	0	b_{14}
1	1	1	1	b_{15}		1	1	1	1	b_{15}		1	1	1	1	b_{15}

In particular, it is sufficient to describe each realization of the component function by its output-bit combination $b_{15...0}$, which is used for Table 1 and Table 2. We can thus search through all possible realizations of the function F by iterating over all 2^{16} possible output-bit combinations for $F1$ and $F2$. The output bit combination of $F3$ then automatically results from $F1$ and $F2$. For the iteration over the realizations for $F2$, we can save half of the iterations because they are already covered by iterating over $F1$. The overall search effort for all possibilities to implement a three-share TI of F is hence 2^{31}.

Part III

RFID System Attacks

Practical Experiences on NFC Relay Attacks with Android[*]
Virtual Pickpocketing Revisited

José Vila[1] and Ricardo J. Rodríguez[2]

[1] Department of Computer Science and Systems Engineering
University of Zaragoza, Spain
[2] Research Institute of Applied Sciences in Cybersecurity
University of León, Spain
594190@unizar.es, rj.rodriguez@unileon.es

Abstract. Near Field Communication (NFC) is a short-range contactless communication standard recently emerging as cashless payment technology. However, NFC has been proved vulnerable to several threats, such as eavesdropping, data modification, and relay attacks. A relay attack forwards the entire wireless communication, thus communicating over larger distances. In this paper, we review and discuss feasibility limitations when performing these attacks in Google's Android OS. We also perform an in-depth review of the Android implementation of the NFC stack. We show an experiment proving its feasibility using off-the-shelf NFC-enabled Android devices (i.e., no custom firmware nor root required). Thus, Android NFC-capable malicious software might appear before long to virtually pickpocket contactless payment cards within its proximity.

Keywords: NFC, security, relay attacks, Android, contactless payment.

1 Introduction

Near Field Communication (NFC) is a bidirectional short-range (up to 10 cm) contactless communication technology based on the ISO-14443 [1] and the Sony FeLiCa [2] Radio Frequency Identification (RFID) standards. It operates in the 13.56 MHz spectrum and supports data transfer rates of 106, 216, and 424 kbps.

NFC defines three operation modes: peer-to-peer, read/write, and card-emulation mode. In peer-to-peer mode, two NFC devices communicate directly with each other. This mode is commonly used to exchange business cards, or credentials for establishing a network link. Read/write mode allows an NFC device to communicate with an NFC tag. Finally, card-emulation mode enables an NFC device to behave as a contactless smartcard, thus allowing to communicate with an NFC reader/writer.

[*] This work was partially supported by the University of León under contract X43.

© Springer International Publishing Switzerland 2015
S. Mangard, P. Schaumont (Eds.): RFIDsec 2015, LNCS 9440, pp. 87–103, 2015.
DOI: 10.1007/978-3-319-24837-0_6

Nowadays, NFC technology is widely used in a disparity of applications, from ticketing, staff identification, or physical access control, to cashless payment. In fact, the contactless payment sector seems the one where NFC has generated more interest, accordingly to market studies [3, 4]. As Fischer envisioned in 2009 [5], the confluence of NFC with smart phones can be the reason behind this fact since NFC is a way to bring "cards" to the mobile [6].

To date, almost 300 different smart phones are (or will be soon) available at the market [7]. Most of them are based on Google's Android OS (or Android for short), while other OS such as Apple's iOS, BlackBerry OS, or Windows Phone OS are less representative. For instance, Apple has just started to add NFC capabilities into its devices: Apple's iPhone 6 is the first model integrated with an NFC chip, although is locked to work only with Apple's contactless payment system [8]. As a recent market research states [9], this trend will keep growing up, expecting to reach more than 500 million of NFC payment users by 2019.

Unfortunately, NFC is insecure as claimed by several works [10–13], where NFC security threats and solutions have been stated. Potential threats of NFC are eavesdropping, data modification (i.e., alteration, insertion, or destruction), and relay attacks. Eavesdropping can be avoided by secure communication, while data modification may require advanced skills and enough knowledge about RF transmission, as well as ad-hoc hardware to perform the attack. A relay attack, defined as a forwarding of the entire wireless communication, allows to communicate over a large distance. A *passive relay attack* forwards the data unaltered, unlike an *active relay attack* [14]. In this paper, we focus on passive relay attacks.

Relay attacks were thought to be difficult from a practical perspective, mainly due to the physical constraints on the communication channel and the specialized hardware (or software) needed. However, the eruption of NFC-enabled mobile phones (or devices) completely changes the threat landscape: Most NFC communication can be relayed – even NFC payment transactions – with NFC-enabled devices. Many works have proved this fact under different attack scenarios, as we reviewed in Section 5.

Mobile malicious software (i.e., malware) usually target user data (such as user credentials or mobile device information), or perform fraud through premium-rate calls or SMS, but we believe that the rise of NFC-enabled devices put NFC in the spotlight for malware developers [15]. To the best of our knowledge, to date there not exist any malware with NFC capabilities although they might appear before long. To prove if an *NFC-capable malware* might exist nowadays, in this paper we study the feasibility of passive relay attacks in Android. Android is used since it leads the global smartphone market [16] and provides a broad set of freely resources for the developers.

The contribution of this paper is threefold: first, we provide an in-depth review of Android implementation of the NFC stack; second, we discuss the implementation alternatives to perform NFC relay attacks in Android; and third, we show a practical implementation of these attacks using two NFC-enabled mobile phones running an off-the-shelf (OTS) Android (i.e., no custom firmware nor root permissions). Our findings put in evidence that these scenarios are nowadays feasible, requiring permission only of NFC and relay communication link chosen (e.g., Bluetooth, WiFi, or GPRS). This issue clearly supposes a high security risk: An NFC-capable malware installed on an Android device can interact with any contactless payment cards in its proximity, being able to conduct illegal transactions. Current limitations and feasibility of some malware attack scenarios are also introduced.

The outline of this paper is as follows. Section 2 introduces previous concepts. In Section 3, we analyse and discuss practical issues of alternatives provided by Android to perform an NFC passive relay attack. Section 4 describes a practical implementation of this attack using OTS Android NFC-enabled devices, discusses threat scenarios, and introduces countermeasures. Section 5 reviews related works. Finally, Section 6 states conclusions and future work.

2   Background

This section first briefly introduces the ISO/IEC 14443 standard [17] since contactless payment cards rely on it. Then, relay attacks and mafia frauds are introduced. Finally, we review the history of NFC support in Android.

2.1   ISO/IEC 14443 Standard

ISO/IEC 14443 is a four-part international standard for contactless smartcards operating at 13.56 MHz [17]. Proximity Integrated Circuit Cards (PICC), also referred to as *tags*, are intended to operate up to 10 cm of a reader antenna, usually termed as Proximity Coupling Device (PCD).

Part 1 of the standard defines the size, physical characteristics, and environmental working conditions of the card. Part 2 defines the RF power and two signalling schemes, Type A and Type B. Both schemes are half duplex with a data rate of 106kbps (in each direction). Part 3 describes initialisation and anticollision protocols, as well as commands, responses, data frame, and timing issues. A polling command is required for waking both card types up and start communication. Part 4 defines the high-level data transmission protocols. A PICC fulfilling all parts of ISO/IEC 14443 is named *IsoDep* card (for instance, contactless payment cards). As response to the polling phase, a PICC reports whether Part 4 is supported. Apart from specific protocol commands, the protocol defined in Part 4 is also capable of transferring Application Protocol Data Units (APDUs) as defined in ISO/IEC 7816-4 [18] and of application selection as defined in ISO/IEC 7816-5 [19]. ISO/IEC 7816-4 and ISO/IEC 7816-5 are part of ISO/IEC 7816, a fifteen-part international standard related to contacted integrated circuit cards, especially smartcards.

2.2   Relay Attacks and Mafia Frauds

Relay attacks were initially introduced by John Conway in 1976 [20], where he explained how a player without knowledge of the chess rules could win to a

Grandmaster. To relate these attacks in detail, let us recall here to the well-known people in the security community Alice, Bob, and Eve.

Consider Grandmasters Alice, Bob, who are both challenged by Eve at the same time to play a correspondence chess game (i.e., chess movements are received and sent via email, postal system, or others long-distance correspondence methods). Eve, who ignores the rules, selects a different colour pieces in each match. When playing, she only needs to relay movements received/sent from one match to the other, until a match ends. Fig. 1 shows the scenario described by Conway. Note that both Alice, Bob, think they are playing against Eve, but in fact they are playing between them.

Fig. 1. Chess game relay

To the best of our knowledge, the first work introducing relay attacks in systems where security is based on the proximity concern is [21]. Desmedt defined the *mafia fraud* as a relay attack where a dishonest prover $\mathcal{P}'$ and a dishonest verifier $\mathcal{V}'$ act together to cheat to a honest verifier $\mathcal{V}$ and a honest prover $\mathcal{P}$, respectively, as $\mathcal{V} \Longleftrightarrow \mathcal{P}' \ll$ *communication link* $\gg \mathcal{V}' \Longleftrightarrow \mathcal{P}$, where $\mathcal{P}', \mathcal{V}'$, communicates one each other through a communication link. Herein, we adhere to this terminology to refer to the contactless payment card (*honest prover*), the legitimate Point-of-Sale (PoS) terminal (*honest verifier*), and the two NFC-enabled Android devices used to perform an NFC passive relay attack (*dishonest prover* and *dishonest verifier*).

2.3   Evolution of NFC Support in Google's Android OS

NFC support in Android began with Android version 2.3 (*Gingerbread* codename), where only peer-to-peer (used by Android Beam) and read/write operation modes were natively supported. This initial limitation was overcome by the following version updates, being incrementally completed up to gaining an NFC full support and a really comprehensive API for developers in Android version 4.4 (*KitKat* codename). In read/write operation mode, different communication protocols and tags are supported, depending on the NFC chip manufacturer. Namely, Android 2.3.3 (API level 10) onward provides (mandatory) support for ISO/IEC 14443-3A (`NfcA`), ISO/IEC 14443-3B (`NfcB`), JIS 6319-4 (`NfcF`), ISO/IEC 15693 (`NfcV`), ISO/IEC 14443-4 (`IsoDep`), and NDEF; while it provides optional support for `NdefFormatable`, `MifareClassic`, and `MifareUltralight` tags. From Android 4.2 (*Jelly Bean*) onward *NfcBarcode* tag was introduced.

Card emulation is the mode with more substantial changes among versions. In the early NFC-enabled Android versions, this mode was only provided via hardware using Secure Elements (SEs) following GlobalPlatform specifications [22]. A SE provides a tamper-proof platform to securely store data and execute applications, thus maintaining confidential data away from an untrusted host. With

SE card emulation, the NFC controller directly routes all communication from external reader (e.g., a PoS terminal) to the tamper-resistant chip, without passing through the OS. That is, NFC communication remains transparent to the OS. SEs are capable to communicate not only with the NFC controller but also with mobile applications running within the OS (such as electronic wallets) and *over-the-air* with the Trusted Service Manager (TSM).

TSM is an intermediary authority acting between mobile network operators and phone manufacturers (or other entities controlling a SE) and enabling the service providers (such as banks) to distribute and manage their applications remotely. This closed, distributed ecosystem guarantees a high level of confidence and has been mainly used by the payment sector. However, it excludes other developers from using the card emulation mode. As a result, many developers asked for an easier access to this resource.

The first solution was provided by BlackBerry Limited (formerly known as Research In Motion Limited) company, which included software card emulation (or "soft-SE") mode in BlackBerry 7 OS [23]. This mode allowed the interaction of RFID readers and mobile phone's applications directly, thus completely opening the card emulation to any developer. Basically, soft-SE (also named as Host Card Emulation, HCE) allowed the OS to receive commands from the NFC controller and to response them by any applications instead of by applets installed on a SE.

HCE feature was unofficially supported to Android in 2011, when Doug Year released a set of patches for Android CyanogenMod OS (version 9.1 onward). These patches provided an HCE mode and a middleware interface adding two new tag technologies (namely, IsoPcdA and IsoPcdB). However, this implementation worked only for a specific NFC controller (particularly, NXP PN544), included at those dates in Google's Android devices such as the Samsung Galaxy Nexus or Asus Nexus 7 (first generation). Finally, Android officially supports HCE mode since October 2013, when Android KitKat was released.

3 Practical Implementation Alternatives in Android

This section first introduces the Android NFC architecture. Then, we focus on implementation issues of read/write and card-emulation operation modes in Android as these modes allow to act as a dishonest verifier and a dishonest prover, respectively, in an NFC attack relay. Finally, we point three limitations out when performing these attacks in Android, and discuss its feasibility.

3.1 Android NFC Architecture: NCI Stack

Android NFC development offers an event-driven framework and extensive API on two native implementations that depends on the NFC chip within the device:

- `libnfc-nxp`, which provides support for NXP PN54x NFC controllers and NXP MIFARE family products. These products are not supported by all

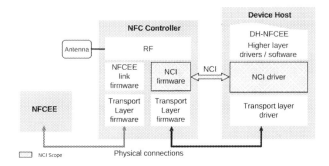

Fig. 2. NFC architecture (taken from [24])

NFC-enabled devices, since they use a proprietary transmission protocol (that is, MIFARE family cards are not IsoDep cards).
– `libnfc-nci`, which provides support for any NFC Controller Interface (NCI) [24] compliant chips, such as Broadcom's BCM2079x family.

Nowadays, NCI leads the NFC development by several reasons: (i) it provides an open architecture not focused on a single family chip; (ii) it offers an open interface between the NFC Controller and the DH; and (iii) it is a standard proposed by NFC Forum, a non-profit industry association that develops NFC specifications, ensures interoperability, and educates the market about NFC technology. In this paper, we focus on NCI by the same reasons.

NCI specification aims at making the chip integration of different manufacturers easier by defining a common level of functionality among the components of an NFC-enabled device. It also provides a logical interface that can be used over different physical channels, such as UART, SPI, and I2C.

A noteworthy fact is that Google dropped NXP in favour of Broadcom's NFC stack in their latest Nexus devices (from LG Nexus 4 onward). Moreover, the Android Open Source Project does not support HCE mode for old NXP PN544 chipsets since they lack of AID dynamic routing capabilities, being only possible to use it in devices with closed-source factory ROMs (e.g., Sony Xperia Z1, Sony Compact Z1, and Sony Z Ultra). Latest NFC chipsets developed by NXP, such as NXP PN547, support HCE mode since they are NCI-compliant.

Three main actors are distinguished in a NCI-compliant NFC scenario, as depicted in Fig. 2: the *NFC Execution Environment* (NFCEE), which is a hardware module in most cases (e.g., embedded SEs or Single Wire Protocol enabled SD-Cards); the *NFC Controller* (NFCC); and the *Device Host* (DH), which refers to the main processor, i.e., the own NFC-enabled device.

The NFCC transmits and receives information over the RF channel and is part of a system-on-chip. It maintains a connection with the DH and others NFCEE using the NCI, which defines a logic interface between them independently of the physical layer. NCI also deals with data packet fragmentation, according to the MTU defined by the physical layer.

NCI defines two message types, packed and transmitted over a particular physical channel: (1) **Control messages**, subdivided in *commands*, *responses*, and *notifications*. Commands are only sent from the DH to the NFCC, whereas the others travel in both directions; and (2) **Data messages**, which carry the information addressed to the NFC endpoint (i.e., a remote tag or reader). These messages are only sent once the logic channel has been established. During initialisation, the default communication channel is set to the RF connection, although more channels can be created with others NFCEEs.

NCI modules, such as the *RF Interface modules*, are a key part of the NCI stack. An RF Interface module defines how the DH communicates with a given NFC endpoint through the NCI. Each RF Interface supports a specific RF protocol and determines how the NCI data-message payload fits on its respective RF message. This layered design allows a modular addition of interfaces implementing new protocols.

3.2   Read/Write Operation Mode

The message flow in reader/writer mode is depicted in Fig. 3. Android applications are not allowed to directly set the device into read/write mode. However, this mode is indirectly reached as follows: first, it registers the set of NFC tags of interest to be detected through the `AndroidManifest.xml` file; and then, the Android NFC service selects and starts the registered application whenever a tag of interest is discovered (i.e., it enters in its proximity communication range). Applications can also ask preference for a discovered tag when they are in foreground mode.

The tag can be discovered by means of the NFCC, which polls the magnetic field. Once a tag is detected, the NFCC first determines the protocol and the technology used. Then, it sends an NCI notification message to the DH with the tag details. The DH (indeed, the `NfcService` in Android) handles this notification and fills a `Tag` object with the data received from the NFCC. Finally, the DH creates and emits an `Intent` with the `EXTRA_TAG` field, which is received by the registered Android application with higher preference.

Android NFC API offers an specific class per RF protocol (i.e., to work with different type of NFC tags) built on top of `TagTechnology` interface. These classes implement the high-level I/O blocking `transceive(byte[] data, boolean raw)` method, which is used to communicate a DH with an NFC tag.

Such a method can work with old NFC implementations (`raw` boolean flag) where some preprocessing is needed before transmitting through the RF channel (e.g., to compute and add CRC payloads to messages). Current `libnfc-nci` implementation ignores this flag, while `libnfc-nxp` implementation uses it to distinguish between ISO/IEC 14443 or NXP proprietary commands. In fact, the `transceive` method executes via Inter Process Communication (IPC) a remote invocation on `TagService` object, defined in `NfcService`. This object is also associated to a `TagEndpoint` object, which references to the remote tag and whose implementation relies on the native library used (`libnfc-nci` or `libnfc-nxp`). Thus, the Android NFC API offers an abstraction of its internal implementation.

Lastly, let us briefly describe low-level issues. The `libnfc-nci` implementation uses a reliable mechanism of queues and message passing named General Kernel Interface (GKI) to easily communicate between layers and modules: Each task is isolated, owning a buffer (or *inbox*) where messages are queued and processed on arrival. This mechanism is used to send messages from the DH to the NFCC chip, and vice versa.

3.3   Host-Card Emulation Operation Mode

The message flow in reader/writer mode is depicted in Fig. 4. Android applications can directly use HCE operation mode by implementing a service to process commands and replies, unlike read/write operation mode, restricted to Android activities. The aforementioned service must extend the `HostApduService` abstract class and implement `processCommandApdu` and `onDeactivated` methods.

The `processCommandApdu` method is executed whenever an NFC reader sends an APDU message to the registered service. Recall that APDUs are the application-level messages exchanged in an NFC communication between a reader/writer and an IsoDep tag, defined by the ISO/IEC 7816-4 specification (see Section 2.1). In fact, an IsoDep-compliant reader initiates the NFC communication by sending an explicit SELECT APDU command to the smartcard to choose a specific Application ID (AID) to communicate with. This command is finally routed by the NFCC to the registered application for the specified AID.

Therefore, each application must previously register the AID list of interest, in order to receive APDU commands. As in the previous case, registration is performed by means of `AndroidManifest.xml` file. Fortunately, Android version 5.0 (*Lollipop* codename) onward enables to dynamically register AIDs.

The Android NFC service (i.e., `NfcService`) populates during initialisation an AID routing table based on the registered AIDs of each HCE application. This table is basically a tree map of AIDs and services.

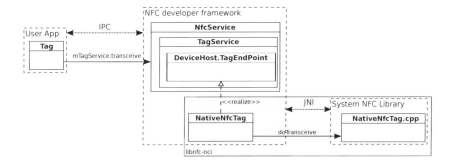

Fig. 3. Message flow in Android NFC stack (reader/writer mode)

When the DH receives a `SELECT` command, the routing table is checked and the corresponding service is set to `defaultService`. Thereafter, subsequent APDU commands are routed to that service until other `SELECT` command is received, or a deactivation occurs (by a `DESELECT` command or a timeout). Routing process is performed by `Messenger` objects sent between the `NfcService` and the `HostApduService`: When the `NfcService` needs to route a message, it sends a `MSG_COMMAND_APDU` to `HostApduService`, which extracts the APDU payload and executes `processCommandApdu`. Similarly, an analogous process occurs with a response, but handling a `MSG_RESPONSE_APDU` instead.

Note that the NFCC also maintains a routing table populated during each `NfcService` activation. Unlike `NfcService`, the NFCC routing table contains information about HCE applications within the DH and about SE applications. In this case, it stores the destination route according to a set of rules: Technology, Protocol, or specific AID. Destination route can be either the DH (default option) or other NFCEE, such as a SE.

3.4   Limitations and Discussion

As previously described, Android NFC architecture is composed by different layers acting at different levels. Table 1 summarises these layers in top-down developer-accessible order, giving also details of implementation languages, on whom depend them, and whether the code is open source software (OSS).

We envisioned three major limitations when performing an NFC relay attack with dishonest parties (i.e., prover and verifier) in Android.

Limitation 1. The scenario envisioned by this limitation depicts an NFC-enabled device with a non-NXP NFCC (the device, for short) acting as a dishonest verifier and communicating with a legitimate proprietary tag such as MIFARE Classic smartcards. The device must be in read/write mode. Since `libnfc-nci` implementation does not allow sending raw ISO/IEC 14443-3 commands, the device is unable to communicate with these proprietary tags. Note that the standard defines a CRC field for each command before sent. We have empirically verified where Android computes this CRC value. After some debugging and code

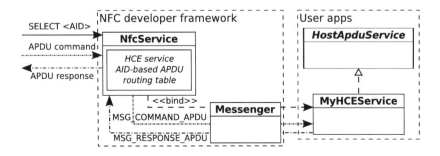

Fig. 4. Message flow in Android NFC stack (host-card emulation mode)

review, we concluded that the entity responsible of this computations is, in fact, the ISO/IEC 14443-3 RF Interface module of the NFCC.

Therefore, this limitation is very unlikely to be circumvented, unless NFCC is modified. On the contrary, since contactless payment cards are IsoDep cards (i.e., fully ISO/IEC 14443-compliant), this issue does not really occur at all.

Limitation 2. In this case, we considered an NFC-enabled device acting as a dishonest prover that communicates with a honest verifier. The device must be in HCE mode, which is natively supported from Android KitKat onward (see Section 2.3). Besides, the specific emulated AID has to be known in advance (see Section 3.3). However, since the routing process is performed in the first layer, it could be surrounded in a device with root permissions. Indeed, there exists an Xposed framework module that addresses this issue. The Xposed framework provides a way to make system-level changes into Android without installing a custom firmware, but needs root permissions instead.

Therefore, an OTS Android (version 4.4) onward, dishonest prover can communicate with a honest verifier emulating any AID when this value is known in advance. Otherwise, an Android device with root permissions is needed.

Limitation 3. Finally, we envisioned a complete NFC passive relay attack scenario where a dishonest prover and a dishonest verifier communicate through a non-reliable peer-to-peer relay channel. Note that the success of the relay attack relies on the delay introduced by this communication link. A good review on NFC relay timing constraints can be found in [25]. ISO/IEC 14443-3 [17] specifies a timings values that were found too low for software emulation on mobile devices [26]. However, ISO/IEC 14443-4 [27] defines the Frame Waiting Time as $FWT = 256 \cdot (16/f_c) \cdot 2^{FWI}, 0 \leq FWI \leq 14$, where $f_c = 13.56$ MHz (i.e., the carrier frequency). Thus, FWT ranges from $500\mu s$ to 5s, which practically solves most timing problems in any relay channel. Moreover, the standard also allows to request additional computation time by the PICC with a `WTX` message, which might potentially be implemented on Android to give an attacker additional time for a relay. We aim at further studying the feasibility of these attacks in Android that we named as *timed-extension NFC relay attack*.

Therefore, an NFC relay attack on ISO/IEC 14443-4 protocol is feasible when the delay on the relay channel is less than 5 seconds. Interestingly, the distance

Table 1. NFC architecture levels in Google's Android OS

Description	Language(s)	Dependency	OSS
NFC developer framework (`com.android.nfc` package)	Java, C++	API level	Yes
System NFC library (`libnfc-nxp` or `libnc-nci`)	C/C++	Manufacturer	Yes
NFC Android kernel driver	C	Hardware and manufacturer	Yes
NFC firmware (`/system/vendor/firmware` directory)	ARM Thumb	Hardware and manufacturer	No

seems to play an insignificant role since delay is reasonable even on geographical scale [28].

Let us remark that FWI is completely generated by the NFCC and not configurable by the Android NFC service on HCE mode (we have reviewed Android source code and its value is not assigned, thus we assume it is assigned by NFCC). Although official documentation defines a $FWI \leq 8$ (i.e., $FWT \leq 78ms$), some PoS devices ignore FWT command sent by the PICC to provide better user responses (and thus, a longer time window). From a read/write mode point of view, this constraint does not happen since Android allows to set a timeout up to 5 seconds. Surprisingly, EMVCo LLC, a public corporation which aims at facilitating worldwide interoperability and acceptance of secure payment transactions, recommends a $FWI \leq 7$ [29]. Thus, FWT would be strictly lower than 5 s. We believe that a mandatory requirement instead of a recommendation would enhance the security of contactless payment cards against NFC relay attacks.

Concluding Remarks. To summarise, any NFC-enabled device running OTS Android version 4.4 onward is able to perform an NFC passive relay attack at APDU level when the specific AID of the honest prover is known and an explicit SELECT is performed. Recall that any other communication involving a APDU-compliant NFC tag (i.e., Type 4 tags such as MIFARE DESFire EV1, Inside MicroPass, or Infineon SLE66CL) can also be relayed.

4 Relay Attack Implementation: Proof-of-Concept

In this section, we first perform an experiment of relay attack at contactless payment cards. Then, we foresee threat scenarios of NFC-capable Android malware that may appear before long. Finally, countermeasures are discussed.

4.1 Proof-of-Concept Experiment

Recall that three parts are involved in an NFC relay attack (see Section 2.2): (i) a peer-to-peer relay communication channel; (ii) a dishonest verifier, which communicates with the honest prover (i.e., a contactless payment card in this case); and (iii) a dishonest prover, which communicates with the honest verifier (i.e., a PoS in this case). The dishonest verifier works in read/write operation mode, while the dishonest prover relies on HCE operation mode.

For ethical reasons we used our own PoS device. Namely, an Ingenico IWL280 with GPRS and NFC support. As dishonest prover and verifier, we used two off-the-shelf Android NFC-enabled mobile devices executing an Android application developed for testing purposes (about 2000 Java LOC, able to act as dishonest verifier/prover depending on user's choice and to communicate point-to-point via WiFi, Bluetooth, or direct TCP/IP socket), having a single constraint: The dishonest prover must execute, at least, an Android KitKat version (first version natively supporting HCE mode, see Section 2.3). The experiment has been successful tested on several mobile devices, such as Nexus 4, Nexus 5 as dishonest provers, and Samsung Galaxy Nexus, Sony Xperia S as dishonest verifiers.

Table 2. Trace of a MasterCard contactless payment relayed

```
V → P 00A4 0400 0E32 5041 592E 5359 532E 4444 4630 3100
P → V 6F30 840E 3250 4159 2E53 5953 2E44 4446 3031 A51E BF0C 1B61 194F 08A0 0000 0004 1010
        0250 0A4D 4153 5445 5243 4152 4487 0101 9000
V → P 00A4 0400 08A0 0000 0004 1010 0200
P → V 6F20 8408 A000 0000 0410 1002 A514 8701 0150 0A4D 4153 5445 5243 4152 445F 2D02 6361
        9000
V → P 80A8 0000 0283 0000
P → V 7716 8202 1880 9410 0801 0100 1001 0100 1801 0200 2001 0200 9000
V → P 00B2 0114 00
P → V 7081 9357 13XX XXXX XXXX XXXX XXXX XXXX XXXX XXXX XXXX XXXX 5A08 XXXX XXXX XXXX XXXX
        5F24 03XX XXXX 5F28 0207 245F 3401 018C 219F 0206 9F03 069F 1A02 9505 5F2A 029A 039C
        019F 3704 9F35 019F 4502 9F4C 089F 3403 8D0C 910A 8A02 9505 9F37 049F 4C08 8E0C 0000
        0000 0000 0000 4203 1F03 9F07 023D 009F 0802 0002 9F0D 05B0 50AC 8000 9F0E 0500 0000
        0000 9F0F 05B0 70AC 9800 9F4A 0182 9000
V → P 00B2 011C 00
P → V 7081 C28F 0105 9F32 0301 0001 9204 3DD0 2519 9081 B034 45XX ...XX62 9000
V → P 00B2 021C 00
P → V 7081 B393 81B0 3445 XXXX XXXX XXXX ...XXXX XXXX XX62 9000
V → P 00B2 0124 00
P → V 7033 9F47 0301 0001 9F48 2A3E XXXX ...XXXX XXXX XX6D 9000
V → P 00B2 0224 00
P → V 7081 949F 4681 9018 XXXX XXXX XXXX ...XXXX XXXX XXF5 9000
V → P 80AE 8000 2B00 0000 0000 0100 0000 0000 0007 2480 0000 8000 0978 1502 2400 37FB 88BD
        2200 0000 0000 0000 0000 001F 03
P → V 7729 9F27 01XX 9F36 02XX XX9F 2608 XXXX XXXX XXXX XXXX 9F10 12XX ...XX90 00
```

The experiment execution workflow is as follows: First, each dishonest party chooses its role (prover or verifier); Then, a peer-to-peer relay channel is established. Finally, the dishonest verifier connects with a contactless payment card, and the dishonest prover relays every APDU from the PoS to the card, and vice versa. Thus, a successful payment transaction is conducted. We presented a live demo during the RFIDsec 2015 event at New York City (USA) relaying a MasterCard contactless payment to Madrid (Spain), i.e., almost 5775 km, using two NFC-capable Android devices and a direct TCP/IP socket.

Table 2 shows a time-ordered excerpt of a MasterCard contactless transaction, indicating the message flow. First, SELECT command (00A4) is sent to ask the payment applications within the card. Then, MasterCard application is selected. We obfuscated some bytes relative to sensitive data. A video demo of the experiment is publicly available at http://vwzq.net/relaynfc/.

4.2   Threat Scenarios

Fig. 5 depicts a pair of threat scenarios using this attack vector. In Fig. 5(a), we envisioned a network of Android infected devices (i.e., a botnet) that communicate with the bot master when a contactless payment card is detected. The bot master can use this smartcard to conduct illegal transactions with a honest verifier, or even multiple transactions at the same time collaborating with multiple dishonest verifiers. We named this attack as *distributed mafia fraud*. Fig. 5(b) foresees the same scenario than before, but with multiple dishonest provers committing fraud at the same time, as a way to hide their real location.

Note that contactless payment cards implement security mechanisms such as PIN after consecutive uses or checking of atypical payment locations. These mechanisms clearly minimise the impact of the second threat scenario envisioned.

(a) Scenario 1: Distributed mafia fraud   (b) Scenario 2: Hiding fraud locations

Fig. 5. Threat scenarios of NFC passive relay attacks by Android malware

Lastly, let us remark a limitation of these attacks performed as an Android malware. Since read/write operation mode in Android is only reachable by activities (see Section 3.2), an NFC-capable Android malware detecting a smartcard in its proximity range starts execution in foreground. That is, when the infected device is screen-locked, the malware cannot begin its execution until screen is unlocked. However, note that a malware with root permissions or behaving as a fake app can bypass this limitation.

In brief, a wide-scale botnet of Android devices running malicious applications that continuously seek contactless payment cards can lead to several problematic situations. For instance, consider a malware that once it detects a contactless payment card within its proximity, it iteratively communicates with it sending incorrect PIN until it blocks. Then, the customer must proceed to reactivate it – besides, s/he would notice the card blocking issue after trying to legitimate use it. Similarly, instead of blocking the card the malware can try to guess the cardholder's PIN using a similar technique as [30], which may lead to a very large scale fraud.

4.3   Relay Attack Resistant Mechanisms

Relay attack resistant mechanisms proposed in several works [10,14,23] are also applicable in these scenarios. For the sake of space, we briefly describe *distance-bounding protocols*, *timing constraints*, and propose *hardware-fingerprinting identification* as practical countermeasure.

Distance-bounding protocols aim at upper bounding the physical distance between two communicating parties based on the Round-Trip-Time of cryptographic challenge-response pairs. Good implementations of these protocols may provide adequate defence mechanisms to relay attacks. However, recent NFC-based bank payment systems, whom actually dropped SE in favour of HCE apps, perform a relay communication with back-end bank servers thus introducing an *allowed* delay within the transmission. This issue puts in evidence the difficulty of establishing a barrier between malicious and non-malicious relay transactions. Similarly, enforcing timing constraints (e.g., timeout responses) in communication protocols can detect the delay of a relayed communication. Unfortunately, timing constraints are not nowadays enforced in NFC-capable systems. Besides, timing extensions allowed by ISO/IEC 14443 might also be problematic. However, these solutions may partially solve a relay attack scenario using a high latency channel or long-distance dishonest parties.

Usually, an NFC chip uses a random unique identifier (UID) for the emulated card in HCE mode. Thus, whitelisting (or blacklisting) UIDs in an NFC-capable system may solve a relay attack scenario. However, this solution is unfeasible in practice since it breaks legitimate mobile payments as well (card UIDs should be previously known). Nonetheless, it may apply in ad-hoc scenarios.

Other physical countermeasures are also applicable, such as card shielding covers acting as Faraday cages, on-card physical button/switch activation, or secondary authentication methods within the cards (e.g., on-card fingerprint scanners).

5   Related Work

Relay attacks on NFC have been widely studied in the literature [14,23,25,31–36]. First works on this topic [14,31] built specific hardware to relay the communication between a smartcard and a legitimate reader. In [31], timing constraints of NFC link are explored, stating that an NFC communication can be relayed up to a distance three orders of magnitude higher than the operating range. Hancke et al. deeply reviewed relay attacks in [14], showing a practical implementation of RFID hardware devices and discussing relay resistant mechanisms (e.g., timing constraints, distance bounding, and additional verification layers).

Following the technological trend, other works perform relay attacks using Nokia mobile phones with NFC capability [23, 32, 33]. Francis et al. described in [32] a relay scenario composed of Nokia NFC-enabled phones and a Java MIDlet application. Similarly, in [23] they relayed legitimate NFC transactions using Nokia NFC-enabled phones and a JavaCard application. Both works also discussed the feasibility of some countermeasures, such as timing, distance bounding, and GPS-based or network cell-based location. In [33], a vulnerability on how Nokia OS handles NFC Data Exchange Format (NDEF) [37] messages is abused to create a Bluetooth link as a backdoor to the phone, thus being able to install third-party software without user content.

Most recently, researchers have focused on relay attacks with Android accessing to SEs [25, 34–36]. SEs are used in mobile devices to securely store data associated with credit/debit cards. In [34–36], Roland et al. described practical attack scenarios to perform Denial-of-Service and sensitive data disclosure in SE of Android devices. However, these attacks require a non OTS Android device, since root permissions are needed. Similarly, Korak and Hutter [25] compared timing on relay attacks using different communication channels (e.g., Bluetooth, GRPS, or WiFi). They also used custom-made hardware and Android devices running custom firmware to build several attack scenarios. Indeed, a custom Android firmware is needed since an Android version prior to KitKat is used (i.e., HCE mode was not natively supported).

Recent works have been published regarding feasibility of relay attacks on long distances. In [38], the proximity assumption is shown to be broken using specific hardware and software to obtain a distance between dishonest parties two orders of magnitude greater than the nominal range (i.e., they reached distances up to 115 centimetres). This limit is overcome in [28], where relay attacks are performed on geographical scale, with a distance between dishonest parties of hundreds of kilometres and very low delay in the relay transmissions.

6   Conclusions and Future Work

NFC is a bidirectional contactless communication technology that brings the opportunity to merge smartcards with mobile smartphones. NFC has a lot of applications, from physical authorisation or identification, to cashless payment. However, NFC has been shown vulnerable in several aspects, such as eavesdropping, data modification, or relay attacks. Unlike eavesdropping or data modification, relay attacks are a threat that may bypass security countermeasures, such as identification of communication parties or cryptography schemes. The rise of mobile phones within an NFC chip inside its hardware put relay attacks in the spotlight: An NFC-enabled phone can be abused to interact with smartcards in its proximity range. This becomes a serious risk when relay attacks in contactless payment cards are feasible, since illegal transactions may be conducted.

In this paper, we perform an in-depth review of the NFC stack implementation in Google's Android and study the implementation alternatives (offered by Android version 4.4) onward to perform an NFC passive relay attack (i.e., data are transmitted unaltered). We discuss some limitations and show a practical implementation of an NFC relay attack using off-the-shelf NFC-enabled Android mobile phone devices (i.e., no custom firmware nor root permissions are required). We finally explain threats scenarios with this attack vector, and countermeasures that may apply.

Our contribution in this paper includes a practical demonstration of a relay attack implementation using NFC-enabled Android mobile phone platform. In our opinion, the combination of high number of potentially exploitable devices, easy development, and fast revenue will cause the *virtual pickpocketing attack* to appear in the wild before long.

As future work, we aim at studying timing constraints of HCE mode in OTS Android devices. Similarly, we aim at analysing whether active relay attacks are feasible in Android.

References

1. International Organization for Standardization: ISO/IEC 18092:2013: Information technology – Telecommunications and information exchange between systems – Near Field Communication – Interface and Protocol (NFCIP-1), March 2013
2. Japanese Industrial Standard: JIS X 6319-4:2010: Specification of implementation for integrated circuit(s) cards – Part 4: High speed proximity cards, October 2010
3. Oak, C.: The year 2014 was a tipping point for NFC payments, January 2015. http://www.finextra.com/blogs/fullblog.aspx?blogid=10382
4. de Looper, C.: Mobile Payment Boasts Rosy Future, But Some Obstacles Remain in Play, January 2015. http://www.techtimes.com/articles/24762/20150106/mobile-payments-worth-130-billion-2020.htm
5. Fischer, J.: NFC in Cell Phones: The New Paradigm for an Interactive World. IEEE Commun. Mag. 47(6), 22–28 (2009)
6. Boysen, A.: NFC is the bridge from cards to the mobile, January 2015. http://www.secureidnews.com/news-item/nfc-is-the-bridge-from-cards-to-the-mobile/
7. NFC World: NFC phones: The definitive list, January 2015.http://www.nfcworld.com/nfc-phones-list/ (accessed at January 26, 2015)
8. Reardon, M., Tibken, S.: Apple takes NFC mainstream on iPhone 6; Apple Watch with Apple Pay, September 2014. http://www.cnet.com/news/apple-adds-nfc-to-iphone-6-with-apple-pay/
9. Juniper Research Limited: Apple Pay and HCE to Push NFC Payment Users to More Than 500 Million by 2019, October 2014. http://www.juniperresearch.com/viewpressrelease.php?pr=483
10. Haselsteiner, E., Breitfuß, K.: Security in near field communication (NFC) – strengths and weaknesses. In: Proceedings of the Workshop on RFID Security and Privacy, pp. 1–11 (2006)
11. Madlmayr, G., Langer, J., Kantner, C., Scharinger, J.: NFC Devices: security and privacy. In: Proceedings of the 3rd International Conference on Availability, Reliability and Security (ARES), pp. 642–647 (2008)
12. Timalsina, S., Bhusal, R., Moh, S.: NFC and its application to mobile payment: overview and comparison. In: Proceedings of the 8th International Conference on Information Science and Digital Content Technology, vol. 1, pp. 203–206 (2012)
13. Damme, G.V., Wouters, K.: Practical experiences with NFC security on mobile phones. In: Proceedings of the 2009 International Workshop on Radio Frequency Identification: Security and Privacy Issues, pp. 1–13 (2009)
14. Hancke, G., Mayes, K., Markantonakis, K.: Confidence in smart token proximity: Relay attacks revisited. Computers & Security 28(7), 615–627 (2009)
15. Felt, A.P., Finifter, M., Chin, E., Hanna, S., Wagner, D.: A Survey of mobile malware in the wild. In: Proceedings of the 1st ACM Workshop on Security and Privacy in Smartphones and Mobile Devices, pp. 3–14. ACM (2011)
16. International Data Corporation: Smartphone OS Market Share, Q3 2014 (2014). http://www.idc.com/prodserv/smartphone-os-market-share.jsp
17. International Organization for Standardization: ISO/IEC 14443-3: Identification cards – Contactless IC cards – Proximity cards – Part 3: Initialization and anti-collision, April 2011
18. International Organization for Standardization: ISO/IEC 7816-4-2013: Identification cards – IC cards – Part 4: Organization, security and commands for interchange (2013)

19. International Organization for Standardization: ISO/IEC 7816-5-2013: Identification cards – IC cards – Part 5: Registration of application providers (2004)
20. Conway, J.H.: On Numbers and Games. Academic Press (1976)
21. Desmedt, Y.: Major security problems with the "unforgeable" (Feige-)Fiat-shamir proofs for identity and how to overcome them. In: Procs. 6th Worldwide Congress on Computer and Comm. Security and Protection, SEDEP Paris, pp. 147–159 (1988)
22. GlobalPlatform: GlobalPlatform Card Specification v2.2.1., January 2011. http://www.globalplatform.org/specificationform.asp?fid=7512
23. Francis, L., Hancke, G., Mayes, K., Markantonakis, K.: Practical relay attack on contactless transactions by using NFC mobile phones. In: Proceedings of the 2012 Workshop on RFID and IoT Security, vol. 8, pp. 21–32. IOS Press (2012)
24. Forum, N.F.C.: NFC Controller Interface (NCI) Technical Specification – version 1.1. Technical report, NFC Forum, Inc ., July 2014
25. Korak, T., Hutter, M.: On the power of active relay attacks using custom-made proxies. In: Proceedings of the 2014 IEEE International Conference on RFID, pp. 126–133 (2014)
26. Hancke, G.: A practical relay attack on ISO 14443 proximity cards. Technical report, University of Cambridge, January 2005
27. International Organization for Standardization: ISO/IEC 14443-4: Identification cards – Contactless IC cards – Proximity cards – Part 4: Transmission protocol, July 2008
28. Sportiello, L., Ciardulli, A.: Long distance relay attack. In: Hutter, M., Schmidt, J.-M. (eds.) RFIDsec 2013. LNCS, vol. 8262, pp. 69–85. Springer, Heidelberg (2013)
29. EMVco: Book D: Contactless Communication Protocol – version 2.4. Technical report, EMVco, LLC, June 2014
30. Emms, M., Arief, B., Little, N., van Moorsel, A.: Risks of offline verify PIN on contactless cards. In: Sadeghi, A.-R. (ed.) FC 2013. LNCS, vol. 7859, pp. 313–321. Springer, Heidelberg (2013)
31. Kfir, Z., Wool, A.: Picking virtual pockets using relay attacks on contactless smartcard. In: Proceedings of the 1st International Conference on Security and Privacy for Emerging Areas in Communications Networks, pp. 47–58 (2005)
32. Francis, L., Hancke, G., Mayes, K., Markantonakis, K.: Practical NFC peer-to-peer relay attack using mobile phones. In: Ors Yalcin, S.B. (ed.) RFIDSec 2010. LNCS, vol. 6370, pp. 35–49. Springer, Heidelberg (2010)
33. Verdult, R., Kooman, F.: Practical attacks on NFC enabled cell phones. In: Proceedings of the 3rd International Workshop on NFC, pp. 77–82 (2011)
34. Roland, M., Langer, J., Scharinger, J.: Practical attack scenarios on secure element-enabled mobile devices. In: Proceedings of the 4th International Workshop on NFC, pp. 19–24 (2012)
35. Roland, M., Langer, J., Scharinger, J.: Relay attacks on secure element-enabled mobile devices. In: Gritzalis, D., Furnell, S., Theoharidou, M. (eds.) SEC 2012. IFIP AICT, vol. 376, pp. 1–12. Springer, Heidelberg (2012)
36. Roland, M., Langer, J., Scharinger, J.: Applying relay attacks to google wallet. In: Proceedings of the 5th International Workshop on NFC, pp. 1–6 (2013)
37. NFC Forum: NFC Data Exchange Format (NDEF) Technical Specification – NDEF 1.0. Technical report, NFC Forum, Inc., July 2006
38. Oren, Y., Schirman, D., Wool, A.: Range extension attacks on contactless smart cards. In: Crampton, J., Jajodia, S., Mayes, K. (eds.) ESORICS 2013. LNCS, vol. 8134, pp. 646–663. Springer, Heidelberg (2013)

Algebraic Cryptanalysis and RFID Authentication

Carlos Cid[1], Loic Ferreira[2], Gordon Procter[1], and Matt J.B. Robshaw[3]

[1] Information Security Group, Royal Holloway University of London
Egham, TW20 OEX, UK
[2] Applied Cryptography Group, Orange Labs
38–40 rue de General Leclerc, 92794 Issy les Moulineaux, France
[3] Impinj, 701 N. 34th Street, Suite 300,
Seattle, WA 98103, USA

Abstract. The standardization group ISO/IEC SC31/WG7 is working on a set of *cryptographic suites* to provide security to wireless devices including UHF RFID tags. These cryptographic suites are presented as independent parts to a single standard ISO/IEC 29167. Within this multi-part standard 29167-15 is based around very simple operations and intended to provide tag, interrogator, and mutual authentication. Here we show that these proposals can be fully compromised using algebraic cryptanalytic techniques; the entire key can be recovered after eavesdropping on just four authentications.

1 Introduction

It is perhaps a sign of commercial maturity that standardization on cryptography for low-cost UHF RFID tags has begun. With such standards to hand tag, interrogator, and mutual authentication, along with secure tag-interrogator communications, can all be considered and securely implemented in the future. Increasingly referred to as RAIN RFID after the foundation of the R*A*dio *I*dentificatio*N* (RAIN) *Industry Alliance* [20], the technology will be widely deployed and is likely to become an integral part of the *Internet of Things (IoT)*. However, such tags pose a major challenge when deploying cryptography since they are very limited in terms of the space available in silicon and the power available for on-tag computation. By comparison HF RFID tags that we find in public transport ticketing and NFC applications are positively luxurious. It is within this context that ISO/IEC 29167-15 has been proposed; to provide security services to resource constrained devices.

One goal of this paper is to highlight the poor—in fact non-existent—security provided by ISO/IEC 29167-15. While the scheme can be compromised in many ways, this paper uses algebraic cryptanalysis to provide an elegant and efficient attack. But an arguably more important goal is to provide a warning of how even technically poor proposals can advance far into the standardization process. Given that there already exist many sound (and standardized) cryptographic designs for HF and UHF RFID tags, we hope our analysis will deter

© Springer International Publishing Switzerland 2015
S. Mangard, P. Schaumont (Eds.): RFIDsec 2015, LNCS 9440, pp. 104–121, 2015.
DOI: 10.1007/978-3-319-24837-0_7

standardization bodies and product developers from adopting schemes that have
had little technical scrutiny.

1.1   The Standardization Landscape for UHF RFID

It may not be immediately apparent why yet another group within ISO/IEC
is standardizing cryptographic mechanisms. To see why this important work is
underway we need to understand the role of other standards in the field.

The commands that can be sent to a (standardized) UHF RFID tag are
defined in two documents that have been published[1] by EPCglobal, part of GS1.
The dominant standard covering all current large-scale deployments is known as
Gen2v1 [8] and the final update to this standard was published in 2008. In 2013,
however, the Gen2v2 standard was published [9] and as the version number
implies, this extends the functionality of Gen2v1. The most significant and far-
reaching additions are optional over-the-air commands that allow the deployment
of security functionality.

Gen2v2 defines the over-the-air commands for UHF RFID but this is all it
does. For instance, a command AUTHENTICATE is defined and this can be used
to develop a solution for tag, interrogator, or mutual authentication. However
all the security commands in Gen2v2, including AUTHENTICATE, have been de-
liberately designed to be both flexible and crypto-agnostic; they are completely
independent of any specific cryptographic technology. By way of illustration, the
format of the AUTHENTICATE command is given below, with the field descrip-
tions, lengths, and possible values given by the three rows of the table. The
`handle` and `CRC-16` are part of the communication protocol while `SenRep` and
`IncRepLen` are application options. The most important fields for our purposes
are marked $\star$ and their values are not defined by Gen2v2. The `CSI` field identifies
the cryptographic algorithm/protocol while the `Length`/`Message` fields identify
the cryptographic payload being carried by the command.

	command	RFU	SenRep	IncRepLen	CSI	Length	Message	RN	CRC
length	8	2	1	1	8	12	*variable*	16	16
value	d5$_x$	00$_b$	0$_b$/1$_b$	0$_b$/1$_b$	$\star$	$\star$	$\star$	handle	CRC-16

For the cryptographic technology itself we would likely turn to the usual
sources. NIST standardizes cryptographic technologies such as the *Advanced
Encryption Standard (AES)* [16]. Other cryptographic technologies have been
standardized within ISO/IEC SC27 and some, such as PRESENT [2,14] and CRYP-
TOGPS [10,15], are explicitly targeted at constrained environments.

However we can see there is an implementation gap between the over-the-air
commands and the cryptographic primitives. For example, the AUTHENTICATE
command says nothing about how to achieve tag authentication using, say, a
challenge-response authentication protocol. It doesn't even say what algorithms
might be supported on the tag or interrogator. Similarly, the AES standard

---

[1] The Gen2v1 specifications are also standardized within ISO/IEC 18000-63 with
Gen2v2 standardization underway as a revision.

(FIPS-197 [16]) doesn't tell us how to use the AES block cipher to perform tag authentication; instead FIPS-197 tells us how a 128-bit output is derived from a 128-bit input and a key. It is the goal of the work in ISO/IEC SC31/WG7, therefore, to provide a mapping between the cryptographic primitive and the generic over-the-air command; that is, to fill in the information marked ⋆ in the command above. This mapping is referred to as a *cryptographic suite* and the ISO/IEC 29167 standard consists of several parts, each describing a cryptographic suite and a solution. If one wishes to perform tag authentication using AES-128 then ISO/IEC 29167-10 is the cryptographic suite of interest. For tag authentication with PRESENT-80, Grain-128a or CRYPTOGPS, parts 29167-11, 29167-13, and 29167-17 are, respectively, the ones to use.

Many cryptographic suites in ISO/IEC 29167 are built on trusted or standardized primitives. Some, however, are built around new and immature proposals. Despite very negative comments during the development of 29167-15, the ISO/IEC voting structure is such that even a technically poor proposal can advance far through the standardization process. The current status of 29167-15 is unclear, though it may be moved to a *Technical Specification*. Technical specifications are sometimes used when there are irreconcilable differences of opinion and they provide the opportunity for public comment. After three years the work in the technical specification is then either abandoned or re-introduced to the standards process. This paper can be viewed, therefore, as input to this process and provides compelling support for the view that future work on this standard should be resisted.

2 Early Versions

One reason for the longevity of ISO/IEC 29167-15 is that patches have been applied at several stages during the process. All variants propose mechanisms for tag authentication, interrogator authentication, and mutual authentication. All variants are simple and built around the supposed difficulty of analyzing the combination of bitwise exclusive-or and integer addition, though first proposals were even simpler; see Table 1.

There are many problems with the proposal in Table 1 but the most pressing is that there is no security. The sole use of a single operator (in this case bitwise exclusive-or) gives a differential attack. By eavesdropping an attacker recovers RI, RT, A, and B. The adversary can then make a fake tag that fools a legitimate reader *without* knowing the secret key K. The attack is outlined in Table 2 where variables in a subsequent run of the protocol are denoted *. To confirm that the fake tag is always accepted as genuine we observe that

$$\text{REVERSE}(\text{T}^*) = \text{REVERSE}(\text{SK}^* \oplus \text{B} \oplus \text{REVERSE}(\text{X}) \oplus \Delta_{SK})$$
$$= \text{REVERSE}(\text{SK} \oplus \text{B}) \oplus \text{X} = \text{REVERSE}(\text{SK} \oplus (\text{SK} \oplus \text{RCI})) \oplus \text{X}$$
$$= \text{CI} \oplus \text{X} = \text{CI} \oplus \Delta_A \oplus \Delta_{SK}$$
$$= (\text{SK} \oplus \text{A}) \oplus (\text{A} \oplus \text{A}^*) \oplus (\text{SK} \oplus \text{SK}^*) = \text{A}^* \oplus \text{SK}^* = \text{CI}^*$$

A tag can be cloned after eavesdropping one legitimate authentication.

Table 1. The first version of the tag authentication scheme where all variables are 64 bits long

Interrogator (secret key K)	**Tag** (secret key K)
Choose random $\texttt{RI}$ $\xrightarrow{\ \texttt{RI}\ }$	
$\xleftarrow{\ \texttt{RT}\ }$	Choose $\texttt{RT}$
$\texttt{SK} = \texttt{K} \oplus \texttt{RI} \oplus \texttt{RT}$	$\texttt{SK} = \texttt{K} \oplus \texttt{RI} \oplus \texttt{RT}$
Choose $\texttt{CI}$	
$\texttt{A} = \texttt{SK} \oplus \texttt{CI}$ $\xrightarrow{\ \texttt{A}\ }$	
	$\texttt{CI} = \texttt{SK} \oplus \texttt{A}$
	$\texttt{RCI} = \text{REVERSE}(\texttt{CI})$
$\xleftarrow{\ \texttt{B}\ }$	$\texttt{B} = \texttt{SK} \oplus \texttt{RCI}$
$\texttt{T} = \texttt{SK} \oplus \texttt{B}$	
$\text{REVERSE}(\texttt{T}) \overset{?}{=} \texttt{CI}$	

Table 2. Fooling a legitimate reader during tag authentication. The attacker has eavesdropped on one run of the protocol in Table 1. The (changing) parameters in this second run are indicated using *.

Interrogator (secret key K)	**Fake Tag**
Choose random $\texttt{RI}^*$ $\xrightarrow{\ \texttt{RI}^*\ }$	
$\xleftarrow{\ \texttt{RT}^*\ }$	Choose $\texttt{RT}^*$
$\texttt{SK}^* = \texttt{K} \oplus \texttt{RI}^* \oplus \texttt{RT}^*$	$\texttt{SK}^*$ is unknown
	$\Delta_I = \texttt{RI} \oplus \texttt{RI}^*$
	$\Delta_T = \texttt{RT} \oplus \texttt{RT}^*$
	Save $\Delta_{SK} = \Delta_I \oplus \Delta_T$
Choose $\texttt{CI}^*$	
$\texttt{A}^* = \texttt{SK}^* \oplus \texttt{CI}^*$ $\xrightarrow{\ \texttt{A}^*\ }$	
	$\texttt{A} \oplus \texttt{A}^* = \Delta_A$
	$\texttt{X} = \Delta_A \oplus \Delta_{SK}$
$\xleftarrow{\ \texttt{B}^*\ }$	$\texttt{B}^* = \texttt{B} \oplus \text{REVERSE}(\texttt{X}) \oplus \Delta_{SK}$
$\texttt{T}^* = \texttt{SK}^* \oplus \texttt{B}^*$	
$\text{REVERSE}(\texttt{T}^*) \overset{?}{=} \texttt{CI}^*$	

Table 3. A second tag authentication scheme. The shared secret key K and all intermediate values are 64 bits long, $\oplus$ denotes bitwise exclusive-or, and $+$ denotes integer addition modulo 2^{64}.

Interrogator (secret key K)	**Tag** (secret key K)
Choose random R	
$S = R \oplus K \xrightarrow{\;S\;} R = S \oplus K$	
$A = R + 0x55 \cdots 55$	
$B = T \oplus K \xleftarrow{\;T\;} T = A \oplus K$	
$B \overset{?}{=} R + 0x55 \cdots 55$	

After this inauspicious start a second proposal is illustrated in Table 3. Interrogator authentication is provided by reversing the roles of the two participants while mutual authentication is derived by interleaving two sessions that establish tag and interrogator authentication.

The weaknesses are immediately apparent and, as before, there are too many problems to list. It is sufficient to show that we can recover the key in a passive attack with high reliability. Indeed, suppose an attacker intercepts S and T from a legitimate authentication session. We then have that

$$S \oplus T = (R + 0x55 \cdots 55) \oplus R.$$

The least significant bit of $S \oplus T$ is always set to 1 and further analysis of $S \oplus T$ is easy to make. For instance, the 2^{32} values of R for which $R \wedge 0x55 \cdots 55 = 0x00 \cdots 00$ will give $S \oplus T = 0x55 \cdots 55$ and other observations based on $S \oplus T$ can be used to recover R and, via S, the shared secret key K.

For an alternative approach we simplify the notation by setting $X = S \oplus T$ and $C = 0x55 \cdots 55$. This means that $X = R \oplus (R + C)$ and considering this equation bit-by-bit gives, for bit position j with $j \geq 0$,

$$X_j = R_j \oplus ((R_j + C_j + c_{j-1}) \bmod 2) = C_j \oplus c_{j-1}$$

where c_{j-1} denotes the carry given at bit $j - 1$ generated within the integer addition $R + C$. Setting $c_{-1} = 0$, the carry bit c_j for $j \geq 0$ is computed as:

$$c_j = \mathrm{MAJ}(R_j, C_j, c_{j-1}) = (R_j \wedge C_j) \oplus (R_j \wedge c_{j-1}) \oplus (C_j \wedge c_{j-1})$$
$$= (R_j \wedge (C_j \oplus c_{j-1})) \oplus (C_j \wedge c_{j-1})$$

where MAJ denotes the *majority function*. Hence, for $j \geq 0$,

$$X_{j+1} = C_{j+1} \oplus (R_j \wedge (C_j \oplus c_{j-1})) \oplus (C_j \wedge c_{j-1})$$
$$= C_{j+1} \oplus (R_j \wedge X_j) \oplus (C_j \wedge (X_j \oplus C_j))$$
$$= C_{j+1} \oplus (R_j \wedge X_j) \oplus (C_j \wedge (X_j \oplus 1))$$

This means that, for $j \geq 0$, we have $R_j \wedge X_j = X_{j+1} \oplus C_{j+1} \oplus (C_j \wedge (X_j \oplus 1))$, which we write, setting $V_j = R_j \wedge X_j$, as

$$V_j = X_{j+1} \oplus C_{j+1} \oplus (C_j \wedge (X_j \oplus 1)) \text{ for } j \geq 0.$$

Looking at the expression for V_j we see that it consists entirely of arguments from X, which is available to an eavesdropper, and C which is fixed and known. Thus if $X_j = 1$ for bit j, which we expect half the time, then we can compute R_j directly and the corresponding bit of the shared secret K is given by

$$K_j = R_j \oplus X_j.$$

Each bit K_j, for $0 \leq j \leq 62$ can be recovered and we expect to be able to recover all but the most significant bit of K_j with two intercepted authentications. The work-effort is negligible. Note that this gives us two possible values for the full 64-bit shared secret K. However these two keys are *equivalent*, that is they behave identically in the authentication protocol, and so they can both be used to impersonate a tag.

3   More Advanced Versions

Those not involved in ISO/IEC standardization may be somewhat mystified by what is happening with ISO/IEC 29167-15. Early versions were clearly weak and offered little promise. Yet voting was such that the scheme moved forward towards standardization anyway. Once we arrive at a *committee draft (CD)* the document should, in theory, be technically mature since each subsequent stage of the process, namely *draft international standard (DIS)* and *final draft international standard (FDIS)* provide little opportunity for technical modification before publication. Yet as we will show in this section, even advanced versions of these schemes were far from being technically mature and were, in fact, completely insecure.

3.1   Applying Algebraic Cryptanalysis

To repair earlier weaknesses a patched version was briefly proposed; see Table 4.

Conventional Observations. Again, we can immediately see that the least significant bit of $S \oplus T$ is always set to 0. It is easy to find other faults and by setting $C = \text{0x55} \cdots 55$ we have $S = (RI + C) \oplus K$ and $T = (K + C) \oplus RI$ so

$$S \oplus K = ((K + C) \oplus T) + C. \tag{1}$$

We can use Equation 1 as a distinguisher to check if a possible value for the key K is a correct candidate. This can be done in several ways, but we illustrate a byte-by-byte approach, first considering the least significant byte of K. Suppose k, a, b are the least significant bytes of K, S, and T respectively. Then any x

Table 4. Another patched version of the tag authentication scheme. All variables are 64 bits long and $C = \mathtt{0x55}\cdots 55$.

Interrogator (secret key K)	**Tag** (secret key K)
Choose RI	
$S = (RI + C) \oplus K \xrightarrow{\ S\ } RI = (S \oplus K) - C$	
$T \oplus RI \stackrel{?}{=} K + C \xleftarrow{\ T\ } T = (K + C) \oplus RI$	

satisfying $a \oplus x = ((x + \mathtt{0x55}) \oplus b) + \mathtt{0x55}$ is a good candidate for k. After eight to sixteen runs, one value should be predicted with close to 100% reliability and the least significant byte of the key is recovered. In *parallel* we can process other bytes of K in the same manner. There is a slight complication due to the possibility of a carry from one byte to another in the integer addition; at the same time the most significant bit of each byte might also need some attention. However, closer analysis when using particular values S and T can be used to avoid significant carry propagation. This allows us to filter incorrect values and the few key candidates that remain can be tested against the tag to find the right one. Passively eavesdropping on eight to sixteen authentication runs appears to be sufficient to recover each byte of the key K with good reliability. The work effort is negligible since all bytes can be treated in parallel.

Algebraic Cryptanalysis. Algebraic attacks are powerful techniques that have been successfully applied against several stream ciphers (*e.g.* [5,6]) and considered against block ciphers and other cryptographic primitives [3,4]. In algebraic attacks, one writes the entire cryptographic operation as a large set of multivariate polynomial equations and then uses equation-solving techniques to recover the value of some of the unknown variables (*e.g.* the encryption key). The scheme in ISO/IEC 29167-15 uses a set of very simple operations and algebraic cryptanalysis proves to be very effective. We describe our attack below.

Let n be the size of the set of all variables in the protocol; in our case we have $n = 64$. We will assume that an attacker can eavesdrop on m runs of a uni-directional (tag or interrogator) authentication protocol. Since the mutual authentication protocol consists of two interleaved runs of a uni-directional protocol, observing m runs of the mutual authentication protocol will give identical results to $2m$ runs of the uni-directional protocol.

Without loss of generality we have implemented the attack on the protocol for uni-directional (tag or interrogator) authentication. Denote the value of S on the tth run of the protocol by S^t, similarly for T and RI. We use variables p_i, st_i, rt_i, sot_i, at_i, and bt_i for $0 \le i \le 63$ and $0 \le t < m$ assuming that all strings are written using big-endian convention with the most significant bit on the left, *i.e* $K = p_{n-1} \ldots p_1 p_0$.

We represent the computation of S^t using the equations

$$s_{t\_i} = p_i + r_{t\_i} + a_{t\_i} + c_i$$

for $0 \leq i < n$, $0 \leq t < m$ and where a_{t_i} is the carry bit during the modular addition of RI^t and C. This gives, for $1 \leq i \leq n$,

$$a_{t\_0} = 0$$
$$a_{t\_i} = \text{MAJ}\big(r_{t\_(i-1)}, c_{i-1}, a_{t\_(i-1)}\big)$$
$$= r_{t\_(i-1)} * c_{i-1} + r_{t\_(i-1)} * a_{t\_(i-1)} + a_{t\_(i-1)} * c_{i-1}$$

Similarly the computation of T^t can be represented, for $1 \leq i < n$ and $0 \leq t < m$, as:

$$b_{t\_0} = 0$$
$$so_{t\_i} = p_i + r_{t\_i} + b_{t\_i} + c_i$$
$$b_{t\_i} = p_{i-1} * c_{i-1} + p_{i-1} * b_{t\_(i-1)} + b_{t\_(i-1)} * c_{i-1}$$

where the b variables denote the carry bits. Finally, we define equations to represent the observed values of S^t and T^t and the defined value of C; $s_{t\_i} = S_i^t$, $so_{t\_i} = T_i^t$, and $c_i = C_i$. Our system is presented as polynomials over the finite field $\mathbb{F}_2$, i.e. all variables and coefficients take values in $\{0, 1\}$. We may therefore include the equations of the form $x^2 = x$ for every variable x.

The complete set of equations can be summarized as follows:

$$
\begin{cases}
s_{t\_i} = p_i + r_{t\_i} + a_{t\_i} + c_i & 0 \leq i < n & 0 \leq t < m \\
a_{t\_(i+1)} = r_{t\_i} * c_i + r_{t\_i} * a_{t\_i} + a_{t\_i} * c_i & 0 \leq i < n-1 & 0 \leq t < m \\
a_{t\_0} = 0 & 0 \leq t < m & \\
so_{t\_i} = p_i + r_{t\_i} + b_{t\_i} + c_i & 0 \leq i < n & 0 \leq t < m \\
b_{t\_(i+1)} = p_i * c_i + p_i * b_{t\_i} + b_{t\_i} * c_i & 0 \leq i < n-1 & 0 \leq t < m \\
b_{t\_0} = 0 & 0 \leq t < m & \\
s_{t\_i} = S_i^t & 0 \leq i < n & 0 \leq t < m \\
so_{t\_i} = T_i^t & 0 \leq i < n & 0 \leq t < m \\
c_i = C_i & 0 \leq i < n & \\
x^2 = x & \text{for all } x &
\end{cases}
$$

This system of polynomial equations includes $5nm + 2n$ variables and $11nm + 3n$ equations of degree at most two. Of course this system can be greatly simplified, by substituting the variables that have a fixed value (e.g. c_i, a_{t_0}, b_{t_0}), as well as the ones observed in the protocol runs (s_{t_i} and so_{t_i}). This reduces the number of variables to $(3n - 2)m + n$, and the number of equations to $(7n - 4)m + n$. For the parameter values of relevance to ISO/IEC 29167-15, the entire system will consist therefore of $444m + 64$ equations in $190m + 64$ variables, which can be constructed for the very small values of m that are required to recover the key. We use Gröbner bases algorithms to solve this system [4].

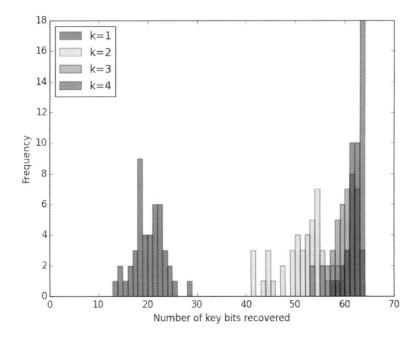

Fig. 1. Results from experiments on the scheme of Section 3.1. The number of protocol runs is given by k in this figure and each set of experiments was repeated 45 independent times.

Results. The average number of key bits recovered and the average time required to solve the system of equations are given in the following table.

Number of protocol runs	1	2	3	4
Average number of key bits recovered	19.7	51.1	59.4	61.7
Average run time (s)	8	83	113	255

The attack was implemented on *SageMathCloud* [21] and timed using Python's `timeit` function; any set-up time is assumed to be pre-computed or amortized over many protocol runs. Figure 1 provides a visualization of the number of key bits recovered after observing m runs of the uni-directional authentication protocol and performing 45 sets of experiments. The values (K, RI^1) were chosen randomly for each trial when $m = 1$. As the number of protocol runs was increased K remains unchanged but fresh random choices were used for RI^2, RI^3, and RI^4 as would be expected in a real-life implementation.

Our experiments suggest that after witnessing four uni-directional runs of the protocol – or just two mutual authentication runs – the attacker would be able to recover 62 out of 64 bits of the secret key in around 84% of the time. While the entirety of the key can often be recovered, we conjecture that the "missing" bits that occur from time-to-time are neutral bits; the values of these bits cannot be determined by that particular instance of the equation system. This is a feature to many cryptanalytic techniques and is often exhibited in the most significant bits of operations such as integer addition. While it might be an interesting exercise to provide an exact explanation of this phenomenon, it is not relevant to the essential message of our cryptanalysis.

3.2   The Most Advanced Version

The fourth iteration to be described in this paper is the mutual authentication protocol outlined in Table 5. As in previous versions tag and interrogator authentication are derived from the relevant halves of the full authentication protocol. Several changes have been made to this latest proposal to complicate the task of the cryptanalyst. The use of the (unknown) bitwise rotation seems to prevent the attacker from aligning bits in the challenge and response in a trivial way. For example a single bit change in the challenge will change the Hamming Weight of the candidate RI derived by the tag; this would result in different rotation amounts being used for the computation of the final response. Despite these complications it is straightforward to compromise the scheme. Our initial analysis suggested that even with the rotation operation, the scheme can be compromised using conventional cryptanalysis after intercepting around 32 uni-directional authentication runs. However, as demonstrated in the previous section, it is more elegant and efficient to use algebraic cryptanalysis against the scheme. This technique allows us again to recover the shared secret key K after eavesdropping on as few as four authentication runs.

Algebraic Cryptanalysis. As before, we need to set up a system of multivariate polynomial equations. The system used to describe this latest scheme is similar to that of Section 3.1. However it is helpful to introduce some additional variables to take account of the rotation: m_{t_i} corresponds to K'_i in the tth protocol run and n_{t_i} corresponds to RI'_i in the tth protocol run. In truth these variables have been introduced to improve the exposition of the attack. It would be straightforward to work without them if there were significant advantage in doing so.

   In this variant of the scheme we need to take account of the unknown rotation amount. The simplest way to do this is to guess the rotation amount, and to solve each set of equations that arise for each guess. To include this within the equation system we introduce an array rot_guess where rot_guess[t] is a guess for the Hamming weight of RI^t.

   The complete set of equations is summarized overleaf and the system includes $7nm + 2n$ variables and $15nm + 3n$ equations of degree at most two. Again, this system can be greatly simplified by substituting fixed/known value variables, as well as redundant ones, to a system with $(3n-2)m+n$ variables, and $(7n-4)m+n$ equations. For the parameter values of relevance to ISO/IEC 29167-15, the entire system consists of $444m + 64$ equations in $190m + 64$ variables, which can be constructed for the small values of m that are required to recover the key.

Table 5. The last version of the mutual authentication scheme. The *Hamming weight* of A is denoted HW(A) while A $\lll$ w (*resp.* A $\ggg$ w) denotes a left (*resp.* right) bitwise rotation of A by w bits. The constant C takes the value 0x55 $\cdots$ 55.

Interrogator (secret key K)	**Tag** (secret key K)
Choose RI	
$S = (RI + C) \oplus K \quad \xrightarrow{\quad S \quad}$	$RI = (S \oplus K) - C$
	$w_i = \text{HW}(RI)$
	$K' = K \lll w_i$
	$RI' = RI \lll w_i$
	$T = (K' + C) \oplus RI'$
	Choose RT
$w_i = \text{HW}(RI) \quad \xleftarrow{\quad T, U \quad}$	$U = (RT + C) \oplus K$
$K' = K \lll w_i$	
$RI' = RI \lll w_i$	
$(T \oplus RI') \overset{?}{=} (K' + C)$	
tag authenticated	
$RT = (U \oplus K) - C$	
$w_t = \text{HW}(RT)$	
$K'' = K \lll w_t$	
$RT'' = RT \lll w_t$	
$V = (K'' + C) \oplus RT'' \quad \xrightarrow{\quad V \quad}$	$w_t = \text{HW}(RT)$
	$K'' = K \lll w_t$
	$RT'' = RT \lll w_t$
	$(V \oplus RT'') \overset{?}{=} (K'' + C)$
	interrogator authenticated

$$
\begin{cases}
s_{t\_i} = p_i + r_{t\_i} + a_{t\_i} + c_i & 0 \leq i < n & 0 \leq t < m \\
a_{t\_(i+1)} = r_{t\_i} * c_i + r_{t\_i} * a_{t\_i} + a_{t\_i} * c_i & 0 \leq i < n - 1 & 0 \leq t < m \\
a_{t\_0} = 0 & 0 \leq t < m \\
m_{t\_i} = p_{(i + \text{rot\_guess}[t]\%n)} & 0 \leq i < n & 0 \leq t < m \\
n_{t\_i} = r_{t\_(i + \text{rot\_guess}[t]\%n)} & 0 \leq i < n & 0 \leq t < m \\
so_{t\_i} = m_{t\_i} + n_{t\_i} + b_{t\_i} + c_i & 0 \leq i < n & 0 \leq t < m \\
b_{t\_(i+1)} = m_{t\_i} * c_i + m_{t\_i} * b_{t\_i} + b_{t\_i} * c_i & 0 \leq i < n - 1 & 0 \leq t < m \\
b_{t\_0} = 0 & 0 \leq t < m \\
s_{t\_i} = S_i^t & 0 \leq i < n & 0 \leq t < m \\
so_{t\_i} = T_i^t & 0 \leq i < n & 0 \leq t < m \\
c_i = C_i & 0 \leq i < n \\
x^2 = x & \forall x
\end{cases}
$$

Guessing the Rotation Amount. The equation-system depends on rot_guess, a guess for the Hamming weight of RI. We expect that a correct guess for the Hamming weight of RI will yield a system of equations that is easily solved to reveal many key bits. The values RI are random and so assuming that they are generated uniformly the random variable HW(RI) will be distributed according to a binomial distribution with parameters $(64, \frac{1}{2})$. It is therefore straightforward to compute the probability that a randomly chosen RI has a particular Hamming weight. Of particular relevance to our attack is the fact that a substantial fraction of all possible RI have a Hamming weight lying within a small range.

x	32	33	34	35	36
$\mathrm{Pr}_{\mathtt{RI}}[\mathrm{HW}(\mathtt{RI}) = x]$	0.10	0.10	0.09	0.08	0.06

This means that the probability HW(RI) lies in the interval $[32 - \delta, 32 + \delta]$ is:

δ	0	1	2	3	4
$\mathrm{Pr}_{\mathtt{RI}}[\mathrm{HW}(\mathtt{RI}) \in [32 - \delta, 32 + \delta]]$	0.10	0.29	0.46	0.62	0.74

Now assume an attacker who eavesdrops on one uni-directional authentication session. He could simply run the equation solving algorithm three times with the guesses of 31, 32, and 33 for the rotation amount. With a probability close to 30% one of these guesses would be correct. Alternatively, he could elect to further try the values 28, 29, 30, 34, 35, and 36 which would require nine runs of the equation solving algorithm. The probability that the eavesdropped session is covered by one of these nine guesses is close to 74%. This has been confirmed by experiments.

It turns out that the polynomial system solving algorithm is a good method to verify whether the guessed rotation amount is correct. Empirically it seems that selecting the wrong rotation makes the system inconsistent, *i.e.* there will be no valid solution and this is quickly detected by the Gröbner bases algorithm. Of course it cannot be ruled out that cases exist when an incorrect guess of rotation results in a system for which solutions exist (corresponding to an incorrect key). However this does not appear to be common; in over 20 experiments we never recovered false solutions for any $\delta \leq 5$. Of course, even if they did occur, false alarms could easily be filtered out using further intercepted authentication attempts or even a forgery attempt.

Results. The average number of key bits recovered and the average time required to solve the system of equations are given in the following table.

Number of protocol runs	1	2	3	4
Average number of key bits recovered	21.3	51.4	60.6	63.2
Average run time (s)	10	53	87	193

Again, the attack was implemented on *SageMathCloud* [21] and timed using Python's `timeit` function; any set-up time is assumed to be pre-computed or amortized over many protocol runs. Figure 2 provides a visualization of the

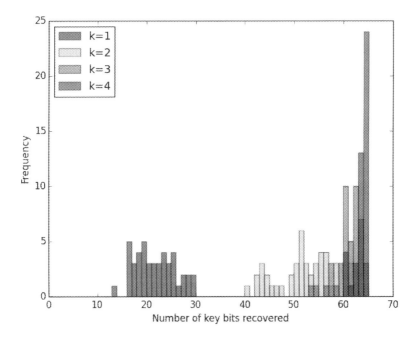

Fig. 2. Results from experiments on the scheme of Section 3.2. The number of protocol runs is given by k in this figure and 45 random instances were generated.

number of key bits recovered after observing m runs of the uni-directional authentication protocol over all 45 sets of experiments. The values $(\mathtt{K}, \mathtt{RI}^1)$ were chosen randomly for each trial when $m = 1$. As the number of protocol runs was increased $\mathtt{K}$ remains unchanged but fresh random choices were used for $\mathtt{RI}^2$, $\mathtt{RI}^3$, and $\mathtt{RI}^4$ as would be expected in a real-life implementation. These results assume a correct guess for $\mathtt{HW}(\mathtt{RI}^j)$, as discussed in the previous section.

Witnessing four uni-directional runs, or two mutual authentication runs, of the scheme in Section 3.2 and guessing the rotation amount correctly gives a probability of approximately 85% for recovering all but two bits of the key. However different attack strategies are possible.

Note that the attack using a single observed run is much faster than the attack with four observed runs, although it would recover a smaller proportion of the secret key bits. Moreover, as discussed above, when attempting to solve the resulting system of equations it is straightforward to recognize when an incorrect rotation has been guessed. Thus an efficient way to perform the full attack is as follows: we try the attack on four individual single authentications with different guesses to $\mathtt{HW}(\mathtt{RI}^t)$. Once we have identified the correct rotation for four runs of the protocol we apply the four-run attack that simultaneously uses the information from all four authentications to recover almost all bits of the key with high probability. For example, using this method, one could mount the full attack to recover all except two bits of the key with probability of approximately 69%, taking around 30 minutes to run on *SageMathCloud*.

4   Results and Discussion

Over the course of this paper we have seen several incremental versions of a tag, reader, and mutual authentication scheme. We have shown that none offer any substantive security. The results are summarized here, with most of the results in this paper being confirmed by implementations.

Version	Type of Attack	Net Result	# Authentications
Table 1	Passive	Tag cloning	1
Table 3	Passive	Key recovery	2
Table 4	Passive	Key recovery	8–16
Table 4	Passive (Algebraic)	Key recovery	4
Table 5	Passive (Algebraic)	Key recovery	4

We have concentrated on uni-directional authentication but mutual authentication consists of two inter-leaved versions of a tag and interrogator authentication. This means that all attacks will also apply to mutual authentication, but often with less effort since twice as much information is leaked during each protocol run. For all but the first variant the long term K key can be recovered.

For completeness we note that there have also been a proposal for a method to provide a secure channel, but first versions of the encryption method were wholly insecure. It might also be noted that there is some ambiguity at times as to whether protocol variables should be considered 64-bit values or 65-bit values. However this is likely to be a case of poor notation since (i) 65-bit values make little mathematical sense and (ii) they carry a significant implementation penalty. Even if we set these objections aside, the discussion quickly becomes academic since our attacks apply in a similar fashion either way.

We note that there will be many other opportunities for the attacker; we happily recognize that our application of algebraic techniques has been straightforward. A little more analysis might yield more efficient attacks, both algebraic and non-algebraic. However, in our view the point is already made and there is little to be gained by adding other incremental attacks to the mix. Those interested at looking at things more will find other work in a similar vein by other authors, *e.g.* [11], as well as other simple proposals [18,19]. Our code is available via www.isg.rhul.ac.uk/~ccid/publications/iso-iec-29167-15.htm.

5   Conclusion

The schemes described in this document are intrinsically weak due to the simple operations used by the tag and the interrogator. Future versions, if based on identical principles, are unlikely to provide additional security (see Appendix A).

In fairness, it should be noted that the combination of exclusive-or, integer addition, and bitwise rotation *can* be a good basis for the design of a secure primitive. So-called ARX designs are rightly popular and they featured prominently in the NIST SHA-3 initiative [17]. However these are typically multi-round algorithms while the most advanced variant of the schemes under analysis has probably just achieved a "single round" of computational complexity (if one can make the analogy).

The project editors for 29167-15 motivate their use of the simplest operations by stating that this will result in a low-area solution. However this is misguided. The bulk of the area for an implementation comes from the cryptographic state which is governed by the size of the variables. So even though ISO/IEC 29167-15 uses simple operations it doesn't lead to a dramatic implementation advantage. More importantly, there are already very good cryptographic solutions for RAIN RFID tags that provide good security; the AES is one option while PRESENT [14,13] or Grain128a [1] provide different implementation trade-offs.

One goal of the paper was to demonstrate that the simple authentication schemes being considered for standardization are flawed; this helps to emphasize the contributions cryptographers can make to a variety of ISO/IEC initiatives [7]. But a second, more important, goal was to stress that cryptography for RFID does not need to be bad cryptography. The state of the art is such that well-studied standardized schemes are available and these can be deployed in even the most demanding environments.

Acknowledgements. The computations in this work were carried out using Sage [21] and *SageMathCloud*, which is supported by National Science Foundation Grant No. DMS-0821725. The figures in this work were generated using Matplotlib [12].

References

1. Ågren, M., Hell, M., Johansson, T., Meier, W.: Grain-128a: A New Version of Grain-128 with Optional Authentication. International Journal of Wireless and Mobile Computing 5(1), 48–59 (2011)
2. Bogdanov, A.A., Knudsen, L.R., Leander, G., Paar, C., Poschmann, A., Robshaw, M., Seurin, Y., Vikkelsoe, C.: PRESENT: An ultra-lightweight block cipher. In: Paillier, P., Verbauwhede, I. (eds.) CHES 2007. LNCS, vol. 4727, pp. 450–466. Springer, Heidelberg (2007)
3. Cid, C., Murphy, S., Robshaw, M.J.B.: Algebraic Aspects of the Advanced Encryption Standard. Springer (2006)
4. Cid, C., Weinmann, R.P.: Block ciphers: algebraic cryptanalysis and Groebner bases. In: Groebner Bases, Coding, and Cryptography, pp. 307–327. Springer (2009)
5. Courtois, N.T.: Cryptanalysis of sfinks. In: Won, D.H., Kim, S. (eds.) ICISC 2005. LNCS, vol. 3935, pp. 261–269. Springer, Heidelberg (2006)
6. Courtois, N., Meier, W.: Algebraic attacks on stream ciphers with linear feedback. In: Biham, E. (ed.) EUROCRYPT 2003. LNCS, vol. 2656, pp. 345–359. Springer, Heidelberg (2003)

7. Degabriele, J.P., Fehr, V., Fischlin, M., Gagliardoni, T., Günther, F., Azzurra Marson, G., Mittelbach, A., Paterson, K.G.: Unpicking PLAID - A Cryptographic Analysis of an ISO-standards-track Authentication Protocol. Cryptology ePrint Archive, Report 2014/728 (2014). http://eprint.iacr.org/

8. EPCglobal. EPC Radio Frequency Identity Protocols, Generation 2 UHF RFID. Specification for RFID Air Interface Protocol for Communications at 860 MHz – 960 MHz Version 1.2.0. Available via.
http://www.gs1.org/gsmp/kc/epcglobal/uhfc1g2

9. EPCglobal. EPC Radio Frequency Identity Protocols, Generation 2 UHF RFID. Specification for RFID Air Interface Protocol for Communications at 860 MHz – 960 MHz Version 2.0.0. Available via.
www.gs1.org/gsmp/kc/epcglobal/uhfc1g2

10. Girault, M., Poupard, G., Stern, J.: On the Fly Authentication and Signature Schemes Based on Groups of Unknown Order. Journal of Cryptology 19(4), 463–488 (2006)

11. Han, D.: Gröbner Basis Attacks on Lightweight RFID Authentication Protocols. Journal of Information Processing Systems 7(4), 691–706 (2011)

12. Hunter, J.D.: Matplotlib: A 2D graphics environment. Computing in Science & Engineering 9(3), 90–95 (2007)

13. ISO/IEC 29167-11:2014 – Information technology – Automatic identification and data capture techniques – Part 11: Crypto suite PRESENT-80 security services for air interface communications

14. ISO/IEC 29192-2:2011 – Information technology – Security techniques – Lightweight cryptography – Part 2: Block ciphers

15. ISO/IEC 29192-4:2013 – Information technology – Security techniques – Lightweight Cryptography – Part 4: Asymmetric Techniques

16. National Institute of Standards and Technology. FIPS 197: Advanced Encryption Standard, November 2001

17. National Institute of Standards and Technology. SHA-3 competition, Available via.
csrc.nist.gov/groups/ST/hash/sha-3/index.html

18. Peris-Lopez, P., Hernandez-Castro, J.C., Estevez-Tapiador, J.M., Ribagorda, A.: M^2AP: A minimalist mutual-authentication protocol for low-cost RFID tags. In: Ma, J., Jin, H., Yang, L.T., Tsai, J.J.-P. (eds.) UIC 2006. LNCS, vol. 4159, pp. 912–923. Springer, Heidelberg (2006)

19. Peris-Lopez, P., Hernandez-Castro, J.C., Estevez-Tapiador, J.M., Ribagorda, A.: EMAP: An efficient mutual-authentication protocol for low-cost RFID tags. In: Meersman, R., Tari, Z., Herrero, P. (eds.) OTM 2006 Workshops. LNCS, vol. 4277, pp. 352–361. Springer, Heidelberg (2006)

20. RAIN RFID. Available via. http://www.rainrfid.org

21. Stein, W.A., et al.: Sage Mathematics Software (Version 6.3), The Sage Development Team (2014). http://www.sagemath.org

Appendix A: Obvious Variants Are Not Secure

It is our belief that the entire rationale for ISO/IEC 29167-15 is misguided. With the hope of discouraging further patches we pro-actively anticipate some modifications that might be made with the hope of increasing security. We show that none of the obvious variants provide a significantly increased level of security.

One variant would be to increase the size of all parameters, using a secret key of size $n = 64 + n'$ bits. The intention would be to increase the size of the equations systems since algebraic cryptanalytic schemes do not scale well. However this is particularly ineffective for the scheme of Table 4 since one can simply discard the n' high bits of the transmitted values and run precisely the same attack, recovering many of the lower 64 bits. We could then guess the value of the carry bit a_{j_64} which would allow the remaining bits to be attacked independently. We view this kind of attack as "slicing" the problem and we will return to this below.

We can apply a similar technique to remove any advantage from increased parameters in the scheme of Table 5. The rotation $r = \mathrm{HW}(\mathtt{RI})$ will, with high probability, lie in an interval $(\frac{n}{2} - \delta, \frac{n}{2} + \delta)$ for small δ. This means we can consider a subset of equations consisting of $\mathtt{S}_0^j \ldots \mathtt{S}_{s-1}^j$ and $\mathtt{T}_r^j \ldots \mathtt{T}_{r+s-1}^j$ (and the corresponding $\mathtt{p_i}, \mathtt{r_{j\_i}}, \mathtt{a_{j\_i}}, \mathtt{b_{j\_i}}$, $etc.$) for some value of the rotation r. This attack requires us to guess the values of the rotations and, additionally, we must guess $\mathtt{b_{j\_r}}$. But this does not significantly affect the complexity of the attack. (In this case we do not need to guess $\mathtt{a_{j\_0}}$, however had we considered a subset of equations not including $\mathtt{S}_0^j$ we would have needed to guess another carry bit.) From two runs of the uni-directional authentication the attacker guesses the value of four bits and, for the correct rotation amount, the number of key bits recovered when using a single 16-bit or 24-bit slice in experiments is shown in Figure 3.

One strategy that may improve the attack would be to first attack a small number of bits (via the slicing attack) for several guessed values of $\mathrm{HW}(\mathtt{RI}^j)$. Then we could carry out a full attack against multiple protocol runs (simultaneously) once the correct rotation values have been identified. This way one could recover almost all the key bits without having to run the full attack many times.

An alternative modification to the protocol might be to change the value of the constant $\mathtt{C}$. We implemented an attack assuming that two runs of the uni-directional authentication protocol were observed. We implemented a 16-bit slice attack and repeated the whole set of experiments for 256 different values of $\mathtt{C}$. The 256 $\mathtt{C}$ values were built up as a single byte pattern repeated eight times. The number of key bits that was recovered in our attacks for different $\mathtt{C}$ is illustrated in Figure 4. Zero is the only value for $\mathtt{C}$ that leaked no key bits. However $00\cdots00$ is a particularly bad choice for $\mathtt{C}$ since this makes $\mathtt{S} = \mathtt{T}$ and forgeries are trivial. Every other choice of $\mathtt{C}$ leads to at least four key bits out of 16 being recovered. This suggests that changing the value of $\mathtt{C}$ is unlikely to improve the security of the proposed protocol.

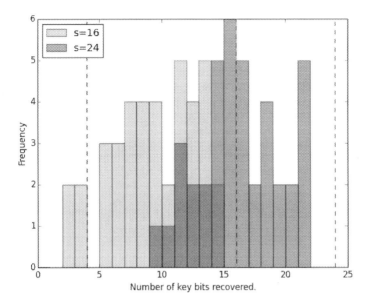

Fig. 3. Implementing the "slicing" attack against the scheme of Table 5 with slices of size s. Dashed lines (green and yellow) highlight the size of the slice used, which is an upper bound on the number of key bits that can be recovered within that slice. In both cases two runs of the uni-directional authentication scheme were used and the value of the four bits were guessed (highlighted by the black, dashed line).

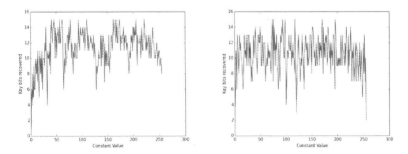

Fig. 4. A set of variants of the scheme in Table 5 were tested where the constant C is varied to take 256 different values (see text). Experiments were run over two instances of the uni-directional authentication scheme and the left and right charts give the results for two randomly generated keys.

An RFID Skimming Gate Using Higher Harmonics

René Habraken[1], Peter Dolron[1], Erik Poll[2], and Joeri de Ruiter[3]

[1] Techno Center, Radboud University Nijmegen
[2] Institute for Computing and Information Sciences, Radboud University Nijmegen
[3] School of Computer Science, University of Birmingham

Abstract. This paper describes a novel antenna design for communicating with ISO/IEC 14443A RFID cards at larger distances than the normal 5-10 cm. The set-up consists of two antennas, one to activate the card at the normal frequency of 13.56 MHz, and another to receive its response at the higher harmonic frequency of 40.68 MHz. The strong field required to power the card at larger distances is likely to drown out its response. By detecting the higher harmonic frequencies originating from the card's response this problem is solved, making communication at larger distances possible. The two antennas, placed 100 cm apart, form an RFID gate that can communicate with cards in the middle of the gate. This is a substantial improvement of the maximum skimming distance of 25 cm reported in literature.

Keywords: RFID, contactless smart card, ISO/IEC 14443, skimming, eavesdropping.

1   Introduction

This paper describes a method to extend the communication range with RFID cards, more specifically ISO/IEC 14443 Type A proximity cards [8]. This type is frequently used and it can be found in electronic passports, national ID cards, contactless bank cards and many systems for building access control. It is also compatible with the NFC (Near Field Communication) technology used in mobile phones. The different types of RFID systems operate at different communication distances. For ISO/IEC 14443 the normal operating range is up to 10 centimeters, but most commercially available card readers only achieve a range that is considerably shorter. Increasing the distance at which an RFID card can be activated improves convenience but is a risk for security and privacy.

One of the limiting factors in achieving larger communication distances is the required power for the card. The cards are passive, meaning they have no battery, so they require a strong fluctuating magnetic field for power. But a powerful antenna set-up to activate the card at large distances will generate a lot of noise, making it hard to receive the card's response. Here we achieve major improvements by using a resonant coil as a 3rd harmonic antenna to receive the card's answer. The spectral and physical separation between the activation

© Springer International Publishing Switzerland 2015
S. Mangard, P. Schaumont (Eds.): RFIDsec 2015, LNCS 9440, pp. 122–137, 2015.
DOI: 10.1007/978-3-319-24837-0_8

and reception paths solves the problem that the high power activation antenna drowns out the answer of the card.

The outline of this paper is as follows. Section 2 gives background information on terminology, attack possibilities and the concepts of near field and far field. Section 2 ends with an overview of related work, giving a summary of earlier results with long range antennas. The next three sections describe the antenna designs and experimental results for three scenarios: activating a card at larger distances (Section 3), eavesdropping at larger distances (Section 4), and finally the combination of the two scenarios, communication with a card (activation and reading) at the maximum distance (Section 5). Finally, our conclusions are summarized in Section 6.

2 Background

2.1 Terminology

RFID (Radio Frequency Identification) technology is a wireless communication technique that uses the inductive coupling of coils to transfer data. ISO/IEC 14443 cards require no battery and are powered (and read) at short ranges via electromagnetic (EM) induction. The ISO/IEC 14443 standard distinguishes two types: A and B, which differ in modulation, coding and protocol initialization. This paper only deals with Type A.

Communication with the data carrier, which is called the transponder, card or tag, is started by a reader. Because this reader initiates the protocol, activates the tag, and reads and writes information, it is also called the initiator or transceiver [4]. For reasons of readability it is referred to as reader throughout this paper. Before a tag is activated it must be brought into an alternating electromagnetic field (EM-field) with the right frequency and power level. The distance at which the tag is activated and can receive commands from the reader is called the *activation distance*. The distance at which the reader can still interpret the answer of the tag is the *reply distance* (see Fig. 1). The maximum distance at which a reader can activate a tag *and* receive its response is called the *skimming distance*.

In this paper the communication path from the reader to the tag is referred to as *Reader-to-Tag-link*. The communication path in the other direction is called the *Tag-to-Reader-link*. When these links are established and a complete initialization protocol is executed, it is possible for the reader to communicate with the tag. As the first step of communication the reader will receive and decode the UID (unique ID) of the tag. In our experiments we checked for successful reception of the UID to see if communication was working.

2.2 Attack Possibilities

Different attack scenarios on RFID tags can be distinguished.

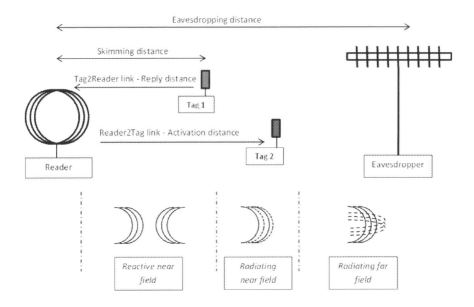

Fig. 1. Terminology

In an **eavesdropping attack**, an attacker intercepts the communication between a tag that is being held close to a normal reader, using a separate eavesdropping antenna. An eavesdropping attack is passive, meaning the eavesdropping antenna that the attacker uses does not have to power the tag, but only listens in on the communication. Because the reader, in contrast to the tag, is an active device and achieves a higher *modulation index* (ratio in signal level between the unmodulated and modulated carrier), the Reader-to-Tag-link is much easier to eavesdrop than the Tag-to-Reader-link.

In a **skimming attack**, an attacker secretly activates a tag and communicates with it. A skimming attack is active, meaning the antenna has to generate a field to power the tag. This limits the maximum distance for a skimming attack compared to an eavesdropping attack. In a skimming attack a compromise must be made between the activation distance and reply distance. This is because increasing the power of an antenna may increase the activation distance but at the same time decreases the reply distance, as the more powerful and noisy signal from the reader makes it harder to detect the tag's response. We refer to the maximum distance at which a skimming device can communicate with a tag as the *skimming distance*.

NB the term skimming for such an attack can be misleading if one thinks of well-known mag-stripe skimming of bank cards. When skimming mag-stripes, the attacker secretly reads the information on the mag-stripe, and can then make copies to create clones of the original bank card that cannot be distinguished from the original. For RFID tags, an attacker will not be able to create clones with a skimming attack, as long as the protocol uses some form of challenge-response.

Still, a skimming attack can be used as part of a **relay attack**, where the communication with the tag is relayed to a genuine terminal. If an attacker can for instance relay the communication from a contactless bank card to a payment terminal, this can be considered a digital form of pickpocketing.

2.3   Near and Far Field

Around an antenna three zones can be distinguished, each with its own properties: the *reactive near field, radiating near field* and *radiating far field* (see bottom of Fig. 1). The boundaries between these zones are hard to determine precisely and depend on the surroundings and characteristics of the antenna. Closest to the antenna a varying magnetic field is generated by the changing current through the antenna. This magnetic field, in its turn, also generates a changing electric field [4]. In close proximity of the reader antenna, the magnetic field is predominant over the electric field and this zone is known as the *reactive near field*. Typically this is the area for RFID technology because tags are powered by this magnetic field and communicate via this field. Moving away from the reader the predominant magnetic component drops quickly by the third power of the distance.

A change in voltage on the antenna terminals cannot result in a direct change in the surrounding EM-field and this delay results in the transmission of electromagnetic waves. Being transmitted from the antenna they cannot retroact on the antenna and this marks the end of the reactive near field and the start of the *radiating near field*. For the antennas presented in this paper the border between the reactive and the radiating near field is approximately at 36 cm from the antenna following:

$$D \approx \frac{2L^2}{\lambda} = \frac{2 \times 2^2}{22.11} = 0.36$$

where L is the length of the antenna, D the distance from the antenna and λ the wavelength.

Far field radiation is the most common view on radio waves, e.g. radiation that occurs when broadcasting a radio program or sending a message with a mobile phone. For the *radiating far field* the intensity is inversely proportional to the distance $(1/D)$. The electric and magnetic components, although perpendicular to each other, are in time phase and equal in energy level. The transition to far field radiation marks the unpassable barrier for RFID technology because it is practically impossible to activate a tag. For the ISO/IEC 14443 RFID protocol with a 13.56 MHz carrier frequency the transition from the radiating near field to the radiation far field starts at approximately 3.5 m following:

$$D \approx \frac{\lambda}{2\pi} = \frac{22.11}{6.28} = 3.52$$

For activation and hence skimming we are typically restricted to the reactive near field, whereas eavesdropping is also possible in the radiating far field. But, as will be shown in this paper, it is possible to go beyond the 36 cm with a skimming set-up.

2.4   Related Work

Kirschenbaum and Wool [10] built a low cost ($100) antenna that achieved a skimming distance of 25 cm. The antenna is a 40 cm diameter copper tube antenna. The whole set-up is powered by a 12 V battery. They expected that their design could be further improved to achieve a skimming distance of approximately 35 cm.

Hancke [6,7] describes activation and eavesdropping experiments with different antenna sizes and power usage. The largest activation distance he reports is 27 cm using an A3-sized antenna powered with 4 W. For the maximum eavesdropping distance he reports 400 cm for the Tag-to-Reader-link using a magnetic field antenna. Hancke notes that activating at a tag at a large distance is bad for the possible eavesdropping distance. When he combines activation and eavesdropping (using two antennas) in a skimming attack he uses a smaller activation distance of 15 cm (using an A5-sized antenna and a 4 W amplifier) where he can eavesdrop at 145 cm.

Earlier, Kfir and Wool [9] already predicted skimming distances that could be achieved with various costs and skills, based on experiments and simulations, but without producing a proof-of-concept. Our experiment results are in line with their predictions, as they predict that skimming up to 50 cm should be possible.

The use of higher harmonic frequencies for eavesdropping is not new. Engelhardt et al. [2] demonstrate that eavesdropping on the Tag-to-Reader-link is possible for ISO/IEC 14443 Type A tags at 18 m using the 3rd harmonic. In this scenario a normal reader is used to power the tag. Engelhardt et al. show that a successful detection of the modulation products in the far field relies on the coupling to nearby cables, and that with proper shielding of the cables the harmonics become undetectable.

Carrying out a relay attack not only involves communication with the victims tag, but also interacting with a genuine terminal. Oren et al. [11] looked into extending the range at which one can interact with an ISO/IEC 14443 reader. They reach a 115 cm range with a relay attack, using an active tag to overcome the short range of a passive tag for the Tag-to-Reader-link.

Francis et al. [5] demonstrated that NFC phones can be used to skim tags and then perform relay attacks. Such phones have a short operating range, but have the advantages of being cheap and readily available.

3 Activation at Greater Distances

3.1 Objective and Test Set-Up

Our first experiments were done on a relatively straightforward skimmer set-up similar to [10] with antenna designs adapted from [12]. Putting two amplifiers in cascade it was possible to power a 50 x 50 cm, transformer-matched, magnetic loop antenna with 60 W. This resulted in a successful skimming distance of approximately 40 cm. The possibility to achieve this distance was already predicted by [9], though we needed a slightly larger and more powerful antenna set-up than predicted. (Kfir and Wool base their prediction on a 40 x 40 cm antenna with the current limited to 4 A). While increasing the amplification, the matching components (necessary to adapt the antenna impedance to a 50 Ω regime for maximum power transfer) heated up to 120° C within two minutes and resulted in a mismatch that eventually broke the antenna and the reader.

By improving the design of the antenna with a gamma matching circuit, it was possible to keep the antenna working over a longer period of time while activating the tag over a long distance. The gamma matching circuit was adapted from [12] and [1] to require the smallest number of high power components compared to other matching strategies (see Fig. 2). We could use this antenna for activation at larger distances, but then the antenna could no longer receive the tag's response. To verify that the tag indeed was activated a pick-up coil was used and held in close proximity to the tag. The signal from this small antenna was fed to the reader to close the communication loop.

Fig. 2. Gamma-matched antenna

3.2   Results

With the gamma-matched activation antenna and a power of approximately 60 W, an activation distance of 60 cm was reached. The tag's UID was received by the separate pick-up coil and decoded by the reader. Because the same reader was used to power the tag and to decode the answer, the received signal from the tag is in phase with the carrier that was sent by the reader (synchronous detection). Receiving the answer with the pick-up coil was only possible up to a distance of 5 cm from the tag.

4   Eavesdropping Using Higher Harmonics

4.1   Objective and Test Set-Up

The limiting factor when communicating with an RFID tag is not the activation of the tag, but receiving its answer. The tag uses load modulation with a sub-carrier (derived from the carrier frequency) to send its answer to the reader. The limitation of this technique is the ability to alter the strong EM-field generated by the reader by switching on and off a small load on the antenna of the tag. If the field from the antenna is too strong, the influence of tag on this field is too small to be observed by the reader. The effect of the reader on the carrier signal is visible as the dips (modulation index of 100%) on the left side in Fig. 3. The effect of the tag as the smaller dips (and the increase of amplitude) on the right side.

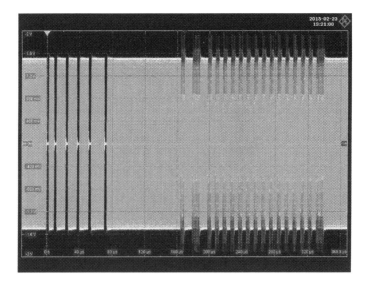

Fig. 3. Reader-to-Tag-link (left) and Tag-to-Reader-link (right)

More power leads to a decrease of the modulation index and signal to noise ratio (SNR), resulting in a smaller effect on the activation antenna. Therefore we started working with two antennas, one for activating the tag, one for receiving its response. This separation is possible because the information from the reader and tag is not only present in the fundamental frequency band (13.56 MHz $\pm$ 847.5 kHz) but also in multitudes of those frequency bands (2 x 13.56 MHz, 3 x 13.56 MHz, 4 x 13.56 MHz, 5 x 13.56 MHz, etc). The sidebands ($f_{harmonic} \pm$ 847.5 kHz) contain the information of the tag.

There are different sources where the multitudes of the fundamental frequency could originate from: the tag, the reader, but also from the saturation of an amplifier. The most likely candidate to produce these frequency components is a non-linear component like the rectifying bridge in the tag, formed by four diodes D1 to D4 as shown in Fig. 4). These diodes load the antenna coil, modelled by L1, and provide a DC voltage for the rest of the circuitry of the tag.

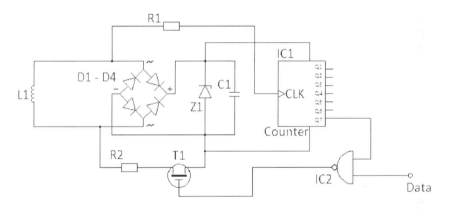

Fig. 4. Electrical circuit of a tag (adapted from: http://rfid-handbook.de/about-rfid.html)

To prove our conjecture that the higher harmonic signals originate from the tag, a self-made replica of a standard ISO/IEC 14443 tag was produced with the same dimension and characteristics as a standard RFID card. A comparison was made between two situations; without the diodes on the replica (Fig. 5) and with diodes mounted on the replica (Fig. 6).

The markers indicate the fundamental, 3rd, and 5th harmonics. Measurements show that by mounting the diodes the power of all the harmonics increases and the power of the fundamental decreases. There is an increase with 15.43 dB for the 3th harmonic and with 29.3 dB for the 5th harmonic. At the same time the loading of the EM-field results in a decrease of the fundamental frequency of 6.17 dB. An overview of all the harmonics is shown in Table 1.

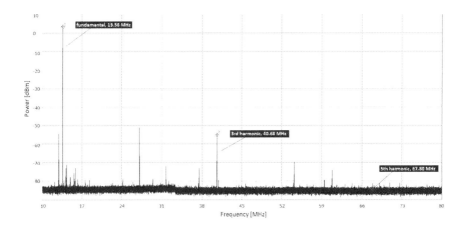

Fig. 5. Without diodes

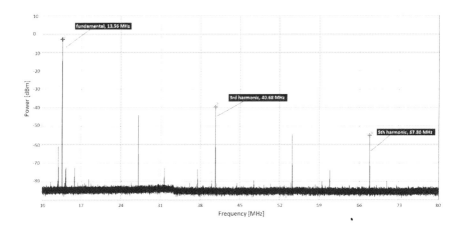

Fig. 6. With diodes

Table 1. Higher order harmonics

	1st 13.56 MHz [dBm]	2nd 27.12 MHz [dBm]	3rd 40.68 MHz [dBm]	4th 54.24 MHz [dBm]	5th 67.80 MHz [dBm]
With diodes	7	-34	-30	-45	-45
Without diodes	13	-41	-45	-60	-74

These harmonics do not yet contain any information from the tag. They have to be modulated with the data from the tag (via IC2 and switch T1 in Fig. 4) before the information will be present in the frequency bands $f_{harmonic} \pm 847.5$ kHz.

A positive side effect when measuring the signal from the tag at these higher frequencies is that there will be less noise from the environment according to [3]. To measure the harmonics (and the modulation products) up to the 5th order (67.80 MHz), a sensitive broadband antenna from the Lofar project[1] was available, that is normally used for astronomical observations. With the activation antenna from Section 3 it was possible to activate the tag at any distance up to 60 cm. The signal coming from the Lofar antenna was digitized with the National Instruments PXIe-5665 spectrum analyzer. In a LabVIEW program the results were digitally filtered and the spectra were extracted from the IQ data stream.

4.2   Results

With this set-up an eavesdropping distance of 3.7 meters was reached at which the answer of the tag (and the request from the reader) could still be retrieved. This distance can be reached measuring at 40.68 MHz (3rd harmonic) and also at 67.80 MHz (5th harmonic). In Fig. 7 the IQ data stream is shown measured with the National Instruments PXIe-5665 spectrum analyzer tuned to 40.68 MHz. The first peaks (until $\pm$ 80 μs) show data from the reader to the tag (REQA, REQuest command, type A [8]). The answer from the tag starts at $\pm$ 160 μs (ATQA, Answer To reQuest, type A). Comparing Fig. 7 with Fig. 3 it is clear that it follows the outline and time base of the AM-signal.

Engelhardt et al. already used higher harmonics for eavesdropping, reporting an eavesdropping range of 18 m, also using the 3rd harmonic of the original signal [2]. They showed that cables attached to the reader were responsible for (re)transmitting the harmonics into free space and that with proper shielding of the reader these harmonics were undetectable. The same phenomenon occurs in our configuration and also [11] reports a high range for the Tag-to-Reader-link due to coupling effects.

Unfortunately, harmonics were only detected by the Lofar antenna if the tag was held in the corner of the activation antenna. Engelhardt et al. report the

---

[1] http://www.lofar.org

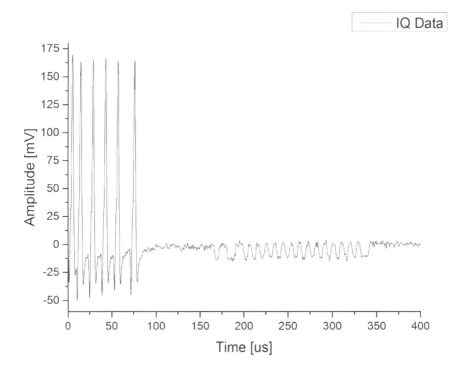

Fig. 7. Response at 40.68 MHz

same effect with the commercial RFID reader they used for activating the tag. They also had to place the tag in the corner of the reader to optimize results.

The observations made in the two paragraphs above, namely that (i) the modulated harmonics cannot be detected in the far field without a coupling effect to neighboring cables, and (ii) these higher harmonics are only present if the tag is held at a very precise location close to the reader, suggest that while the use of higher harmonics may be useful for passive eavesdropping attacks, it is not useful for active skimming attacks. After all, in a skimming attack the tag must be activated at a large distance. Concluding, the achieved eavesdropping distance looks promising but this set-up cannot be used in a skimming attack scenario.

5   Skimming Using Higher Harmonics

5.1   Objective and Test Set-Up

The RFID signal originates from the chip inside the reader as a square wave and contains all the harmonics according to the Fourier series. Together with the fundamental frequency these harmonics are amplified, reach the activation antenna and, despite the fact that it is not tuned for these frequencies, they are still transmitted (mainly in the reactive near field). Besides the carrier, the tag modulates these harmonics resulting in a combined effect with the harmonics generated by the diodes on the tag (Section 4.1). Placed in the far field, the Lofar antenna could only receive the answer of the tag if this signal coupled into a nearby cable. It was not possible to place the Lofar antenna closer to the tag and activation antenna (in the near field) because it was too sensitive for the fundamental frequency. Although this fundamental frequency was outside the bandwidth of the antenna, the high power in the 13.56 MHz band still saturated the Lofar antenna and made a sensitive measurement impossible.

Measurements with a small pick-up coil in the near field of the tag showed that higher harmonics were still detectable at activation distances up to 20 cm. Besides that, we observed the decrease of power of the fundamental in the pick-up coil when placing the rectifying diodes in the self-made replica. This led to the idea of amplifying the third harmonic in the antenna of the tag by placing a second resonant coil in its near-field (< 3.5 m) and use it as a receiving antenna. To prove this idea a new magnetic loop receiving antenna was made resonant at 40.68 MHz (undamped, resulting in a high Q-factor). Measurements with the receiving antenna placed at 12 cm from the tag showed an increase of the third harmonic of approximately 22 dB.

5.2   Results

Receiving the tag's response at a different frequency than the activation frequency makes it easier to retrieve the answer of the tag in the received signal. With the high power activation antenna and the selective receive antenna it is possible to use the maximum power available to activate the tag over a long distance, without the risk of damaging the receiving back-end and measurement equipment. With these two different antennas, tuned to two different frequencies, we made an RFID skimmer gate, shown in Fig. 8.

The square activation antenna, on the left side in the photo, is tuned to 13.56 MHz and activates the tag. The round receiving antenna, on the right side in the photo, is tuned to 40.68 MHz, enhances the 3rd harmonic and receives the reply of tag. It was also possible to tune the receiving antenna to the 5th harmonic, but this did not result in a better reception of the answer. Albeit attenuated strongly, the carrier frequency is also received by the receiving antenna and, in contrast to the other antenna designs, without saturating the low-noise amplifier or reception circuit of the reader. The answer of the tag is decoded real time without any significant latency or delay.

The two main parameters in the configuration of our RFID gate are the width of the gate, i.e. the distance between the two antennas, and the activation power, i.e. the power from the amplifiers to the activation antenna. Each combination of width and power level results in a different communication range over which a tag can be activated and its response can be picked up. This communication range is determined at one end by the maximum activation distance and at the

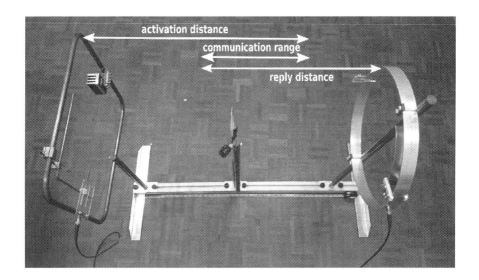

Fig. 8. RFID Skimming gate

Table 2. Results for RFID gate, where communication range is measured from the side of the gate formed by the activation antenna, i.e. the left side of the gate in Fig. 8

Gate width [cm]	Power [W]	Activation distance [cm]	Reply distance [cm]	Communication range [from activation side of gate]
70	14-22	60	60	from 10 to 60 cm
90	14-22	75	20	from 70 to 75 cm
100	75-88	52.5	52.5	from 47.5 to 52.5 cm

other end by the maximum reply distance. Table 2 gives the results achieved for three different widths of the gate, using different power levels:

– *An RFID gate of 70 cm.* Communication with a tag is possible over a range of 50 cm between the antennas, i.e. almost the full width of the gate except very close to either end. This is a major improvement compared to the earlier reported skimming distance of 25 cm [10].
– *An RFID gate of 90 cm.* This set-up achieves a long activation distance (of 75 cm from the activation antenna), while keeping the possibility to communicate with the tag at 20 cm of the receiving antenna. This is a substantial improvement of the maximum activation distances reported in the literature so far (27 cm) [6]. However, skimming – i.e. activating the card *and* receiving its response – is only possible over a very small range, 5 cm wide, in this configuration.

- *An RFID gate of 100 cm.* This configuration requires a large amount of power, and allows both activation and reception at just over 50 cm. It reaches the maximum skimming distance: interaction with the tag is possible if it is held close to the middle of the gate.

The results above are obtained without the use of additional DSP software (Digital Signal Processing), using hardware from a standard card reader. We have strong indications that with better filtering techniques and a different amplifier longer distances and communication ranges are possible. The experiments were carried out using a standard ISO/IEC 14443A tag, where we used the reception of the card's UID upon activation as evidence that the card was working.

We also experimented with various types of cards to confirm that after sending their UID they can also carry out their normal functionality. They generally did, except that, as expected, the range may be reduced if this functionality requires a lot of computing power, esp. for asymmetric cryptography. For example, experiments using a programmable Java Card showed that, when using the same amount of activation power, the range over which the RFID gate can power an RSA computation on the card is smaller than the range over which it can power a DES or AES encryption. When gradually sliding the tag away from the activation antenna first RSA fails, followed by both DES and AES, which fail together with all functionality of the card. So for this card only RSA, and not AES and DES, required a shorter distance. Of course, such characteristics will be highly depend on the specific processor hardware inside a card.

We also observed the effect of the orientation of the tag by changing the position relative to the antennas. Ideally the tag is parallel with the antennas, for optimal inductive coupling. However, placing a tag at an angle of 45° with respect to the antennas still resulted in successful communication. Increasing the angle above 50° communication quickly deteriorated because of the reduced coupling.

Depending on the skimming scenario (secretly activate a tag and start a communication session) it is possible to tune the antenna arrangement. The most practical scenario will be the 70 cm gate. With this set-up a large communication range within the gate is achieved and not much power is needed (22 W compared to 88 W in the 100 cm set-up). The 70 cm gate width is wide enough to let people pass, and when the victim is forced to make a turn between the antennas (for example in a voting booth or fitting room), the chance of a successful readout is significantly increased. More compact solutions are also possible by placing the antennas close together (see Fig. 9). Here the tag does not have to be between the two antennas, but it can be held near them. Because the antennas are tuned to different frequencies there is little influence on each other and a skimming distance of 60 cm is achieved.

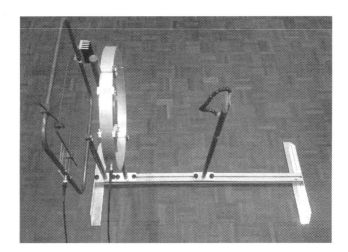

Fig. 9. Compact configuration of the antenna set-up, with activation and receiving antennas close together (on the left)

Currently, no commercial RFID readers are found achieving similar results for the ISO/IEC 14443A protocol. There are manufacturers that also use dual frequency technologies, but this requires non-standard tags equipped with two antennas. The advantage of the method presented in this paper is that widely available tags can be used without any adaption on the side of the tag and at the data rates the protocol specifies.

6   Conclusions

We presented several antenna set-ups to study the practical communication limits of ISO/IEC 14443 Type A RFID technology. The final result is a new antenna design that significantly increases the communication range of RFID tags. The set-up is an RFID gate formed by two antennas, one activating the card at 13.56 MHz and another antenna receiving its response at the third harmonic frequency at 40.68 MHz. This RFID skimming gate is the first working prototype using higher harmonics for communicating with a tag over a long range in the near field.

The activation antenna can withstand 100 W, enough to activate the tag over a large distance. Normally when activating a tag over larger distances its answer cannot be received anymore due to the reduced coupling with the activation antenna. This is solved by enhancing and receiving the third harmonic of the tag's answer by placing a undamped loop antenna in the near field.

The two antennas can be placed in several configurations, for example to form

- a gate with a width of 100 cm, which can communicate with a tag held near the center between the two antennas, or

– a gate with a width of 70 cm, which can communicate with a tag over almost the entire range between the antennas.

Our results so far have been obtained without using any additional DSP (Digital Signal Processing) software. We have strong indications that with better filtering techniques and a different low-noise amplifier longer distances and wider communication ranges are possible.

References

1. The ARRL Antenna Book. The American Radio Relay League (2000)
2. Engelhardt, M., Pfeiffer, F., Finkenzeller, K., Biebl, E.: Extending ISO/IEC 14443 type a eavesdropping range using higher harmonics. In: Proceedings of 2013 European Conference on Smart Objects, Systems and Technologies (SmartSysTech), pp. 1–8. IEEE (2013)
3. European Radiocommunications Committee (ERC): ERC report 69 – propagation model and interference range calculation for inductive systems 10 kHz - 30 MHz (1999)
4. Finkenzeller, K.: RFID Handbook: Fundamentals and Applications in Contactless Smart Cards and Identification, 3rd edn. Wiley (2010)
5. Francis, L., Hancke, G., Mayes, K., Markantonakis, K.: Practical NFC peer-to-peer relay attack using mobile phones. In: Ors Yalcin, S.B. (ed.) RFIDSec 2010. LNCS, vol. 6370, pp. 35–49. Springer, Heidelberg (2010)
6. Hancke, G.P.: Practical attacks on proximity identification systems. In: IEEE Symposium on Security and Privacy (S&P 2006), pp. 328–333. IEEE (2006)
7. Hancke, G.P.: Practical eavesdropping and skimming attacks on high-frequency RFID tokens. J. Comput. Secur. 19(2), 259–288 (2011)
8. ISO/IEC: ISO/IEC 14443-3:2011, Identification cards – Contactless integrated circuit cards – Proximity cards – Part 3: Initialization and anticollision (2011)
9. Kfir, Z., Wool, A.: Picking virtual pockets using relay attacks on contactless smartcard. In: First International Conference on Security and Privacy for Emerging Areas in Communications Networks (SecureComm 2005), pp. 47–58. IEEE (2005)
10. Kirschenbaum, I., Wool, A.: How to build a low-cost, extended-range RFID skimmer. In: Proceedings of the 15th USENIX Security Symposium, pp. 43–57. Usenix (2006)
11. Oren, Y., Schirman, D., Wool, A.: Range extension attacks on contactless smart cards. In: Crampton, J., Jajodia, S., Mayes, K. (eds.) ESORICS 2013. LNCS, vol. 8134, pp. 646–663. Springer, Heidelberg (2013)
12. Texas Instruments: HF antenna cookbook - technical application report 11-08-26-001, March 2001

Part IV

Efficient Implementations

Efficient E-cash with Attributes on MULTOS Smartcards

Gesine Hinterwälder, Felix Riek, and Christof Paar*

Horst Görtz Institute for IT Security, Ruhr-University Bochum, Germany
{gesine.hinterwaelder,christof.paar}@rub.de,
felix.riek@googlemail.com

Abstract. Ever since its invention in the 1980s, e-cash has been considered a promising solution for privacy-preserving electronic payments. However, the computational capabilities, required for the processing of e-cash protocols, are demanding. Only recent works show the feasibility of implementing e-cash on constrained platforms. A particularly challenging, while at the same time extremely attractive platform, are *smartcards*. Smartcards are, next to magnetic stripe cards, the dominant platform used to execute electronic payments, and they enjoy wide user acceptance. In this paper we present an implementation of two e-cash schemes on MULTOS smartcards. We base the schemes on elliptic curve cryptography, which is supported by the API of the platform of choice. Our results are promising: When relying on a 160-bit elliptic curve, spending a coin, which encodes two attributes that are not revealed, can be executed in less than 800 ms with both considered schemes.

Keywords: Privacy-preserving payment schemes, E-cash, Elliptic curve cryptography, MULTOS smartcards.

1 Introduction

When compared to traditional cash payments, electronic payments have many benefits. As such, they can increase security, they reduce maintenance cost, as no cash has to be physically carried and collected, and spending and collecting is considerably faster. A crucial drawback of e-payment, however, is that user privacy can be greatly affected. For example, widely used schemes such as debit or credit card payments, reveal crucial information towards the vendor and the bank. This allows to collect personal information about a user and her habits and thus directly impacts her privacy. Apart from societal consequences that a loss of privacy of individuals has, two arguments for not handing over personal information to commercial entities are: (1) Providing a company with sensitive personal information requires that a user trusts the company to store the information securely, and to prevent malicious parties to have access to it. For example the store chain Target reported in late 2013 that credit card and debit card information of 40 million customers had been stolen. This information included the customers' names,

---

* This work was supported in part by the German Federal Ministry for Economic Affairs and Energy (Grant 01ME12025 SecMobil).

their credit card numbers, expiration dates and the three-digit security codes [19]. This incident demonstrates that it can be risky to provide a company with sensitive personal information, even if the company itself does not try to use the information in a questionable way. (2) It gives entities, especially financial institutions, the power of interpretation of vast amounts of personal data. Users are very often not even aware that such data is collected and how it is being interpreted. As an example for the possibilities of abuse (admittedly not from the e-payment world), it was found that employers are far less willing to hire someone who has an arrest record, even if this person has been found to be innocent [16].

There exist cryptographic protocols which overcome this drawback, namely electronic cash schemes. Electronic cash, or e-cash, has been introduced in 1982 by David Chaum [9]. Following his idea, e-cash has become an area of cryptographic research and many schemes were proposed [6,10,4,7,8]. A scheme known for its efficiency during the spending phase was proposed by Brands in 1993 [6]. However, Brands' untraceable off-line cash scheme has never been proven secure. Further, its proof of security has been shown to be impossible under currently known techniques [3]. Recently, Baldimtsi *et al.* proposed Anonymous Credentials Light (ACL), an anonymous credential scheme, which extends Abe's credential scheme [1] to allow the encoding of attributes. This scheme can easily be adapted to be used as an e-cash scheme [2]. It has a full security proof, at the expense of a slightly lower efficiency compared to Brands' scheme.

An implementation of Brands e-cash scheme with attributes and ACL, based on the relatively powerful CPU of a smartphone, has been shown in [13]. In practice, however, it is highly desirable to execute payment applications on a secure device, such as a smartcard or the secure element of a smartphone, instead of a smartphone's main processor. Both smartcards and secure elements are usually equipped with a relatively small microprocessor. As an additional hurdle in practice, it is suprisingly difficult for researchers to have free access to smartcards, i.e., to program smartcards using native code. Usually, if at all, only high-level access is provided [25]. This has made it quite difficult to analyze the performance of non-standard cryptographic protocols on smartcards. While certain cryptographic primitives (such as AES or 3DES encryption), which are required for many security applications, is supported by many smartcard APIs, advanced cryptographic protocols, especially those requiring the execution of computationally complex arithmetic, cannot easily be executed on these platforms in an acceptable execution time. In summary, the motivation for the work at hand is that realizing privacy-preservering payment schemes, which support proving user attributes during a payment, on low-cost smart cards is of great practical interest, but poses at the same time many computational and technical challenges.

1.1   Related Work

Multiple works present an implementation of anonymous credentials on smartcards. Bichsel *et al.* presented an implementation of the Camenish-Lysyanskaya anonymous credential system on a Java Card [5]. However, their best result requires more than 7 sec for the issuance of a credential. Sterckx *et al.* presented an implementation of the Direct Anonymous Attestation scheme on Java Cards [22], where their execution of the signing protocol requires 4.2 sec. Vullers *et al.* presented an implementation of an

Idemix based credential scheme on a MULTOS smartcard, which they called IRMA card [26]. When encoding two attributes, their implementation, which is based on a 1024-bit modulus, executes in 1.1 sec if not revealing an attribute and 0.9 sec, when revealing both attributes. Finally, Mostowski and Vullers presented an implementation of the U-Prove system on MULTOS smartcards in [17]. Their issuance of a U-Prove token requires 3.6 sec, when allowing the encoding of two attributes into the token, while showing the credential without revealing the encoded attributes requires 550 ms.

Only few implementations of full e-cash schemes on mobile platforms exist. While Brands' untraceable offline cash scheme or variations of it has been implemented on mobile platforms, no implementation of ACL on a constrained device has been presented in the literature. Clemente-Cuervo *et al.* presented an implementation of an e-cash scheme based on Brands' on a PDA [11], while Hinterwälder *et al.* presented an implementation of Brands' and ACL including the encoding of attributes on a Blackberry smartphone, which supports NFC-communication [13]. In real-world applications it is desirable to execute security-critical protocols on a trusted platform, which can be assumed to be much more constrained in size and performance than a powerful smartphone CPU. In [12] Hinterwälder *et al.* showed that Brands' untraceable offline cash scheme (without the encoding of attributes) can be executed efficiently even on extremely constrained microcontrollers, which can be used on a passively powered computational RFID tag.

1.2 Contribution

In this paper we show in practice that Brands' untraceable off-line cash scheme including the encoding of two attributes into coins can be implemented efficiently on low-cost smartcards, meeting the stringent timing requirements of modern payment systems. In public transportation payment systems a payment should be executable within 300 ms to allow making a payment while slowly passing turnstiles [20]. In many other payment scenarios a bit longer transaction times are acceptable, however a payment transaction should be executable within a couple of hundreds of miliseconds. We implemented the scheme on a UbiVelox MULTOS smartcard achieving an execution time of the time-critical spending phase in 800 ms. While Brands' credential scheme has been implemented on off-the-shelf smartcards before, this paper is the first to present a smartcard implementation of Brands' e-cash scheme supporting the encoding of attributes into electronic coins. These results highlight that privacy-preserving e-cash schemes are indeed practical.

We further present an implementation of the Anonymous Credentials Light scheme (ACL), to be used as e-cash, also encoding two attributes into coins, on the same platform. For both schemes we present performance results at two security levels, namely at a level comparable to 80-bit symmetric security and a level comparable to 128-bit security. While 80-bit security offers sufficient security for low-value payment systems, we show that the presented implementations achieve an acceptable performance for high-security applications. We further analyze and compare the performance of both schemes on the chosen platform.

1.3 Organization

In Section 2 we review basics about e-cash schemes and describe the withdrawal and spending protocols of the schemes that we implemented in detail. We introduce the smartcard that we chose as our target platform in Section 3 and describe our implementation in Section 4. Finally, our implementation results are presented in Section 5 followed by a discussion in Section 6.

2 Review of Electronic Cash

Electronic cash denotes cryptographic protocols that map the system of physical cash into the digital world. Apart from its inbuilt preservation of a customer's privacy, the benefit of electronic cash in comparison to other electronic payment protocols is that payments can be executed offline. In contrast to this other payment schemes, such as the bitcoin payment scheme, require an online connection to a peer-to-peer network, or a central authority, such as credit card payments, for verification of a payment. Allowing offline verification has benefits in a domain, where devices accepting a payment might not have a constant connection to the Internet. For completeness of description of our implementation, we review the basics of the implemented protocols, namely Brands' untraceable off-line cash scheme and Anonymous Credentials Light (ACL), allowing the encoding of attributes, in this section. The protocols have been presented in [13].

There are three players involved in an electronic cash scheme, namely the bank B, users U, and shops S. In the considered payment schemes these players execute the following protocols:

- Setup, in which system parameters are generated and the bank generates a private and public key pair.
- Registration, in which a user registers at the bank. After authentication by means of a passport or credit card, the user generates a private and public key pair and proves possession of his private key to the bank. The bank stores the user information together with the user's public key, to be later used for identification purposes in case of fraud.
- Withdrawal, in which a user receives electronic coins (the currency in an electronic cash scheme) from the bank, who is the only entity able to generate these coins. The user's bank account is debited the amount of money he received in electronic coins.
- Spending, in which a user spends electronic coins to a shop in exchange for goods. This process happens offline, i. e. a shop checks by cryptographic means, whether she received a valid coin from the user. She cannot check, whether the user has already spent the coin before.
- Deposit, in which a shop deposits coins she received from users to her bank account. During this process the bank checks, whether it receives a valid coin from the shop, and adds its value to the shop's bank account. Later it checks whether this coin had already been deposited before. If so, it executes the double-spending detection protocol.
- Double-Spending Detection, in which the bank checks, whether the shop is trying to double-deposit the coin, or whether a user has double-spent the coin. If it detects that a user has double-spent a coin, it reveals his identity from the coin.

In the considered payment schemes an electronic coin consists of a serial number and a double-spending tag, which are blindly signed by the bank. The serial number ensures that a coin can be identified later on. This is required in order to identify, whether a coin was spent multiple times, otherwise a user could just copy the coin data and spend it over and over again. The double-spending tag requires a user to reveal partial information about his identity during the spending process such that, if he reveals this information twice, *i. e.* if he spends the same coin multiple times, the pieces of information can be combined and his identity can be extracted from them. If he behaves *correctly* (in terms of the system rules), and spends each coin only once, his identity remains hidden during payments. Even further, in a privacy-preserving electronic cash scheme coins are unlinkable, meaning that it remains hidden, whether two spendings originate from the same user.

The security of an e-cash scheme is based on the *unforgeability* of the underlying blind signature scheme. While anyone in possession of the bank's public key is able to validate a coin, *i. e.* its blind signature, the bank is the only entity able to generate blind signatures and thus to generate electronic coins. Privacy is ensured by *blindness* of the underlying blind signature scheme, which means that contents are blinded in a way that the bank does not know the contents it generates a signature for. Thus, when a coin is deposited later on, the bank does not know, which user it had given to this particular coin. The considered schemes further ensure that a coin is bound to the private key of a user, i.e. only an entity in possession of the private key can spend the coin later on.

Certain e-cash schemes, and in particular the ones that were implemented for this paper allow the encoding of attributes. A user commits to these attributes during the registration process. An attribute could for example be a user's age, zip code, or his eligibility to receive a certain discount. He can later on prove possession of these attributes, which can be used for discount systems or the collection of meaningful data about customer behavior in a payment system.

In this work we focus on the withdrawal and spending protocols, as those are the time critical protocols of an e-cash scheme, i.e. they are executed at points of sale in the worst case when there is high user-traffic, while the other protocols are either executed only once per user, or can be executed at any point in time. In the following we review the withdrawal and spending protocols of both schemes for the case of encoding and revealing two attributes. This has been presented in [13].

2.1 Brands' E-Cash Scheme for the Encoding of Two Attributes

In Brands' e-cash scheme [6] when allowing the encoding of two attributes $\mathcal{B}$ generates five generators $\hat{g}, g, g_0, g_1, g_2$ of a cyclic group G of prime order q during system setup. It then generates a private key $sk_{\mathcal{B}} \in_{\mathcal{R}} \mathbb{Z}_q$ and computes its public key $pk_{\mathcal{B}} = g^{sk_{\mathcal{B}}}$. During registration $\mathcal{U}$ generates a private key $sk_{\mathcal{U}} \in_{\mathcal{R}} \mathbb{Z}_q$ and computes his public key as $pk_{\mathcal{U}} = g_0^{sk_{\mathcal{U}}}$. He further commits to the two attributes $L_1, L_2 \in \mathbb{Z}_q$ and computes the commitment $C = g_0^{sk_{\mathcal{U}}} g_1^{L_1} g_2^{L_2}$. $\mathcal{U}$ then provides a proof of knowledge of his secret key, that he knows an opening of the commitment C and that the same value $sk_{\mathcal{U}}$ has been used for the commitment and $pk_{\mathcal{U}}$. The bank checks this proof of knowledge, stores $\mathcal{U}$'s information, computes $z = (C\hat{g})^{sk_{\mathcal{B}}}$, and sends z to $\mathcal{U}$.

Withdrawal Protocol. For each coin $\mathcal{U}$ and $\mathcal{B}$ engage in the protocol described in Table 1, after which $\mathcal{U}$ knows the representation of a coin as $A, B, \text{sign}(A, B) = A, B, \hat{z}, \hat{a}, \hat{b}, \hat{r}$, where $\text{sign}(A, B)$ denotes a signature on A and B. Additionally to the coin, the user stores s, x, x_0, x_1 and x_2, which he will later need for spending the coin.

Table 1. Brands' withdrawal protocol when encoding two attributes

$\mathcal{B}$		$\mathcal{U}$
$w \in_R \mathbb{Z}_q, a = g^w, b = (C\tilde{g})^w$	$\xrightarrow{\quad a,b \quad}$	$s \in_R \mathbb{Z}_q^*, \; A = (C\tilde{g})^s, \; \hat{z} = z^s$
		$x, x_0, x_1, x_2, u, v \in_R \mathbb{Z}_q$
		$B = A^x g_0^{x_0} g_1^{x_1} g_2^{x_2}$
		$\hat{a} = a^u g^v, \; \hat{b} = b^{su} A^v$
		$\hat{c} = \mathcal{H}(A, B, \hat{z}, \hat{a}, \hat{b})$
	$\xleftarrow{\quad c \quad}$	$c = \hat{c}/u$
$r = c \times sk_{\mathcal{B}} + w$	$\xrightarrow{\quad r \quad}$	$g^r \overset{?}{=} pk_{\mathcal{B}}^c a, \; (C\tilde{g})^r \overset{?}{=} z^c b$
		$\hat{r} = r \times u + v$

Spending Protocol. To spend a coin with representation $A, B, \text{sign}(A, B)$, which encodes two attributes, the protocol presented in Table 2 is executed between $\mathcal{U}$ and $\mathcal{S}$. In this protocol $id_{\mathcal{S}}$ denotes the ID of the shop and ts a time stamp of the current time and date. We present the specific case of revealing the attribute L_1. The other possible cases can be derived from this case. The verification of $\text{sign}(A, B)$ checks whether $g^{\hat{r}} \overset{?}{=} pk_{\mathcal{B}}^{\hat{c}} \hat{a}$ and $A^{\hat{r}} \overset{?}{=} \hat{z}^{\hat{c}} \hat{b}$. If the signature verifies, $\mathcal{S}$ accepts the payment and saves the payment transcript $A, B, \text{sign}(A, B), (R, r_0, r_1, r_2)$. The interested reader is referred to [13] for further details.

Table 2. Brands' with attributes spending protocol when revealing attribute L_1

$\mathcal{U}$		$\mathcal{S}$
	$\xrightarrow{\quad A,B,\hat{z},\hat{a},\hat{b},\hat{r} \quad}$	$A \overset{?}{\neq} 1$
$r_0 = -d \times sk_{\mathcal{U}} + x_0$	$\xleftarrow{\quad d \quad}$	$d = \mathcal{H}_0(A, B, id_{\mathcal{S}}, ts)$
$r_2 = -d \times L_2 + x_2$		
$R = d/s + x$	$\xrightarrow{\quad (R,r_0,r_2)(L_1,x_1) \quad}$	$r_1 = -d \times L_1 + x_1$
		$g_0^{r_0} g_1^{r_1} g_2^{r_2} \tilde{g}^{-d} \overset{?}{=} A^{-R} B$
		verify $\text{sign}(A, B)$

2.2 ACL E-Cash for the Encoding of Two Attributes

In the ACL e-cash scheme [2], when allowing the encoding of two attributes, $\mathcal{B}$ first chooses the generators $z, g, \hat{g}, \tilde{g}, g_0, g_1, g_2$ in the cyclic group G of order q. $\mathcal{B}$ then generates a private and public key pair, by choosing a private key $sk_\mathcal{B} \in_\mathcal{R} \mathbb{Z}_q$ and computing the public key as $pk_\mathcal{B} = g^{sk_\mathcal{B}}$. During registration $\mathcal{U}$ first chooses a private key $sk_\mathcal{U} \in_\mathcal{R} \mathbb{Z}_q$ and computes his public key as $pk_\mathcal{U} = g_0^{sk_\mathcal{U}}$. He then commits to his attributes $L_1, L_2 \in \mathbb{Z}_q$ by computing the commitment $C = \tilde{g}^R g_0^{sk_\mathcal{U}} g_1^{L_1} g_2^{L_2}$, where $R \in_\mathcal{R} \mathbb{Z}_q$. Similar to Brands e-cash $\mathcal{U}$ then proves knowledge of his secret key, that he knows an opening to the commitment C and that the same value $sk_\mathcal{U}$ has been encoded in his public key and in his commitment.

Withdrawal Protocol. For each coin $\mathcal{U}$ and $\mathcal{B}$ run the withdrawal protocol depicted in Table 3. After the execution of this protocol $\mathcal{U}$ knows a representation of a coin as coin $= (\zeta, \zeta_1, \rho, \omega, \hat{\rho}_1, \hat{\rho}_2, \hat{\omega})$. He stores it together with the values r, τ and γ, which he will need later on for spending the coin.

Table 3. ACL e-cash withdrawal protocol with encoding of two attributes

$\mathcal{B}$	$\mathcal{U}$
$r, u, \hat{c}, \hat{r}_1, \hat{r}_2 \in_\mathcal{R} \mathbb{Z}_q$	
$z_1 = Cg^r, \ z_2 = z/z_1$	
$a = g^u$	
$\hat{a}_1 = g^{\hat{r}_1} z_1^{\hat{c}}, \ \hat{a}_2 = \hat{g}^{\hat{r}_2} z_2^{\hat{c}} \quad \xrightarrow{r, a, \hat{a}_1, \hat{a}_2}$	Check whether $a, \hat{a}_1, \hat{a}_2 \in G$
	$z_1 = Cg^r$
	$\gamma, \tau, t_1, t_2, t_3, t_4, t_5 \in_\mathcal{R} \mathbb{Z}_q$
	$\zeta = z^\gamma, \ \zeta_1 = z_1^\gamma, \ \zeta_2 = \zeta/\zeta_1$
	$\eta = z^\tau, \ \alpha = ag^{t_1} sk_\mathcal{B}^{t_2}$
	$\hat{\alpha}_1 = \hat{a}_1^\gamma g^{t_3} \zeta_1^{t_4}, \ \alpha'_2 = \hat{a}_2^\gamma \hat{g}^{t_5} \zeta_2^{t_4}$
	$\varepsilon = \mathcal{H}(\zeta, \zeta_1, \alpha, \hat{\alpha}_1, \hat{\alpha}_2, \eta)$
$c = e - \hat{c} \quad \xleftarrow{\quad e \quad}$	$e = \varepsilon - t_2 - t_4$
$x = u - c \times sk_\mathcal{B} \quad \xrightarrow{c, x, \hat{c}, \hat{r}_1, \hat{r}_2}$	$\rho = x + t_1$
	$\omega = c + t_2, \ \hat{\rho}_1 = \gamma \times \hat{r}_1 + t_3$
	$\hat{\omega} = \hat{c} + t_4, \ \hat{\rho}_2 = \gamma \times \hat{r}_2 + t_5$

Spending Protocol. In Table 4 we present the spending protocol for the case when revealing the attribute L_1. Revealing attribute L_2 can be done in a similar fashion. If $\mathcal{U}$ does not wish to prove possession of an attribute, he stops the protocol execution at the first intermediate line in Table 4. For further details, please refer to [13].

3 Multi Application Card Operating System (MULTOS)

MULTOS International Pte Ltd. is one of the leading providers of technology and solutions for the smartcard industry [18]. The consortium provides MULTOS modules, or

Table 4. ACL e-cash spending protocol when revealing attribute L_1

$\mathcal{U}$		$\mathcal{S}$
$\epsilon_p = \mathcal{H}(z^\tau, \mathrm{coin}, d)$	$\xleftarrow{\quad d \quad}$	$d = \mathcal{H}(id_\mathcal{S}, ts)$
$\mu_p = \tau - \epsilon_p \times \gamma$	$\xrightarrow{\quad \epsilon_p, \mu_p, \mathrm{coin} \quad}$	$\zeta \overset{?}{\neq} 1,\ \epsilon_p \overset{?}{=} \mathcal{H}(z^{\mu_p}\zeta^{\epsilon_p}, \mathrm{coin}, d)$
		$\omega + \hat{\omega} \overset{?}{=}$
		$\mathcal{H}(\zeta, \zeta_1, g^\rho sk_\mathcal{B}{}^\omega, g^{\hat{\rho}_1}\zeta_1^{\hat{\omega}}, (\hat{g})^{\hat{\rho}_2}\zeta_2^{\hat{\omega}}, z^{\mu_p}\zeta^{\epsilon_p})$

$\mathcal{U}$		$\mathcal{S}$
$r', \hat{x}, x', \tilde{x}, x_0, x_1, x_2 \in_\mathcal{R} \mathbb{Z}_q$		
$\hat{C} = g_1^{L_1\gamma} g^{r'\gamma},\ \tilde{C} = g_1^{x_1} g^{x'}$		
$\widetilde{\zeta}_1 = \tilde{g}^{\tilde{x}} g_0^{x_0} g_1^{x_1} g_2^{x_2} g^{\hat{x}}$		
$c = \mathcal{H}(\zeta_1, \tilde{\zeta}_1, \hat{C}, \tilde{C}, ts)$		
$\tilde{s} = \tilde{x} + c \times R \times \gamma$		
$s_0 = x_0 + c \times sk_\mathcal{U} \times \gamma$		
$s_1 = x_1 + c \times L_1 \times \gamma$		
$s_2 = x_2 + c \times L_2 \times \gamma$		
$\hat{s} = \hat{x} + c\, r\, \gamma$	$\xrightarrow{\quad L_1, \widetilde{\zeta}_1, \hat{C}, \tilde{C} \quad}$	
$s' = x' + c\, r'\, \gamma$	$\xrightarrow{\quad \tilde{s}, s_0, s_1, s_2, \hat{s}, s' \quad}$	$c = \mathcal{H}(\zeta_1, \widetilde{\zeta}_1, \hat{C}, \tilde{C}, ts)$
		$\widetilde{\zeta}_1 \zeta_1^c \overset{?}{=} \tilde{g}^{\tilde{s}} g_0^{s_0} g_1^{s_1} g_2^{s_2} g^{\hat{s}},\ \tilde{C}\hat{C}^c \overset{?}{=} g_1^{s_1} g^{s'}$

chips to card manufacturers. Their application ranges from banking, over transit payments to government ID. The hardware of MULTOS cards may differ for different types of MULTOS cards, depending on the chip manufacturer, but it has to be ensured that it supports a specified MULTOS operating system. Communication with the card and provision of the virtual machine, which handles code execution on the card as well as memory management and loading and deletion of applications, are provided by the MULTOS operating system [15]. It is claimed by the MULTOS consortium that they provide "the world's most secure multi-application smartcard operating system" [18]. A multi-application smartcard has many benefits, as it can host multiple applications in a single device. It can thus combine several payment and authentication services, such as transit payments, credit card payments and government ID in a single card. Besides security the focus lies on an open access, which is why those cards were chosen for this work. In particular we use UbiVelox UBM 21-Z48 cards as the API of these MULTOS smartcards support a variety of cryptographic primitives, in particular elliptic curve cryptography, allowing the implementation of advanced cryptographic protocols on them.

To allow the secure execution of multiple applications on the card, the operating system provides an application separating firewall, ensuring that applications on the card cannot interfere with each other. This firewall provides each application with memory area for code, data and session data. The firewall ensures that the code memory space cannot be read or written by another application. Application data, which has to persist in memory over multiple executions of the application is stored in data memory. Code and data are stored in EEPROM of the chip. Session data, which is only needed within an execution of a specific application, is held in the much faster RAM on the card.

Information is exchanged between reader and card using Application Protocol Data Units (APDU). A reader sends a command APDU to which the card answers with a corresponding APDU response. A command APDU has a 4 byte header. This header encodes a class byte CLS, which selects the class within an instruction, an instruction byte INS, which selects the instruction within a class and two parameter bytes P1 and P2, which specify parameters within the instruction. It further has an optional body consisting of a byte Lc, which specifies the length of the command data that follows, the command data itself and a byte Le, which indicates the expected length of the cards response.

We used a UBM21-Z48 developer card manufactured by UbiVelox for our analysis. This card, which supports MULTOS version 4.2.1, contains an ST23ZL48 chip from STMicroelectronics[1]. The ST23ZL48 chip has a 8/16-bit ST23 CPU core, 300 kB of ROM, 6 kB of RAM, and 48 kB of EEPROM. The CPU can be operated at frequencies of up to 27 MHz. It further has an AIS-31 class P2 compliant true random number generator and an enhanced NESCRYPT crypto-processor [24]. The coprocessor provides high-performance native support for $GF(p)$ and $GF(2^n)$ arithmetic and includes dedicated instructions to accelerate execution of the SHA-1 and SHA-2 family of hash functions. It thus allows high-performance implementations of public-key cryptosystems [23]. We chose this card due to its Elliptic Curve Cryptography (ECC) support, which we base the implemented e-cash schemes on. In particular supports the chosen target addition, multiplication, inversion and an equality check of points on the elliptic curve. It further supports modular arithmetic in the field underlying an elliptic curve.

MULTOS requires that the function getRandomNumber is supported by its approved platforms but leaves its implementation to the card manufacturer. While the NESCRYPT coprocessor offers true random number generation, it is not clear, whether this is used to generate random numbers directly, or whether it is used as seed for a pseudo random number generator (PRNG). We checked the statistical properties of the generated random numbers on the card using the National Institute of Standards and Technology's test suite [21]. We generated a 126 MB random number sequence and ran all tests on it. Based on these tests, we found no violations against true random behavior irrespective of the test. We conclude that the statistical properties of the generated random numbers are good.

4   Implementation

In our implementation the terminal, which is represented by an HP ProBook 650G1 notebook with an Intel i5-4200M processor having 8 GB RAM and running Windows 7 (64 Bit), represents the bank as well as the shop. Communication is executed with the notebook's integrated Alcor Micro Smart Card Reader. The terminal implementation is based on Java and was developed using the Eclipse Luna Service Release 1. While a C implementation would lead to faster execution times, our main focus is on evaluating the execution time of the computation on the smartcard side. Terminals could easily

---

[1] http://www.multos.com/products/approved_platforms/

be equipped with stronger or dedicated hardware, greatly reducing the execution time on the terminal. Java provides the *javax.smartcardio* package allowing a comfortable implementation of communication with smartcards via APDUs. This package provides an API to set up connection with the smartcard reader as well as sending APDUs to and receiving from a smartcard. For the implementation of cryptographic functionality we relied on the Bouncy Castle library version 1.5.1. This library provides a great variety of cryptographic functionality, including the implementation of elliptic curve cryptography and hash generation. We further relied on the MySQL 5.5 database management system to log the execution times of each protocol.

We developed code for the smartcard using the MULTOS SmartDeck application development system for MULTOS cards and loaded the application to the card using MULTOS Utility (MUtil). SmartDeck contains the required compiler, a generator to generate Application Load Units (ALUs) and a debugger for code development. A developer key is required to load the application to the card. key. Code for the card can be written in MULTOS Assembly Language or in a higher level language (C or Java) which is then translated by the compiler. We choose C as programming language, since the set up is easier than the one for Java and code can be written much more efficiently than in MULTOS Assembly Language. While more efficient code could be written in MULTOS Assembly Language we anticipate that the speed-up would be limited as we mostly relied on functionality provided by the card's API.

Our implementation is based on the Brainpool elliptic curves. Those curves, which were proposed by the Brainpool consortium, are for example implemented in the German identity card and have recently been standardized for use in TLS [14]. While we measured execution times for elliptic curves of four security levels, namely brainpoolP160r1 (reaching a security level comparable to 80-bit symmetric security), brainpoolP192r1 (reaching a security level comparable to 96-bit symmetric security), brainpoolP224r1 (reaching a security level comparable to 112-bit symmetric security), and brainpoolP256r1 (reaching a security level comparable to 128-bit symmetric security), we only present implementation results for brainpoolP160r1 and brainpoolP256r1. Since e-cash mostly targets micro-payments as well as low-value payments, *i. e.* payments of up to $100, use of a 160-bit elliptic curve presents a sufficient level of security, and to further increase security, system parameters could be updated on a regular basis.

5   Results

In this section we first present the execution times of the two implementations and then give estimates for the number of coins that could be stored in the chosen smartcard. Our analysis targets the evaluation of the execution time of the withdrawal and spending protocols. While registration is executed only once, withdrawal and spending are executed repeatedly over a period of time, and thus greatly determine user acceptance. We obtained the execution times by executing the protocols 100 times and averaging the results.

The execution times for the withdrawal protocol for Brands and ACL encoding two attributes into coins are presented in Table 5. We separately present the times for

Table 5. Execution timings of the withdrawal protocols of Brands' untraceable offline cash scheme [6] and Anonymous Credentials Light (ACL) [2] for the case of encoding two attributes in a coin based on brainpoolP160r1 (160-bit) and brainpoolP256r1 (256-bit) elliptic curves.

Scheme	Terminal	Communication	Card	Total
Brands (160-bit)	118 ms	194 ms	2114 ms	2426 ms
ACL (160-bit)	158 ms	360 ms	2430 ms	2948 ms
Brands (256-bit)	179 ms	279 ms	2996 ms	3454 ms
ACL (256-bit)	204 ms	544 ms	3438 ms	4186 ms

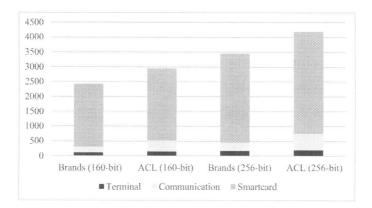

Fig. 1. Execution times of Brands' and ACL withdrawal protocols at the 80-bit and 128-bit security levels, encoding two attributes (visualization of the results presented in Table 5). The time scale is given in miliseconds.

computations on the card, computations on the terminal, the communication overhead, and the total execution time. Results are presented at two security levels, namely at the 80-bit security level and the 128-bit security level.

As mentioned above should 80-bit security be sufficient for the implementation of a low-value payment scheme, and thus the withdrawal of a coin can be executed in under 2.5 seconds and 3 seconds respectively. While for both protocols the computation on the card clearly presents the bottleneck in the scheme, we observe a noticeable difference between the execution times of the two withdrawal protocols. ACL requires the communication of a greater number of elements as well as the computation of more elements in G on the card. Please note however, that ACL has a full prove of security, which comes at the expense of only slightly less efficiency. We would further like to emphasize that the withdrawal process is not time critical and could be executed at home. A user could be provided with a desktop banking application, which would allow him to charge his payment device using his personal smartcard reader. He could start the charging process and could leave the card inserted in the reader until the withdrawal process is completed. Even if this takes multiple minutes this could be acceptable for users.

The timings for spending a coin, not revealing an attribute, are presented in Table 6. Note that in our study we present timings of the spending protocols without revealing attributes only. In that case 9 exponentiations and 3 comparisons in G have to be executed for Brands' spending protocol on the Terminal, while only 8 exponentiations in G and 3 comparisons in $\mathbb{Z}_q$ have to be executed on the terminal for the ACL scheme, leading to lower computation times on the terminal. Additionally, in Brands' spending protocol the communication is split in two parts, and the communicated data is 5 elements in G and 5 elements in $\mathbb{Z}_q$, while ACL requires only the communication of 2 elements in G and 7 elements in $\mathbb{Z}_q$, thus leading to lower communication times for ACL. For the 256-bit curve based Brands' spending protocol the communicated data needs to be split into a greater number of APDUs thus leading to proportionally higher communication times. Overall, when not revealing an attribute both spending protocols can be executed within 800 ms when relying on a 80-bit security level.

If an attribute was revealed during spending, we would save on one modular multiplication and addition on the card side for Brands' protocol, which would then have to be executed on the terminal side, but would have to send one more element in $\mathbb{Z}_q$. This would only slightly increase the communication time. By measurements we figured out that the communication of one byte requires 1.18 ms plus an initial 26 ms for the initialization of an APDU. The communication would thus increase by less then 50 ms. If an attribute was revealed during the spending of ACL's scheme, 7 random numbers in $\mathbb{Z}_q$ would have to be generated, 9 exponentiations in G, 14 modular multiplications and 6 modular additions in $\mathbb{Z}_q$, as well as one hash function would have to be computed. Additionally, 3 elements in G and 7 elements in $\mathbb{Z}_q$ would have to be sent to the terminal, resulting in an increase in communication time of about 330 ms, when relying on the 160-bit elliptic curve. Thus when revealing an attribute the spending of the ACL scheme would be outperformed by Brands' spending protocol.

Table 6. Execution timings of the spending protocols of Brands' untraceable offline cash scheme [6] and Anonymous Credentials Light (ACL) [2] for the case that two attributes are encoded in a coin, but no attribute is revealed based on brainpoolP160r1 (160-bit) and brainpoolP256r1 (256-bit) elliptic curves.

Scheme	Terminal	Communication	Card	Total
Brands (160-bit)	110 ms	433 ms	259 ms	769 ms
ACL (160-bit)	76 ms	310 ms	407 ms	793 ms
Brands (256-bit)	257 ms	660 ms	297 ms	1063 ms
ACL (256-bit)	92 ms	466 ms	510 ms	1068 ms

Those results demonstrate that keeping the number of encoded attributes to a minimum is required to save time. However, we would like to emphasize that an attribute in the 160-bit implementation encodes 160 bits of data, while attribute data, if it encodes for example a zip code is requires a low bit size. One could hence encode multiple attribute values into one coin attribute. For example could two attributes of 64 bits and another one of 32 bits be encoded in one coin attribute. This would greatly limit the number of attributes that would have to be encoded into a coin.

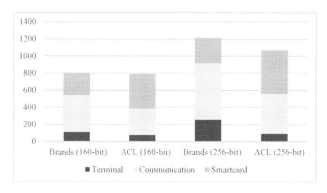

Fig. 2. Execution times of Brands' and ACL spending protocols at the 80-bit and 128-bit security levels, encoding two attributes but revealing no attribute (visualization of the results presented in Table 6). The time scale is given in miliseconds.

5.1 Storage Estimation

While the EEPROM size of the chip integrated in the card is given as 48 kB, we found out that only 44.7 kB are available for writing on the used card.

The implementation of Brands' protocol requires 7 kB of code space, leaving 37.7 kB available for storing electronic coins. A coin in Brands' protocol, encoding two attributes, requires to store 5 elements in G and 6 elements in $\mathbb{Z}_q$. For the 160-bit implementation this adds up to 320 byte per coin, while 512 byte are required for storing a coin based on the 256-bit implementation. Next to other data, such as the keying material and so on, this allows to store around 110 of Brands' coins on the card, when relying on a 160-bit implementation and 65 when relying on the 256-bit implementation, if no other application would be implemented.

ACL requires 8.4 kB of code space, thus leaving 36.3 kB available for storing electronic coins. Storing coin data in ACL requires storing 2 elements in G and 8 elements in $\mathbb{Z}_q$. For the 160-bit implementation this adds up to 240 byte that have to be stored on the card per coin, while 384 byte have to be stored per coin using the ACL scheme based on a 256-bit implementation. Thus around 150 of ACL coins can be stored on the card, when relying on the 160-bit key size, while only 90 coins can be stored when relying on the 256-bit key size, if the card is solely used for this payment application.

6 Discussion

We presented an implementation of two e-cash schemes on an off-the-shelf MULTOS smartcard. Due to their support of elliptic curve cryptography and open API access, we used the UBM21-Z48 developer cards from UbiVelox for our investigations. We implemented both schemes in a way that the encoding of two attributes was allowed, while we did not reveal them during spending. We however give estimates of the execution times, when allowing revealing an attribute.

Our results are promising. When relying on an implementation, of which the security is comparable to 80-bit symmetric security, which is sufficient for low-value payment schemes, a spending can be executed within 800 ms for both schemes, while the cards would allow storing 110 and 150 coins respectively for both schemes. We further presented execution times at a high security level, namely comparable to 128-bit symmetric security, and show that the performance of our implementation is acceptable for high-security applications.

Acknowledgements. We would like to express our gratitude towards Chris Torr for his support with the MULTOS platform and UBIVELOX for providing us with a UBM21-Z48 developer card.

References

1. Abe, M.: A secure three-move blind signature scheme for polynomially many signatures. In: Pfitzmann, B. (ed.) EUROCRYPT 2001. LNCS, vol. 2045, pp. 136–151. Springer, Heidelberg (2001)
2. Baldimtsi, F., Lysyanskaya, A.: Anonymous credentials light. In: Proceedings of the 20th ACM Conference on Computer and Communications Security – ACM CCS 2013, pp. 1087–1098. ACM, New York (2013)
3. Baldimtsi, F., Lysyanskaya, A.: On the security of one-witness blind signature schemes. In: Sako, K., Sarkar, P. (eds.) ASIACRYPT 2013, Part II. LNCS, vol. 8270, pp. 82–99. Springer, Heidelberg (2013)
4. Belenkiy, M., Chase, M., Kohlweiss, M., Lysyanskaya, A.: Compact E-cash and simulatable vRFs revisited. In: Shacham, H., Waters, B. (eds.) Pairing 2009. LNCS, vol. 5671, pp. 114–131. Springer, Heidelberg (2009)
5. Bichsel, P., Camenisch, J., Groß, T., Shoup, V.: Anonymous credentials on a standard java card. In: Proceedings of the 16th ACM Conference on Computer and Communications Security – ACM CCS 2009, pp. 600–610. ACM, New York (2009)
6. Brands, S.: Untraceable off-line cash in wallets with observers (extended abstract). In: Stinson, D.R. (ed.) CRYPTO 1993. LNCS, vol. 773, pp. 302–318. Springer, Heidelberg (1994)
7. Camenisch, J.L., Hohenberger, S., Lysyanskaya, A.: Compact E-cash. In: Cramer, R. (ed.) EUROCRYPT 2005. LNCS, vol. 3494, pp. 302–321. Springer, Heidelberg (2005)
8. Chan, A.H., Frankel, Y., Tsiounis, Y.: Easy come - easy go divisible cash. In: Nyberg, K. (ed.) EUROCRYPT 1998. LNCS, vol. 1403, pp. 561–575. Springer, Heidelberg (1998)
9. Chaum, D.: Blind signatures for untraceable payments. In: Chaum, D., Rivest, R., Sherman, A. (eds.) Advances in Cryptology – CRYPTO 1982, pp. 199–203. Springer US (1983)
10. Chaum, D., Fiat, A., Naor, M.: Untraceable electronic cash. In: Goldwasser, S. (ed.) CRYPTO 1988. LNCS, vol. 403, pp. 319–327. Springer, Heidelberg (1990)
11. Clemente-Cuervo, E., Rodríguez-Henríquez, F., Arroyo, D.O., Ertaul, L.: A PDA implementation of an off-line e-cash protocol. In: Proceedings of the 2007 International Conference on Security & Management, SAM 2007, Las Vegas, Nevada, USA, June 25-28, pp. 452–458 (2007)
12. Hinterwälder, G., Paar, C., Burleson, W.P.: Privacy preserving payments on computational RFID devices with application in intelligent transportation systems. In: Hoepman, J.-H., Verbauwhede, I. (eds.) RFIDSec 2012. LNCS, vol. 7739, pp. 109–122. Springer, Heidelberg (2013)
13. Hinterwälder, G., Zenger, C.T., Baldimtsi, F., Lysyanskaya, A., Paar, C., Burleson, W.P.: Efficient E-cash in practice: NFC-based payments for public transportation systems. In: De Cristofaro, E., Wright, M. (eds.) PETS 2013. LNCS, vol. 7981, pp. 40–59. Springer, Heidelberg (2013)

14. Lochter, D.M.: ECC brainpool standard curves and curve generation v. 1.0 (2005).
http://www.ecc-brainpool.org/download/Domain-parameters.pdf
15. MAOSCO Limited. MULTOS developer's guide (2014).
http://www.multos.com/uploads/MDG.pdf
16. McFarland, M.: Why we care about privacy (2012).
http://www.scu.edu/ethics/practicing/focusareas/technology/
internet/privacy/why-care-about-privacy.html
17. Mostowski, W., Vullers, P.: Efficient U-prove implementation for anonymous credentials on
smart cards. In: Rajarajan, M., Piper, F., Wang, H., Kesidis, G. (eds.) SecureComm 2011.
LNICST, vol. 96, pp. 243–260. Springer, Heidelberg (2012)
18. Multos international Pte Ltd. Company profile & an introduction to MULTOS technology.
http://www.multosinternational.com/media/4992/
multos_international.pdf
19. Perlroth, N.: Target struck in the cat-and-mouse game of credit theft (2013).
http://www.nytimes.com/2013/12/20/technology/target-stolen-
shopper-data.html?pagewanted=all
20. Rankl, W., Effing, W.: Smart Cards in Transportation Systems, pp. 869–891. John Wiley &
Sons, Ltd. (2010)
21. Rukhin, A., Soto, J., Nechvatal, J., Smid, M., Barker, E., Leigh, S., Levenson, M., Vangel, M.,
Banks, D., Heckert, A., Dray, J., Vo, S.: Special publication 800 - 22 revision 1a – a statistical
test suite for random and pseudorandom number generators for cryptographic applications
(2010). http://csrc.nist.gov/groups/ST/toolkit/rng/
documents/SP800-22rev1a.pdf
22. Sterckx, M., Gierlichs, B., Preneel, B., Verbauwhede, I.: Efficient implementation of anonymous credentials on java card smart cards. In: 1st International Workshop on Information
Forensics and Security – WIFS 2009, pp. 106–110, December 2009
23. STMicroelectronics. ST23ZL48 data brief (2009).
https://www.commoncriteriaportal.org/files/epfiles/
ANSSI-CC-cible_2010-02en.pdf
24. STMicroelectronics. SA23YR48B / SB23YR48B / SA23YR80B / SB23YR80B security target - public version - common criteria for it security evaluation (2013).
http://www.st.com/st-web-ui/static/active/en/resource/
technical/document/data_brief/CD00239124.pdf
25. Tews, H., Jacobs, B.: Performance issues of selective disclosure and blinded issuing protocols
on java card. In: Markowitch, O., Bilas, A., Hoepman, J.-H., Mitchell, C.J., Quisquater, J.-J.
(eds.) Information Security Theory and Practice. LNCS, vol. 5746, pp. 95–111. Springer,
Heidelberg (2009)
26. Vullers, P., Alpár, G.: Efficient selective disclosure on smart cards using idemix. In: Fischer-
Hübner, S., de Leeuw, E., Mitchell, C. (eds.) IDMAN 2013. IFIP AICT, vol. 396, pp. 53–67.
Springer, Heidelberg (2013)

Efficient and Secure Delegation of Group Exponentiation to a Single Server

Bren Cavallo[1], Giovanni Di Crescenzo[2],
Delaram Kahrobaei[3], and Vladimir Shpilrain[3]

[1] Graduate Center, City University of New York
bcavallo@gc.cuny.edu
[2] Applied Communication Sciences
gdicrescenzo@appcomsci.com
[3] City University of New York
DKahrobaei@gc.cuny.edu, shpil@groups.sci.ccny.cuny.edu

Abstract. We consider the problem of delegating computation of group operations from a computationally weaker client holding an input and a description of a function, to a *single* computationally stronger server holding a description of the same function. Solutions need to satisfy natural correctness, security, privacy and efficiency requirements. We obtain delegated computation protocols for the following functions, defined for an *arbitrary* commutative group:

1. Group inverses, with security and privacy holding against any computationally unrestricted malicious server.
2. Group exponentiation, with security and privacy holding against any computationally unrestricted "partially honest" server.
3. Group exponentiation, with security and privacy holding against any polynomial-time malicious server, under a pseudorandom generation assumption, and security holding with constant probability.

1 Introduction

Efficient implementation of cryptographic protocols on RFID tags is a challenging research area, due to their limited power, storage and computational resources. Among all types of cryptographic protocols, public-key, or asymmetric, protocols are especially hard to deal with, because their demands in terms of costs, area and power, are typically higher than their symmetric, or private-key, counterparts (see, e.g., [3] and references therein for a detailed treatment of deployment issues in the implementation of public-key cryptography over RFID tags). An active research direction addressing these challenges consists of modifying known cryptographic protocols into a lightweight version that can be executed by computationally weaker devices, such as RFID tags. Another (perhaps dual, in some sense) research direction addresses these challenges by delegated (also called outsourced, or server-aided) computation of cryptographic primitives. In this latter direction, a computationally weaker client, holding an input and a description of a function, wants to delegate much of the computation to one or more computationally stronger servers holding a description of the same

© Springer International Publishing Switzerland 2015
S. Mangard, P. Schaumont (Eds.): RFIDsec 2015, LNCS 9440, pp. 156–173, 2015.
DOI: 10.1007/978-3-319-24837-0_10

function. Solutions typically come with the following requirements: correctness (i.e., if the client and servers are honest, the client obtains the output of the function evaluated on its input), security (i.e., servers cannot convince the client of a false computation output), privacy (i.e., servers cannot learn any information about the client's input), and efficiency (i.e., the client's running time is much smaller than the servers' running time or the time to non-interactively compute the function). In this paper, we study delegated computation to a *single* server of an operation that is a component of a large number of cryptographic primitives and/or protocols: exponentiation in a (multiplicative) group. The goal in such delegated protocols is for the client to perform a smaller number of group multiplications than in a non-delegated group exponentiation. This problem is expected to be of great interest, given that very recent advances [1] show how to practically implement group multiplication, for a specific group, and a related public-key cryptosystem, using RFID tags.

Related Work. Delegating computation has been and continues to be an active topic, with the increased importance of new computation paradigms, such as computing with low-power (including RFID) devices, cloud computing, etc. A number of solutions had been proposed and then broken in follow-up papers.

An elegant solution for a client to provably delegate any polynomial-time circuit to a single (semi-honest) server was given in [7], using garbled circuits [13] and fully-homomorphic encryption. Due to its generality, this solution is asymptotically efficient, but not so in practical settings, such as low-power devices.

Solutions that provably and efficiently delegate variable-base exponentiation were given in [8,5,6,12] under a pseudo-random powers generation assumption, in turn based on the hidden-subset-sum hardness assumption [4,11], and [10], under the (stronger) subset sum hardness assumption.

In [8], motivated by efficiency for RFID tags, the authors presented a protocol where a client only performs $O(\log^2 \ell)$ multiplications, where ℓ is the bit length of the exponent, to detect, with constant probability, an untrusted response from either two servers, of which at most one is untrusted, or from one server, which is trusted on average inputs. A different solution with two servers and similar features, but improved constants for client running time, was later given in [5], who explicitly posed the open problem of provable and efficient delegation of modular exponentiation to a single, untrusted, server. Batch exponentiation was first studied in [9] and later improved in [10], where a client can delegate t exponentiations to servers, by performing $O(t + \ell)$ modular multiplications, assuming the hardness of the subset sum problem. In [12] the authors present protocols to delegate variable-exponent, variable-base exponentiation to a single, untrusted, server. In [6], the authors provide efficient and secure solutions, where the base is known to the server (thus, not addressing our privacy requirement).

Our Contributions. In this paper we first of all provide *rigorous definitions* for the requirements of correctness, privacy, security and efficiency for delegated computation protocols in the single, malicious, server model. We then construct three protocols that provably satisfy these requirements while delegating, to a *single* malicious server, computations over *any* arbitrary commutative group G.

Although our main objective is to delegate group exponentiation, our first protocol is a simple protocol for the delegation of group inverses, where both security and privacy hold against a computationally unrestricted, malicious, server. We were surprised to notice that the need for such a protocol has been overlooked in the literature, even though almost all previous solutions (as well as ours) for delegated exponentiation do require inverse computations from the client, and even given the fact that in both theoretical algorithms and practical implementations, a non-delegated inverse computation is more expensive than a non-delegated multiplication. Our protocol for inverses works for any (even non-commutative) group, only requires the client to perform 3 group multiplications, and satisfies both security (with negligible detection error) and privacy *even in the presence of a computationally unrestricted adversary corrupting the server.*

Our second protocol is for the delegation of group exponentiation to a single, "partially-honest", server. This protocol only requires the client to perform $2m + 4$ group multiplications, where m can be any super-logarithmic and sublinear function in $\ell = \log |G|$, and satisfies both security (in a one-wayness sense, with negligible detection error) and privacy *even against a computationally unrestricted adversary corrupting the server.* Proving the security of this protocol also requires establishing a new lemma of independent interest about the number of distinct group products. No previous protocol was proved to achieve these strong security or privacy guarantees, even against a trusted server.

Our third protocol is for the delegation of group exponentiation to a single, malicious, server. This protocol only requires the client to perform $2m_r + 5$ group multiplications, where m_r is the number of multiplications required by the pseudo-random power generator (recommended to be set to $O((\log \ell)^2)$), and satisfies both security (with constant detection error) and privacy under the hidden-subset-sum assumption, as used in [4,11]. This protocol improves over previous solutions with a single, untrusted, server *by requiring no inverses and reducing the number of client multiplications,* as detailed in Table 1.

Table 1. Comparison of our third protocol with previous similar solutions delegating variable-base exponentiation to a single, untrusted, server

	Ma et. al. [10]	Wang et. al. [12]	Our Third Protocol
Mod Mult	$O(\log k)$	$7m_r + 12 + O(\log \ell)$	$2m_r + 5$
Mod Inv	2	4	0

Our protocols are written so to delegate function $F_{G,exp,k}(x) = x^k$ (i.e., fixed-exponent, variable-base exponentiation), but can be reformulated so to delegate function $F_{G,exp,x}(k) = x^k$ (i.e., variable-exponent, fixed-base exponentiation).

2 Definitions and Preliminaries

In this section we formally define delegation protocols, and their correctness, security, privacy and efficiency requirements (building on the approaches in [7] and [8]). We start with some basic notations.

Basic Notations. The expression $y \leftarrow T$ denotes the probabilistic process of randomly and independently choosing y from set T. The expression $y \leftarrow A(x_1, x_2, \ldots)$ denotes the (possibly probabilistic) process of running algorithm A on input $x_1, x_2, \ldots$ and any necessary random coins, and obtaining y as output. The expression $(z_A, z_B, tr) \leftarrow (A(x_1, x_2, \ldots), B(y_1, y_2, \ldots))$ denotes the (possibly probabilistic) process of running an interactive protocol between algorithm A, taking as input $x_1, x_2, \ldots$ and any necessary random coins, and algorithm B, taking as input $y_1, y_2, \ldots$ and any necessary random coins, where tr is the sequence of messages exchanged by A and B as a result of this execution, and z_A, z_B are A and B's final outputs, respectively.

System Scenario, Entities, and Protocol. We consider a system with two types of parties: clients and servers, where a client's computational resources are expected to be more limited than a server's ones, and therefore clients are interested in delegating (or outsourcing) the computation of specific functions to servers. In all our solutions, we consider a single *client*, denoted as C, and a single *server*, denoted as S.

Let σ be a security parameter, expressed in unary notation (i.e., 1^σ), and let $F : Dom(F) \rightarrow CoDom(F)$ be a function, where $Dom(F)$ denotes F's domain, $CoDom(F)$ denotes F's co-domain, and $desc(F)$ denotes F's description. Assuming $desc(F)$ is known to both C and S, and input x is known only to C, we define a *client-server protocol for the delegated computation of F* as a 2-party communication protocol between C and S, denoted as $(C(1^\sigma, desc(F), x), S(1^\sigma, desc(F)))$. A *delegated computation of the value $y = F(x)$* is an execution, using independently chosen random bits for C and S, of the above client-server protocol, and is denoted as

$$(y_C, y_S, tr) \leftarrow (C(1^\sigma, desc(F), x), S(1^\sigma, desc(F))),$$

meaning that at the end of the execution C learns $y_C = y$, S learns y_S (usually an empty string in this paper), and tr is the transcript of the communication exchanged between C and S. (We will often omit $desc(F)$ and 1^σ for brevity of description.) Executions of delegated computation protocols can happen *sequentially* (each execution starting after the previous one is finished) or *concurrently* (S runs at the same time one execution with each one of many clients). [1]

Correctness Requirement. Informally, the (natural) correctness requirement states that if both parties follow the protocol, C obtains some output at the end of the protocol, and this output is equal to the value obtained by evaluating function F on C's input. A formal definition follows.

Definition 1. Let σ be a security parameter, and F be a function, and let (C, S) be a client-server protocol for the delegated computation of F. We say that (C, S) satisfies *correctness* if for any x in F's domain, it holds that

$$\mathrm{Prob}\left[(y_C, y_S, tr) \leftarrow (C(1^\sigma, desc(F), x), S(1^\sigma, desc(F))) : y = F(x)\right] = 1.$$

---

[1] We assume that the communication link between each client and S is private or not subject to confidentiality, integrity, or replay attacks, and note that such attacks can be separately addressed using known techniques in cryptography and security.

Security Requirement. Informally, the most basic security requirement would state the following: if C follows the protocol, a malicious adversary corrupting S cannot convince C to obtain, at the end of the protocol, some output y' different from the value y obtained by evaluating function F on C's input x. To define a stronger and more realistic security requirement, we augment the adversary's power so that the adversary can even choose C's input x, and even take part in a polynomial number of protocol executions, with inputs again chosen by the adversary, before attempting to convince C of an incorrect output.

We also define a natural "partially-honest variant" of this definition, where the adversary can arbitrarily choose the inputs to all protocol executions but can only honestly run the protocols.

For simplicity, we only consider sequential protocol executions, but note that the definition adapts naturally to the case of concurrent protocol executions. A formal definition follows.

Definition 2. Let σ be a security parameter, and F be a function, and let (C, S) be a client-server protocol for the delegated computation of F.

We say that (C, S) satisfies (t_s, ϵ_s)-*security against a malicious adversary* if for any algorithm A running in time t_s, it holds that

$$\text{Prob}\left[\, out \leftarrow \text{SecExp}_{F,A}(1^\sigma) \; : \; out = 1 \,\right] \leq \epsilon_s,$$

for some small ϵ_s, where experiment *SecExp* is detailed below.

We say that (C, S) satisfies (t_s, ϵ_s)-*security against a partially-honest adversary* if for any algorithm A running in time t_s, it holds that

$$\text{Prob}\left[\, out \leftarrow \text{phSecExp}_{F,A}(1^\sigma) \; : \; out = 1 \,\right] \leq \epsilon_s,$$

for some small ϵ_s, where experiment *phSecExp* is detailed below.

$\text{SecExp}_{F,A}(1^\sigma)$
1. $i = 1$
2. $(a, x_1, aux) \leftarrow A(1^\sigma, desc(F))$
3. while $(a \neq \text{"}attack\text{"})$ do
    $(y_i, (a, x_{i+1}, aux), tr_i) \leftarrow (C(x_i), A(aux))$
    $i = i + 1$
4. $x \leftarrow A(aux)$
5. $(y', aux, tr_i) \leftarrow (C(x), A(aux))$
6. if $y' \neq \bot$ and $y' \neq F(x)$ then
    return: 1
7. if $y' = \bot$ or $y' = F(x)$ then
    return: 0.

$\text{phSecExp}_{F,A}(1^\sigma)$
1. $i = 1$
2. $(a, x_1, aux) \leftarrow A(1^\sigma, desc(F))$
3. while $(a \neq \text{"}attack\text{"})$ do
    $(y_i, \cdot, tr_i) \leftarrow (C(x_i), S)$
    $(a, x_{i+1}, aux) \leftarrow A(aux)$
    $i = i + 1$
4. $x \leftarrow A(aux, tr_1, \ldots, tr_{q(\sigma)})$
5. $(y', \cdot, tr) \leftarrow (C(x), S)$
6. if $y' \neq \bot$ and $y' \neq F(x)$ then
    return: 1
7. if $y' = \bot$ or $y' = F(x)$ then
    return: 0.

Privacy Requirement. Informally, the most basic privacy requirement would state the following: if C follows the protocol, a malicious adversary corrupting S cannot obtain any information about C's input x from a protocol execution. This is formalized by extending the indistinguishability-based approach used in formal definitions for encryption schemes in the cryptography literature. That is, the adversary can pick two inputs x_0, x_1, then one of these two inputs is chosen at random and used by C in the protocol with the adversary acting as S, and then the adversary tries to guess which input was used by C. To define a stronger and more realistic privacy requirement, we augment the adversary's power so that the adversary can even take part in a polynomial number of protocol executions, where it chooses C's input before attempting to guess C's input in one last execution.

We also define a natural "partially-honest variant" of this definition, where the adversary chooses the inputs to a polynomial number of protocols but can only honestly run the protocols, and later tries to guess a randomly chosen x' such that $F(x') = F(x)$, where x is C's input.

For simplicity, we only consider sequential protocol executions, but note that the definition adapts naturally to the case of concurrent protocol executions. A formal definition follows.

Definition 3. Let σ be a security parameter, and F be a function, and let (C, S) be a client-server protocol for the delegated computation of F.

We say that (C, S) satisfies (t_p, ϵ_p)-privacy (in the sense of indistinguishability) against a malicious adversary if for any algorithm A running in time at most t_p, it holds that

$$\text{Prob}\left[out \leftarrow \text{PrivExp}_{F,A}(1^\sigma) : out = 1 \right] \leq \epsilon_p,$$

for some small ϵ_p, where experiment $PrivExp$ is detailed below.

We say that (C, S) satisfies (t_p, ϵ_p)-privacy (in the sense of one-wayness) against a partially-honest adversary if for any algorithm A running in time at most t_p, it holds that

$$\text{Prob}\left[out \leftarrow \text{phPrivExp}_{F,A}(1^\sigma) : out = 1 \right] \leq \epsilon_p,$$

for some small ϵ_p, where experiment $phPrivExp$ is detailed below.

$\text{PrivExp}_{F,A}(1^\sigma)$
1. $(a, x_1, aux) \leftarrow A(1^\sigma, desc(F))$
2. while $(a \neq \text{``attack''})$ do
   $(y_i, (a, x_{i+1}, aux), \cdot) \leftarrow (C(x_i), A(aux))$
   $i = i + 1$
3. $(x_0, x_1, aux) \leftarrow A(aux)$
4. $b \leftarrow \{0, 1\}$
5. $(y', b, tr) \leftarrow (C(x), A(aux))$
6. if $b = d$ then **return:** 1
7. if $b \neq d$ then **return:** 0.

$\text{phPrivExp}_{F,A}(1^\sigma)$
1. $(a, x_1, aux) \leftarrow A(1^\sigma, desc(F))$
2. while $(a \neq \text{``attack''})$ do
   $(y_i, \cdot, tr_i) \leftarrow (C(x_i), S)$
   $(a, x_{i+1}, aux) \leftarrow A(aux)$
   $i = i + 1$
3. $x \leftarrow Dom(F)$
4. $(\cdot, x', \cdot) \leftarrow (C(x), A(aux, tr_1, \ldots, tr_{q(\sigma)}))$
5. if $F(x') = F(x)$ then **return:** 1
6. if $F(x') \neq F(x)$ then **return:** 0.

Efficiency Metrics and Requirements. Let (C, S) be a client-server protocol for the delegated computation of function F, We say that (C, S) has *efficiency parameters* $(t_F, t_C, t_S, cc, mc))$, if F can be computed using $t_F(\sigma)$ atomic operations, C can be run using $t_C(\sigma)$ atomic operations, S can be run using $t_S(\sigma)$

atomic operations, C and S exchange a total of at most mc messages, of total length at most cc. In our analysis, we only consider group operations as atomic operations (e.g., group multiplications, inverses, and/or exponentiation), and neglect lower-order operations (e.g., equality testing between group elements). Our goal is to design protocols where $t_C(\sigma)$ is smaller than $t_F(\sigma)$, and $t_S(\sigma)$ is not significantly larger than $t_F(\sigma)$, with the following underlying assumptions, that are consistent with the state of the art in cryptographic implementations at least for many group types:

1. group multiplication require significantly less computing resources than group inverses;
2. group multiplication require significantly less computing resources than group exponentiation.

Naturally, we also try to minimize other typical protocol efficiency metrics, such as message complexity mc and communication complexity cc.

3   Delegation of Inverses

In this section we present a client-server protocol for delegated computation of group inverses. Our protocol is especially simple, works for any (even not commutative) group and for any computationally unrestricted adversary, and will be used as a subprotocol in our two protocols for delegated computation of modular exponentiation.

Notations and Formal Theorem Statement. Let $(G, *)$ be a group, where the group operation $*$ is also referred as *multiplication*, and 1 denotes G's *identity* element. For any $a \in G$, let $b = a^{-1}$ denote the *inverse* of a; i.e., the value b such that $a * b = 1$. Let $F_{G,inv} : G \rightarrow G$ denote the function that maps every $a \in G$ to its inverse a^{-1}. Formally, we show the following

Theorem 1. There exists (constructively) a client-server protocol (C, S) for delegated computation of function $F_{G,inv}$ which satisfies

1. correctness;
2. (t_s, ϵ_s)-security (in the sense of indistinguishability) against any malicious adversary, for $t_s = \infty$ and $\epsilon_s = 0$;
3. (t_p, ϵ_p)-privacy (in the sense of indistinguishability) against any malicious adversary, for $t_p = \infty$ and $\epsilon_p = 0$;
4. efficiency with parameters (t_F, t_C, t_S, cc, mc), where
   - t_F and t_S are $= 1$ inversion in G;
   - t_C is $= 3$ multiplications in G;
   - $cc = 2$ elements in G and $mc = 2$.

We remark that Theorem 1 satisfies very strong versions of the security and privacy requirements (i.e., the adversary can arbitrarily deviate from S' program and is not even restricted to run in polynomial time), and of the efficiency requirement (t_C only requires running 3 multiplications in G). In what follows, we describe the protocol satisfying Theorem 1 and its properties.

Description of Protocol (C, S). Informally speaking, the protocol claimed in Theorem 1 for delegated computation of $F_{G,inv}$ goes as follows. On input $x \in G$, C uses the group operation to mask x with a random group element, and sends the masked value to S. The latter inverts the masked element and sends it to C. Finally, C uses the group operation to check that the received value is a valid inverse for the masked value and to derive an inverse for its input x. A formal description follows.

Input to S: 1^σ, $desc(F_{G,inv})$

Input to C: 1^σ, $desc(F_{G,inv})$, $x \in G$

Protocol Instructions:

1. C randomly chooses $c \in G$, computes $d = x * c$ and sends d to S;
2. S computes $e = d^{-1}$ and sends e to C;
3. C checks whether $d * e = 1$;
   if no, C returns failure symbol $\perp$;
   if yes, C computes $y = c * e$ and returns: y.

Properties of protocol (C,S) are detailed in Appendix A.

4   Delegation of Exponentiation in the Presence of a Partially-Honest Adversary

In this section we present a client-server protocol for delegated computation of group exponentiation, in the model where the adversary corrupting the server is partially honest and polynomial-time bounded. Our protocol works for any commutative group and does not rely on any additional complexity assumptions.

Notations and Formal Theorem Statement. Let $(G, *)$ be a commutative group, let $\ell = \lceil \log |G| \rceil$ and let $b = a^k$ denote the *exponentiation* of a to the k-th power; i.e., the value $b \in G$ such that $a * \cdots * a = b$, where the multiplication operation $*$ is applied $k-1$ times. Let $k > 0$ be an integer (assumed, for simplicity, smaller than G's order), and let $F_{G,exp,k} : G \to G$ denote the function that maps every $a \in G$ to the exponentiation of a to the k-th power. Formally, we show the following

Theorem 2. Let m be a function super-logarithmic and sub-linear in ℓ. There exists (constructively) a client-server protocol (C, S) for delegated computation of function $F_{G,exp,k}$ which satisfies

1. correctness;
2. (t_s, ϵ_s)-security (in the sense of indistinguishability) against any partially-honest adversary, for $t_s = \infty$ and ϵ_s negligible in ℓ;
3. (t_p, ϵ_p)-privacy (in the sense of one-wayness) against any partially-honest adversary, for $t_s = \infty$ and $\epsilon_s = 2^{-m}+$ a quantity negligible in ℓ;
4. efficiency with parameters (t_F, t_C, t_S, cc, mc), where
   - t_F is $= 1$ exponentiation in G;
   - t_S is $= m + 1$ exponentiations and 1 inversion in G;

- t_C is $\leq 2m + 4$ multiplications in G;
- $cc = 2m + 4$ elements in G and $mc = 4$.

We remark that Theorem 2 only considers privacy in the sense of one-wayness and partially-honest adversaries for security and privacy. In this model, it does satisfy a strong version of the security and privacy requirements, in that the adversary is not restricted to run in polynomial time. The parameter m can be set as the output of a function of ℓ, that is: (1) super-logarithmic, so to obtain an ϵ_s negligible in ℓ, and (2) sub-linear, so to obtain a t_C sub-linear in ℓ. In the rest of this section, we describe the protocol satisfying Theorem 2 and its properties.

Informal Description of Protocol (C, S). Informally speaking, the protocol claimed in Theorem 2 for delegated computation of $F_{G,exp,k}$ is based on the following ideas. Direct attempts to produce a protocol for group exponentiation as the natural extension of the protocol for group inverses underlying Theorem 1 fail for efficiency reasons: a small number of multiplications in G do not seem to suffice for C to derive an exponentiation for input value x from an exponentiation for a masked value produced by S. To deal with this problem, we require C to do the following: first, C asks S for a number of exponentiations of random group elements; then, C produces a masked value for x by combining it with a random subset of the previously used random group elements; finally, C obtains an exponentiation for the masked value from S and divides it by the (now known) exponentiations of the random group elements in the subset to obtain the exponentiation of its own value x. Division is delegated to S by using a few group multiplications and the inverse delegation protocol from Section 3. A formal description follows.

Formal Description of Protocol (C, S). Let (C_{inv}, S_{inv}) denote the protocol satisfying Theorem 1 for delegated computation of inverses in group G. That is, on input a value in G to be inverted, C_{inv} returns a group value d to be sent to S_{inv}; and, on input d, S_{inv} returns a group value e to be sent to C_{inv}.

Let m be a value obtained by applying a super-logarithmic and sublinear function to ℓ, or, more practically speaking, a value such that 2^{-m} is a s sufficiently small probability and m is sufficiently smaller than ℓ. We do not further specify m to allow for security/efficiency trade-off analysis.

Input to S: 1^σ, $desc(F_{G,exp,k})$, 1^m

Input to C: 1^σ, $desc(F_{G,exp,k})$, $x \in G$, 1^m

Protocol Instructions:

1. C randomly chooses $u_1, \ldots, u_m \in G$, and sends them to S
2. S computes $v_i = u_i^k$ and sends v_i to C, for $i = 1, \ldots, m$;
3. C randomly chooses a subset U of $\{1, \ldots, m\}$;
   C computes $z = x * \prod_{i \in U} u_i$ and $p = \prod_{i \in U} v_i$;
   C runs C_{inv} on input p, thus obtaining d
   C sends z, d to S;

4. S computes $w = z^k$;
   S runs S_{inv} on input d, thus obtaining e;
   S sends w, e to C
5. C runs C_{inv} on input p, d, e to compute p^{-1};
   if this execution of (C_{inv}, S_{inv}) returned $\perp$ as output
       C **returns:** $\perp$ and the protocol halts;
   C computes $y = w * p^{-1}$ and **returns:** y

Properties of Protocol (C,S). The efficiency properties are verified by protocol inspection: C runs $\leq 2m + 4$ multiplications in G, and S runs $m + 1$ exponentiations and 1 inversion in G. Thus, if m is sub-linear in the size of elements in G, C's running time improves by a factor of about ℓ/m over the non-delegated computation of an exponentiation in G. With respect to round complexity, the protocol only requires two rounds, each round being one message from C to S followed by one message from S to C. With respect to communication and message complexity, the protocol requires the transfer of $2m + 4$ group elements and a total of 4 messages.

The correctness properties follows by observing that if C and S follow the protocol, C's output y is not $\perp$, by the correctness of (C_{inv}, S_{inv}), and satisfies

$$y = w * p^{-1} = z^k * \left(\prod_{i \in U} v_i \right)^{-1} = \left(x * \prod_{i \in U} u_i \right)^k * \left(\prod_{i \in U} u_i^k \right)^{-1} = x^k,$$

which implies that $y = F_{G,exp,k}(x)$ for each $x \in G$.

The security property follows by combining the following two observations: (1) in each execution of (C, S), if S follows the protocol, then the equality $y = F_{G,exp,k}(x)$ holds for each $x \in G$; (2) seeing multiple executions of (C, S) does not help the adversary violate the equality $y = F_{G,exp,k}(x)$ in a future execution, even when C's inputs in these executions are chosen by the adversary. Both observations (1) and (2) are based on the fact that the correctness property holds for any $x \in G$. Moreover, observation (2) is based on the fact that a partially-honest adversary is defined to follow the protocol, even when maliciously choosing the input x for it.

We now show that the privacy property is satisfied. First, for each $x \in G$, let n_z be the number of z values that C can compute in step 3 of the protocol as the product of a random subset from the $u_1, \ldots, u_m$ values computed in step 1. Note that C can choose at most 2^m subsets U in step 3 and therefore it holds that $n_z \leq 2^m$. Then we show the following two facts: (1) when input x is randomly chosen from G, the probability that an adversary playing as S can compute x' such that $F_{G,exp,k}(x') = F_{G,exp,k}(x)$ at the end of a single execution of (C, S), is $1/n_z$; (2) if m is super-logarithmic in ℓ, except with negligible (in ℓ) probability, it holds that $n_z = 2^m$.

To see that fact (1) holds, note that the adversary, playing as S, receives the following information from C: the m-tuple $(u_1, \ldots, u_m)$, the value d as part of the execution transcript of subprotocol (C_{inv}, S_{inv}) on input $p = \prod_{i \in U} v_i$, and the value z which directly involves x. Then we make the following observations:

1. the values $u_1, \ldots, u_m$ received by the adversary at step 1 are randomly chosen in G and thus do not leak any information about x; and
2. even conditioned on $u_1, \ldots, u_m$ and $v_1, \ldots, v_m$, because of what proved in Theorem 1, the execution of subprotocol (C_{inv}, S_{inv}) does not leak any information about p, and thus about x, to the adversary.

Given the above two observations, the only protocol value that may leak any information about x to S is z. In fact, each possible z determines exactly one possible x value, specifically $x = z * (\prod_{i \in U} u_i)^{-1}$, as the value used by C to compute z. Thus, we obtain that for each z sent by C in step 3, and conditioned on $u_1, \ldots, u_m, v_1, \ldots, v_m$ and the communication transcript of (C_{inv}, S_{inv}), the number of possible x that might have been used to compute z is n_z. When x is randomly chosen, this implies fact (1).

Fact (2) follows from a new lemma of independent interest about the number of distinct group products, and is detailed in Appendix B.

Facts (1) and (2) imply that the probability of A guessing x' such that $F_{G,exp,k}(x') = F_{G,exp,k}(x)$ is $\leq 2^{-m}$ plus a negligible (in ℓ) amount.

This concludes the proof of Theorem 2.

A Protocol Extension. We can achieve a stronger privacy notion, in the sense of indistinguishability instead of one-wayness, by assuming the hardness of the subset-sum problem in groups. This however imposes one further lower bound on the number m, due to ensuring that the subset-sub problem is hard, which decreases the efficiency of the protocol.

5   Delegation of Exponentiation in the Presence of a Malicious Adversary

In this section we present a client-server protocol for delegated computation of group exponentiation, in the model where the adversary corrupting the server can be malicious. Our protocol works for any commutative group, and is based on a pseudo-random generation assumption, which in previous work was instantiated using the hidden-subset-sum assumption.

Notations and Formal Theorem Statement. Let $(G, *)$ be a commutative group, let $\ell = \lceil \log |G| \rceil$, and let $k > 0$ be an integer not larger that G's order.

Let σ be a security parameter. We say that $Rand_{G,k}$ is a *pseudo-random* (G, k)-*powers generator* if it is a stateful probabilistic polynomial-time algorithm with the following syntax and properties:

1. on input $i = 0$, $Rand_{G,k}$ returns an auxiliary state information aux;
2. on input integer $i > 0$, and auxiliary state information aux, $Rand_{G,k}$ returns a pair (u_i, u_i^k), where $u_i \in G$, and an updated state aux;
3. for any polynomial p, the tuple $\{(u_1, u_1^k), \ldots, (u_{p(\sigma)}, u_{p(\sigma)}^k)\}$, obtained as part of the output of algorithm $Rand_{G,k}$, is computationally indistinguishable from the tuple $\{(z_1, z_1^k), \ldots, (z_{p(\sigma)}, z_{p(\sigma)}^k)\}$, where $z_1, \ldots, z_{p(\sigma)}$ are random and independent elements from G.

A generator with these properties was first designed in [4], then refined in [11], and since then used in a number of works, including previous work in outsourcing modular exponentiation (see, e.g., [8]). We recall that this generator can be designed based on the hidden-subset-sum assumption in groups. Using this same design, the running time of $Rand_{G,k}$ is comparable to about m_r group multiplications, where, based on previously recommended parameter settings, $m_r = O(\log^2 \ell)$ (see, e.g., [8]). The security parameter σ and the group element length ℓ are, in turn, typically set to be the same value.

Formally, we show the following

Theorem 3. Let σ be a security parameter, let k be a positive integer and assume the existence of a pseudo-random (G, k)-powers generator. There exists (constructively) a client-server protocol (C, S) for delegated computation of function $F_{G,exp,k}$ which satisfies

1. correctness;
2. (t_s, ϵ_s)-security against any malicious adversary, for $t_s = \text{poly}(\sigma)$ and $\epsilon_s = 1/2 + \epsilon_0$, where ϵ_0 is negligible in σ;
3. (t_p, ϵ_p)-privacy against any malicious adversary, for $t_p = \text{poly}(\sigma)$ and ϵ_p negligible in σ;
4. efficiency with parameters (t_F, t_C, t_S, cc, mc), where
   - t_F is $= 1$ group exponentiation in G;
   - t_S is $= 2$ group exponentiations and 1 group inverse in G;
   - t_C is $= 5 + 2 \cdot m_r$ multiplications in G, where m_r denotes the number of multiplications in one execution of $Rand_{G,k}$ with input > 0;
   - $cc = 6$ elements in G and $mc = 2$.

We remark that the result in Theorem 3 does not restrict to partially-honest adversaries, as done in Theorem 2, but holds for malicious adversaries, under the assumption of the existence of procedure $Rand(G, k)$. In the rest of this section, we describe the protocol satisfying Theorem 3, together with its properties.

Informal Description of Protocol (C, S). One approach to construct the protocol claimed in Theorem 3 for delegated computation of $F_{G,exp,k}$ could be to produce a protocol secure and private against a malicious adversary by building on the protocol secure and private against a partially-honest adversary underlying Theorem 2. Although general conversion techniques are known in the cryptography literature to transform a protocol secure against a honest adversary into one secure against a malicious adversary, these techniques do not perform well with respect to many efficiency metrics, typically because of their generality. Instead, we propose the following approach.

Instead of C delegating to S the computation of a k-th power of a random group element, as done in the protocol from Section 4, C uses the procedure $Rand_{G,k}$ to generate two pairs $(u_0, v_0), (u_1, v_1)$ of random group elements u_0, u_1 and their k-th powers v_0, v_1, respectively. Then, one of these two pairs is used to verify that answers from S are correct, and the other pair is used to mask C's input x and allow C to compute a k-th power of x, using the answers received from S. Again, as before, division is delegated by using one group operation and the inverse delegation protocol from Section 3. The privacy property follows from the fact that the message sent by C to S is computationally indistinguishable from random elements in G with their k-th powers, in turn based on the properties of $Rand_{G,k}$, and thus leaks no information about x. The security property follows from the fact that the message sent by C to S does not reveal which of the two pairs of group elements is used for verification and which is used for computation and therefore any dishonest answer from S will be detected by C with probability at least $1/2$. A formal description follows.

Formal Description of Protocol (C, S)**.** Let (C_{inv}, S_{inv}) denote the protocol satisfying Theorem 1 for delegated computation of inverses in group G. That is, on input a value x in G to be inverted, C_{inv} returns a group value d to be sent to S_{inv}; then, on input d, S_{inv} returns a group value e to be sent to C_{inv}; finally, based on x, d, e, algorithm C_{inv} computes value x^{-1}.

Also, let $Rand_{G,k}$ denote a pseudo-random (G, k)-powers generator. We assume that C computes $aux = Rand_{G,k}(0)$ once and at setup time, before running any delegated computation protocol.

Input to S: 1^σ, $desc(F_{G,exp,k})$

Input to C: 1^σ, $desc(F_{G,exp,k})$, $x \in G$, $aux = Rand_{G,k}(0)$

Protocol Instructions:

1. C computes $(u_i, v_i, aux) = Rand_{G,k}(i, aux)$, for $i = 0, 1$;
   C randomly chooses $b \in \{0, 1\}$;
   C sets $z_b = u_b$, $z_{1-b} = x * u_{1-b}$;
   C runs C_{inv} on input v_{1-b}, thus obtaining d;
   C sends z_0, z_1, d to S;
2. S computes $w_i = z_i^k$ for $i = 0, 1$;
   S runs S_{inv} on input d, thus obtaining e;
   S sends w_0, w_1, e to C
3. C runs C_{inv} on input t, d, e to compute v_{1-b}^{-1};
   if this execution of (C_{inv}, S_{inv}) returned $\perp$ as output
       C **returns:** $\perp$ and the protocol halts;
   if $w_b \neq v_b$ then
       C **returns:** $\perp$ and the protocol halts;
   C computes $y = w_{1-b} * v_{1-b}^{-1}$ and **returns:** y

Properties of Protocol (C,S). The efficiency properties are verified by protocol inspection. With respect to round complexity, the protocol only requires one round, consisting of one message from C to S followed by one message from S to C. With respect to communication complexity, the protocol requires the transfer of 6 group elements. With respect to runtime complexity, S runs 2 exponentiation operations and 1 inversion operation in G, and C runs 2 multiplication operations in G, 1 execution of the inverse delegation protocols (requiring 3 multiplications) and 2 executions of procedure $Rand_{G,k}$.

The correctness properties follows by observing that if C and S follow the protocol, C's equality verification in step 3 will be satisfied, and thus C's output y is $\neq \perp$ and satisfies

$$y = w_{1-b} * v_{1-b}^{-1} = (x * u_{1-b})^k * ((u_{1-b})^k)^{-1} = x^k * (u_{1-b})^k * (u_{1-b})^{-k} = x^k,$$

which implies that $y = F_{G,exp,k}(x)$ for each $x \in G$.

The privacy property follows by combining the following two observations: (1) on a single execution of (C, S), the message z_0, z_1, d sent by C does not leak any information about x; and (2) seeing multiple executions of (C, S) does not help the adversary in obtaining information about the input x in a new execution, even when C's inputs in these executions are chosen by the adversary. To show observation (1), first observe that (u_0, u_1) is computationally indistinguishable from a pair of random group elements, by property 3 of the pseudo-random (G, k)-powers generator. Thus, the same holds for pair (z_0, z_1), since $z_b = u_b$ and $z_{1-b} = x * u_{1-b}$ for some $b \in \{0, 1\}$. Then, the fact that the entire message z_0, z_1, d sent by C does not leak any information about x follows from Theorem 1 and the fact that the value d (and, in fact, the entire transcript of the execution of protocol (C_{inv}, S_{inv})), do not depend on x. Because protocol (C, S) is a one-round protocol, the analysis done to show observation (1) extends across multiple executions of the same protocol, thus showing observation (2).

To see that the security property is satisfied, first consider a single execution of (C, S), where C follows the protocol, and, for any probabilistic polynomial-time adversary corrupting S, consider the values w_0, w_1, e returned by the adversary to C. The value e is associated with an execution of the inverse delegation protocol from Section 3, which is secure against any probabilistic polynomial-time adversary, as shown in Theorem 1. Thus, if the adversary deviates from the protocol in computing an e that allows C to compute v_{1-b}^{-1}, C will detect this fact and return the failure symbol $\perp$. Now, consider values w_0, w_1, and let n_A be the number in $\{0, 1, 2\}$ of $i \in \{0, 1\}$ such that $w_i = z_i^k$. We have two cases: (a) $n_A = 2$, and (b) $n_A \leq 1$. If (a) happens, then C will not return the failure symbol and can compute y as in the last line of protocol step 3, and it will satisfy

$$y = w_{1-b} * v_{1-b}^{-1} = (z_{1-b})^k * v_{1-b}^{-1} = (x * u_{1-b})^k * ((u_{1-b})^k)^{-1} = x^k,$$

On the other hand, if (b) happens, since $v_b = u_b^k$ and, assuming property 3 of the pseudo-random (G, k)-powers generator, S cannot guess random bit b, the verification $w_b = v_b$ will be passed with probability at most $1/2$. Seeing multiple executions of (C, S) does not help the adversary increase this probability in the next execution, since no information is leaked to S in any execution, assuming property 3 of the pseudo-random (G, k)-powers generator, as discussed when showing the privacy property.

This concludes the proof of Theorem 3.

A Protocol Extension. We can extend protocol (C, S) to decrease the $\epsilon_s = 1/2$ in the security property by a suitable parallel repetition of it, as follows: first of all, t executions of the protocol are executed in parallel, then, in step 3, C also returns the failure symbol $\perp$ if the value y computed in step 3 is not the same in each parallel execution. The resulting protocol satisfies the security property with $\epsilon_s = 2^{-t}$, and the efficiency property with $t_C = t(5 + 2 \cdot m_r)$ multiplications in G. Thus, only small values for t can be used until the value t_C becomes as large as the number of multiplications in a non-delegated computation of $F_{G,exp,k}$.

6   Performance Results

In this section we report our software evaluation of improvements in delegated computation from non-delegated computation. The experiments were carried out on a Gateway DX4300 desktop with an AMD Phenom(tm) II X4 820 2.80 GHz processor with 6GB of RAM running Ubuntu version 15.04. The experiments were also programmed in Python 2.7 using the gmpy2 package and both input 1024-bit and 2048-bit input lengths. Running times are grouped in the three tables and two pictures below, as follows. The leftmost table contains the times (in seconds) to perform modular multiplication (MM), modular inversion (MI) with gmpy2.invert, modular exponentiation (ME) with gmpy2.powmod, and modular inversion using the client-server protocol (P1) from Section 3. The middle table and the leftmost picture contain the running times for the client-server protocol from Section 4 as parameter m varies. Analogously, the rightmost table and the rightmost picture contain the running times for the client-server protocol from Section 5, as parameters m_r varies.

Operation	1024-bit	2048-bit
MM	2.8126e-6	3.6781e-6
MI	1.5029e-5	3.1179e-5
ME	5.6877e-4	3.9004e-3
P1	1.3101e-5	1.8432e-5

m	1204-bit	2048-bit
100	2.7657e-4	4.5698e-4
150	3.8839e-4	6.3672e-4
200	4.6488e-4	7.6977e-4
250	4.9629e-4	8.8256e-4
300	6.8792-4	1.2126e-3

m	1204-bit	2048-bit
100	4.1224e-4	6.3293e-4
150	5.0923e-4	1.2045e-3
200	6.5394e-4	1.3220e-3
250	9.0009e-4	1.7628e-3
300	1.0210e-3	2.0004e-3

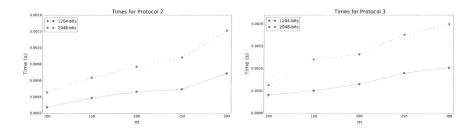

7   Conclusions

Towards making public-key cryptography more accessible to RFID tags, we considered the problem of delegating group exponentiation to a single, untrusted, server. We showed protocols that provably satisfy formal correctness, privacy, security and efficiency requirements. With our protocols, we highlighted the importance of delegating the group inverse operation, the possibility of achieving strong privacy and security properties against computationally unrestricted adversaries, and approaches to further improving client computation time even in the presence of a malicious adversary corrupting the server.

Acknowledgement. Research of Delaram Kahrobaei was partially supported by a PSC-CUNY grant from the CUNY research foundation, as well as the City Tech foundation. Research of Vladimir Shpilrain was partially supported by the NSF grant CNS-1117675. Research of Delaram Kahrobaei and Vladimir Shpilrain was also supported by the ONR (Office of Naval Research) grant N000141210758.

References

1. Arbit, A., Livne, Y., Oren, Y., Wool, A.: Implementing public-key cryptography on passive RFID tags is practical. Int. J. Inf. Sec. 14(1), 85–99 (2015)
2. Barrett, P.: Implementing the Rivest Shamir and Adleman public key encryption algorithm on a standard digital signal processor. In: Odlyzko, A.M. (ed.) CRYPTO 1986. LNCS, vol. 263, pp. 311–323. Springer, Heidelberg (1987)
3. Batina, L., Guajardo, J., Kerins, T., Mentens, N., Tuyls, P., Verbauwhede, I.: Public-Key cryptography for RFID-tags. In: Fifth Annual IEEE International Conference on Pervasive Computing and Communications - Workshops (PerCom Workshops 2007), White Plains, New York, USA, March 19–23, pp. 217–222 (2007)
4. Boyko, V., Peinado, M., Venkatesan, R.: Speeding up discrete log and factoring based schemes via precomputations. In: Nyberg, K. (ed.) EUROCRYPT 1998. LNCS, vol. 1403, pp. 221–235. Springer, Heidelberg (1998)
5. Chen, X., Li, J., Ma, J., Tang, Q., Lou, W.: New algorithms for secure outsourcing of modular exponentiations. In: Foresti, S., Yung, M., Martinelli, F. (eds.) ESORICS 2012. LNCS, vol. 7459, pp. 541–556. Springer, Heidelberg (2012)
6. Dijk, M., Clarke, D., Gassend, B., Suh, G., Devadas, S.: Speeding Up Exponentiation using an Untrusted Computational Resource. Designs, Codes and Cryptography 39(2), 253–273 (2006)
7. Gennaro, R., Gentry, C., Parno, B.: Non-interactive verifiable computing: Outsourcing computation to untrusted workers. In: Rabin, T. (ed.) CRYPTO 2010. LNCS, vol. 6223, pp. 465–482. Springer, Heidelberg (2010)
8. Hohenberger, S., Lysyanskaya, A.: How to securely outsource cryptographic computations. In: Kilian, J. (ed.) TCC 2005. LNCS, vol. 3378, pp. 264–282. Springer, Heidelberg (2005)
9. Jakobsson, M., Wetzel, S.: Secure server-aided signature generation. In: Kim, K. (ed.) PKC 2001. LNCS, vol. 1992, pp. 383–401. Springer, Heidelberg (2001)
10. Ma, X., Li, J., Zhang, F.: Outsourcing computation of modular exponentiations in cloud computing. Cluster Computing 16, 787–796 (2013)
11. Nguyen, P.Q., Shparlinski, I.E., Stern, J.: Distribution of modular sums and the security of the server aided exponentiation. In: Cryptography and Computational Number Theory, pp. 331–342. Springer (2001)

12. Wang, Y., Wu, Q., Wong, D.S., Qin, B., Chow, S.S.M., Liu, Z., Tan, X.: Securely outsourcing exponentiations with single untrusted program for cloud storage. In: Kutyłowski, M., Vaidya, J. (eds.) ICAIS 2014, Part I. LNCS, vol. 8712, pp. 326–343. Springer, Heidelberg (2014)
13. Yao, A.C.: Protocols for secure computations. In: Proceedings of the 23rd Annual Symposium on Foundations of Computer Science, pp. 160–168. IEEE Computer Society (1982)

A   Properties of Our First Protocol

Properties of Protocol (C,S). The efficiency properties are verified by protocol inspection: C runs at most 3 multiplications in G, and S runs the inversion operation in G once. With respect to round complexity, the protocol only requires one message from C to S, followed by one message from S to C. With respect to communication complexity, the protocol only requires the transfer of one group element in each of the 2 messages.

The correctness properties follows by observing that if C and S follow the protocol, C's check $d * e = 1$ is satisfied and C's output y satisfies

$$y = c * e = c * d^{-1} = c * c^{-1} * x^{-1} = x^{-1}.$$

The privacy property follows by combining the following two observations: (1) on a single execution of (C, S), the message d sent by C does not leak any information about x; and (2) seeing multiple executions of (C, S) does not help the adversary, even when C's inputs in these executions are chosen by the adversary. Both observations are consequences of the fact that in each execution of (C, S), the value d is uniformly distributed in G and independent from all previous executions.

The security property follows by combining the following two observations: (1) on a single execution of (C, S), C's verification in step 3 forces the adversary to send a honestly computed value e in step 2; and (2) seeing multiple executions of (C, S) does not help the adversary, even when C's inputs in these executions are chosen by the adversary. Observation (1) follows by the fact that there is a single value e satisfying C's check "$e * d = 1$" and it is $e = d^{-1}$; that is, the same value that an honest S sends. Observation (2) follows from the privacy property.

This concludes the proof of Theorem 1.

B   Number of Distinct Group Products

Let $X \subset G$ where G is a commutative group. We say that X is *not collision free* (NCF) if there exist distinct subsets $S_1, S_2 \subset X$ such that

$$\prod_{i \in S_1} i = \prod_{j \in S_2} j.$$

Alternatively if all subsets of X have distinct products, we say that X is collision free (CF).

Lemma 1. Let m be super-logarithmic and sub-linear in $\ell = \log |G|$. Then the probability that a random subset $X \subset G$ where $|X| = m$ has a collision is negligible in ℓ.

Proof. Let $X = \{x_1, \cdots, x_m\}$ and $X_i = \{x_1, \cdots, x_i\}$, for $i = 1, \ldots, m$. Then

$$
\begin{aligned}
\Pr(X \text{ is NCF}) &= \Pr(X \text{ is NCF} \mid X_{m-1} \text{ is CF}) * \Pr(X_{m-1} \text{ is CF}) + \\
&\quad \Pr(X \text{ is NCF} \mid X_{m-1} \text{ is NCF}) * \Pr(X_{m-1} \text{ is NCF}) \\
&\leq \Pr(X \text{ is NCF} \mid X_{m-1} \text{ is CF}) + \Pr(X_{m-1} \text{ is NCF}) \\
&\leq \sum_{i=1}^{m} \Pr(X_i \text{ is NCF} \mid X_{i-1} \text{ is CF}) \\
&\leq \sum_{i=1}^{m} \frac{3^{i-1}}{|G|} \\
&= \frac{3^m - 1}{2|G|},
\end{aligned}
$$

which is negligible in ℓ as long as $m = o(\ell)$, and where the probability derivations are explained as follows.

The first equality is obtained by an application of the probability conditioning rule. The first inequality follows by upper bounding $\Pr(X_{m-1} \text{ is CF})$ with 1 and observing that, by definition, $\Pr(X \text{ is NCF} \mid X_{m-1} \text{ is NCF}) = 1$. The second inequality is obtained by iterating the first inequality to the $\Pr(X_{m-1} \text{ is NCF})$ term. The second equality is obtained by a geometric summation calculation. To see how the third inequality is obtained, observe that we compute an upper bound for $\Pr(X_i \text{ is NCF} \mid X_{i-1} \text{ is CF})$ as follows. First note that the only way X_i can have a collision is if $\exists a, b$ that are products of distinct elements of X_i such that

$$ax_i = b.$$

Therefore, x_i must avoid all distinct elements of the form ba^{-1}. Note that any element of the form ba^{-1} can be written as

$$x_{j_1} \cdots x_{j_k} x_{j_{k+1}}^{-1} \cdots x_{j_l}^{-1}$$

where all elements in the above product are distinct and for each x_j that appears, x_j^{-1} does not appear. There are a total of 3^{i-1} such strings and therefore x_i must avoid at most 3^{i-1} distinct elements. We then have that

$$\Pr(X_i \text{ is NCF} \mid X_{i-1} \text{ is CF}) \leq \frac{3^{i-1}}{|G|}.$$

$\square$

Author Index

Becker, Georg T.   17
Burleson, Wayne   3, 53

Cavallo, Bren   156
Cid, Carlos   104

de Ruiter, Joeri   122
Di Crescenzo, Giovanni   156
Dolron, Peter   122

Ferreira, Loic   104
Forte, Domenic   32

Gross, Hannes   68

Habraken, René   122
Hinterwälder, Gesine   141
Holcomb, Daniel E.   3

Kahrobaei, Delaram   156
Kumar, Raghavan   53

Paar, Christof   141
Poll, Erik   122
Procter, Gordon   104

Riek, Felix   141
Robshaw, Matt J.B.   104
Rodríguez, Ricardo J.   87
Rührmair, Ulrich   3

Shpilrain, Vladimir   156

Tehranipoor, Mark   32
Tobisch, Johannes   17

Vila, José   87

Xu, Xiaolin   3

Yang, Kun   32

Printed in the United States
By Bookmasters